Praise for Michael and Mimi Donaldson

"I negotiate all day long. This book is terrific. It is packed with good information. We all need to focus more on negotiation and less on the courts to resolve our disputes and disagreements. We need to spend more energy finding the common ground."

> — Ralph Munro, Secretary of State, State of Washington

"Mimi and Michael's clearly delineated six skills of negotiating will make a difference in all aspects of life — business and personal."

> — Sarina Simon, President, Philips Media, Home & Family Entertainment

"This book gives you everything you need to know about negotiating. The Donaldsons share it all. They believe there are no secrets — no tricks."

> — Tom Sullivan, actor, writer, composer, singer, and speaker

"Mimi's practical information on men and women combined with Mike's insight into negotiating provide positive tools you can use every day — plus it's positively entertaining."

> — Spike Jones, Jr., Goldberg & O'Reily, TV Producer

"The Donaldsons are unparalleled in their ability to focus a diverse audience on the most effective techniques for win-win negotiations that are fun to learn and put into action — as they have done time after time in their sold out classes at UCLA Extension."

> — Ronnie Rubin, Director, Department of Entertainment Studies & Performing Arts, UCLA Extension

"My spa guests are sophisticated, intelligent decision makers/business and household executives. They expect a lot from a speaker. They get a lot from the Donaldsons. Negotiating, communicating, and relating skills presented in a dynamic captivating, and humorous manner."

> — Sheila T. Cluff, Owner/President, The Oaks at Ojai, The Palms at Palm Springs, health and fitness spas

"Michael and Mimi have written an interesting and valuable book for people in every occupation I can imagine, including homemaking. Its easy, common-sense approach to getting what you need while respecting your counter-part's needs makes success even sweeter when you realize that they, too, must feel the same satisfaction."

> —Barbara Bosson

"Not just another quick fix that falls apart. *Negotiating For Dummies* shows you in a no-nonsense, get-to-the-point way how to really negotiate. I strongly suggest you don't loan your copy out — you'll never see it again.

> —Dr. Judith Briles, author of *Gender Traps* and *The Confidence Factor*

"We thoroughly enjoyed Mimi and Michael's presentation on negotiating in Milan. They gave us valuable tips and were very entertaining."

> —Diane Fryman, Former President, Toastmasters Chapter of Milan, Italy, and Internal Program Director for the Professional Women's Association (Milan, Italy)

Praise for Michael Donaldson

"Michael Donaldson has negotiated in personal, political, and business environments. I have watched him in all three areas for over 30 years. He knows what he is doing."

> —Bob Beverly, State Senator, State of California

"Michael Donaldson is a premiere negotiator. I have the utmost respect for him. I trust him, and I'm thrilled with the deal he made for me."

> —Jess Walton, Actress, "Jill Foster Abbott" on *The Young and The Restless* series CBS-TV

"Michael Donaldson has the talent to take a non-commercial project that you do for yourself and find a way to negotiate a very good financial deal for everyone."

> —Chuck Workman, Oscar winning filmmaker

"Michael is simply the best lawyer in town. He is honest. He knows what he is doing — and he is absolutely unflappable at the negotiating table."

> —Norma Connolly Rodman, Actress, "Aunt Ruby" on *General Hospital* series ABC-TV

"I've worked with Michael for many years. I've seen him negotiate in all kinds of situations. He knows how to keep it simple, and he's always a gentleman."

— Kent McCray, Producer, *Bonanza, Little House on the Prairie, Highway to Heaven*

Praise for Mimi Donaldson

"One vital key to success is strategic negotiating. Mimi's insights will definitely sharpen your skills."

— Betsy Myers, Deputy Assistant to the President, White House, Office for Women's Initiatives & Outreach

"Mimi taught our managers how to negotiate for results with employees and clients. Her techniques, like her warm personality, are entertaining, innovative, and accessible to all."

— Nan Tepper, Vice President, Human Resources, CBS West Coast

"I've listened to Mimi for more than 20 years. She's amazing. Few people are both hilarious and insightful simultaneously. Mimi is. Now she's in print. Don't miss this!"

— Tom Koenig, President, CEO, Koenig & Strey Realtors, Chicago, Illinois

"It was no surprise to me that Mimi was a smash hit at the Million Dollar Round Table to an audience of 7,500 people. She is fantastic, vibrant, and wise."

— Tom Richards, General Agent, Northwestern Mutual Life, and President of Northwestern Mutual Life General Agents Association

"After 20 years of being a speaker, I have heard the best — Mimi has you laughing because of what she says — and HOW she says it really strikes home."

— Rosita Perez, President, Creative Living Programs, Inc.

"Mimi has a way of presenting the idea that it's possible to put your foot down when necessary without stamping it."

— Esther Williams, Actress/Entrepreneur

NEGOTIATING
FOR
DUMMIES™

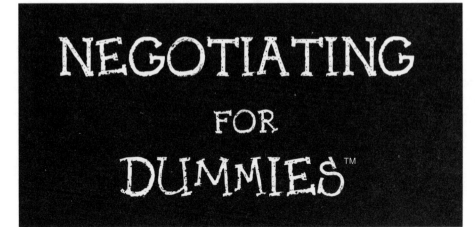

NEGOTIATING FOR DUMMIES™

by Michael C. Donaldson
and Mimi Donaldson

Foreword by David Frohnmayer
President, University of Oregon

IDG Books Worldwide, Inc.
An International Data Group Company

Foster City, CA ♦ Chicago, IL ♦ Indianapolis, IN ♦ Southlake, TX

Negotiating For Dummies™

Published by
IDG Books Worldwide, Inc.
An International Data Group Company
919 E. Hillsdale Blvd.
Suite 400
Foster City, CA 94404

Library of Congress Catalog Card No.: 96-76251

ISBN: 1-56884-867-6

Printed in the United States of America

10 9 8 7 6 5 4 3 2 1

1O/QY/QX/ZW/IN

Distributed in the United States by IDG Books Worldwide, Inc.

Distributed by Macmillan Canada for Canada; by Contemporanea de Ediciones for Venezuela; by Distribuidora Cuspide for Argentina; by CITEC for Brazil; by Ediciones ZETA S.C.R. Ltda. for Peru; by Editorial Limusa SA for Mexico; by Transworld Publishers Limited in the United Kingdom and Europe; by Academic Bookshop for Egypt; by Levant Distributors S.A.R.L. for Lebanon; by Al Jassim for Saudi Arabia; by Simron Pty. Ltd. for South Africa; by Pustak Mahal for India; by The Computer Bookshop for India; by Toppan Company Ltd. for Japan; by Addison Wesley Publishing Company for Korea; by Longman Singapore Publishers Ltd. for Singapore, Malaysia, Thailand, and Indonesia; by Unalis Corporation for Taiwan; by WS Computer Publishing Company, Inc. for the Philippines; by WoodsLane Pty. Ltd. for Australia; by WoodsLane Enterprises Ltd. for New Zealand. Authorized Sales Agent: Anthony Rudkin Associates for the Middle East and North Africa.

For general information on IDG Books Worldwide's books in the U.S., please call our Consumer Customer Service department at 800-762-2974. For reseller information, including discounts and premium sales, please call our Reseller Customer Service department at 800-434-3422.

For information on where to purchase IDG Books Worldwide's books outside the U.S., contact IDG Books Worldwide's International Sales department at 415-655-3078 or fax 415-655-3281.

For information on foreign language translations, contact IDG Books Worldwide's Foreign & Subsidiary Rights department at 415-655-3018 or fax 415-655-3281.

For sales inquiries and special prices for bulk quantities, contact IDG Books Worldwide's Sales department at 415-655-3200 or write to the address above.

For information on using IDG Books Worldwide's books in the classroom or for ordering examination copies, contact IDG Books Worldwide's Educational Sales department at 800-434-2086 or fax 817-251-8174.

For authorization to photocopy items for corporate, personal, or educational use, please contact Copyright Clearance Center, 222 Rosewood Drive, Danvers, MA 01923, or fax 508-750-4470.

 is a trademark under exclusive license to IDG Books Worldwide, Inc., from International Data Group, Inc.

About the Authors

Michael C. Donaldson

Michael C. Donaldson is a founding partner of Berton & Donaldson, a Beverly Hills, California, firm specializing in entertainment and copyright law with an emphasis in the representation of independent film producers. He is the author of *Do It Yourself! Trademarks & Copyrights,* which was released in June of 1995, and also wrote the introduction to *Conversations with Michael Landon.* He is currently writing *Clips, Clearance & Copyright — Everything the Filmmaker Needs to Know.*

Donaldson earned his law degree in 1967 at the University of California at Berkeley. He is a member of the Beverly Hills Bar Association (where he was formerly co-chairman of the Entertainment Section), the Los Angeles County Bar Association, the State Bar of California, and the American Bar Association. He is listed in the current edition of *Who's Who in American Law.*

Mimi Donaldson

Mimi Donaldson is an international management consultant specializing in quality communications training. She has been training managers and employees to negotiate with each other for more than 20 years. She has worked with over 100,000 executives, managers, and staff members from a wide variety of fields, including aerospace, engineering, manufacturing, hospitality, insurance, finance, and entertainment.

In addition to her consulting work, Mimi is greatly sought after by companies and associations as a dynamic keynote speaker. She has brought audiences of 7,500 to their feet with her hilarious insights on negotiating with bosses, coworkers, spouses, and kids. Her clients for training and speaking include CBS Television, Paramount Studios, American Honda Motor Corporation, Toyota Motor Sales of USA, Inc., Xerox, IBM, Hewlett-Packard, Northwestern Mutual Life, Prudential, and the Marriott Corporation, to name a few. Mimi is Past President of the Los Angeles Chapter of the National Association of Women Business Owners.

ABOUT IDG BOOKS WORLDWIDE

WINNER
Eighth Annual
Computer Press
Awards 1992

WINNER
Ninth Annual
Computer Press
Awards 1993

IDG BOOKS WORLDWIDE

Welcome to the world of IDG Books Worldwide.

IDG Books Worldwide, Inc., is a subsidiary of International Data Group, the world's largest publisher of computer-related information and the leading global provider of information services on information technology. IDG was founded more than 25 years ago and now employs more than 7,700 people worldwide. IDG publishes more than 250 computer publications in 67 countries (see listing below). More than 70 million people read one or more IDG publications each month.

Launched in 1990, IDG Books Worldwide is today the #1 publisher of best-selling computer books in the United States. We are proud to have received 8 awards from the Computer Press Association in recognition of editorial excellence and three from Computer Currents' First Annual Readers' Choice Awards, and our best-selling *...For Dummies*® series has more than 19 million copies in print with translations in 28 languages. IDG Books Worldwide, through a joint venture with IDG's Hi-Tech Beijing, became the first U.S. publisher to publish a computer book in the People's Republic of China. In record time, IDG Books Worldwide has become the first choice for millions of readers around the world who want to learn how to better manage their businesses.

Our mission is simple: Every one of our books is designed to bring extra value and skill-building instructions to the reader. Our books are written by experts who understand and care about our readers. The knowledge base of our editorial staff comes from years of experience in publishing, education, and journalism — experience which we use to produce books for the '90s. In short, we care about books, so we attract the best people. We devote special attention to details such as audience, interior design, use of icons, and illustrations. And because we use an efficient process of authoring, editing, and desktop publishing our books electronically, we can spend more time ensuring superior content and spend less time on the technicalities of making books.

You can count on our commitment to deliver high-quality books at competitive prices on topics you want to read about. At IDG Books Worldwide, we continue in the IDG tradition of delivering quality for more than 25 years. You'll find no better book on a subject than one from IDG Books Worldwide.

John J. Kilcullen

John Kilcullen
President and CEO
IDG Books Worldwide, Inc.

IDG Books Worldwide, Inc., is a subsidiary of International Data Group, the world's largest publisher of computer-related information and the leading global provider of information services on information technology. International Data Group publishes over 250 computer publications in 67 countries. Seventy million people read one or more International Data Group publications each month. International Data Group's publications include: **ARGENTINA:** Computerworld Argentina, GamePro, Infoworld, PC World Argentina; **AUSTRALIA:** Australian Macworld, Client/Server Journal, Computer Living, Computerworld, Digital News, Network World, PC World, Publishing Essentials, Reseller; **AUSTRIA:** Computerwelt, PC TEST; **BELARUS:** PC World Belarus; **BELGIUM:** Data News; **BRAZIL:** Annuário de Informática, Computerworld Brazil, Connections, Super Game Power, Macworld, PC World Brazil, Publish Brazil, SUPERGAME; **BULGARIA:** Computerworld Bulgaria, Networkworld/Bulgaria, PC & MacWorld Bulgaria; **CANADA:** CIO Canada, ComputerWorld Canada, InfoCanada, Network World Canada, Reseller World; **CHILE:** Computerworld Chile, GamePro, PC World Chile; **COLUMBIA:** Computerworld Colombia, GamePro, PC World Colombia; **COSTA RICA:** PC World Costa Rica/Nicaragua; **THE CZECH AND SLOVAK REPUBLICS:** Computerworld Czechoslovakia, Elektronika Czechoslovakia, PC World Czechoslovakia; **DENMARK:** Communications World, Computerworld Danmark, Macworld Danmark, PC World Danmark, PC World Danmark Supplements, TECH World; **DOMINICAN REPUBLIC:** PC World Republica Dominicana; **ECUADOR:** PC World Ecuador, GamePro; **EGYPT:** Computerworld Middle East, PC World Middle East; **EL SALVADOR:** PC World Centro America; **FINLAND:** MikroPC, Tietoverkko, Tietoviikko; **FRANCE:** Distributique, Golden, Info PC, Le Guide du Monde Informatique, Le Monde Informatique, Reseaux & Telecoms; **GERMANY:** Computer Business, Computerwoche, Computerwoche Extra, Computerwoche Focus, Electronic Entertainment, GamePro, I/M Information Management, Macwelt, PC Welt; **GREECE:** GamePro, Macworld & Publish; **GUATEMALA:** PC World Centro America; **HONDURAS:** PC World Centro America; **HONG KONG:** Computerworld Hong Kong, PCWorld Hong Kong, Publish in Asia; **HUNGARY:** ABCD CD-ROM, Computerworld Szamitastechnika, PC & Mac World Hungary, PC-X Magazine; **INDIA:** Computerworld India, PC World India, Publish in Asia; **INDONESIA:** InfoKomputer PC World, Komputek Computerworld, Publish in Asia; **IRELAND:** ComputerScope, PC Live!; **ISRAEL:** PC World 32 BIT, People & Computers; **ITALY:** Computerworld Italia, Computerworld Italia Special Editions, Lotus Italia, Macworld Italia, Networking Italia, PC Shopping, PC World Italia, PC World/Walt Disney; **JAPAN:** Macworld Japan, Nikkei Personal Computing, SunWorld Japan, Windows World Japan; **KENYA:** East African Computer News; **KOREA:** Hi-Tech Information/Computerworld, Macworld Korea, PC World Korea; **MACEDONIA:** PC World Macedonia; **MALAYSIA:** Computerworld Malaysia, PC World Malaysia, Publish in Asia; **MEXICO:** Computerworld Mexico, GamePro, Macworld, PC World Mexico; **MYANMAR:** PC World Myanmar; **NETHERLANDS:** Computable, Computer! Totaal, LAN Magazine, Macworld, Net Magazine; **NEW ZEALAND:** Computer Buyer, Computerworld New Zealand, MTB, Network World, PC World New Zealand; **NICARAGUA:** PC World Costa Rica/Nicaragua; **NIGERIA:** PC World Africa; **NORWAY:** Computerworld Norge, Computerworld Privat, CW Rapport Klient/Tjener, CW Rapport Nettverk & Telecom, CW Rapport Offentlig Sektor, IDG's KURSGUIDE, Macworld Norge, Multimedia World, PC World Ekspress, PC World Nettverk, PC World Norge, PC World's Produktguide, Windows Spesial; **PAKISTAN:** Computerworld Pakistan, PC World Pakistan; **PANAMA:** GamePro, PC World Panama; **PARAGUAY:** PC World Paraguay; **P. R. OF CHINA:** China Computerworld, China Infoworld, Computer & Communication, Electronic Product World, Electronics Today, Game Camp, PC World China, Popular Computer Week, Software World, Telecom Product World; **PERU:** Computerworld Peru, GamePro, PC World Profesional Peru, PC World Peru; **POLAND:** Computerworld Poland, Computerworld Special Report, Macworld, Networld, PC World Komputer; **PHILIPPINES:** Computerworld Philippines, PC Digest, Publish in Asia; **PORTUGAL:** Cerebro/PC World, Correio Informático/Computerworld, Mac•In/PC•In Portugal; **PUERTO RICO:** PC World Puerto Rico; **ROMANIA:** Computerworld Romania, PC World Romania, Telecom Romania; **RUSSIA:** Computerworld Rossiya, Network World Russia, PC World Russia; **SINGAPORE:** Computerworld Singapore, PC World Singapore, Publish in Asia; **SLOVENIA:** MONITOR; **SOUTH AFRICA:** Computing S.A., Network World S.A., Software World; **SPAIN:** Computerworld España, COMUNICACIONES WORLD, Dealer World, Macworld España, PC World España; **SWEDEN:** CAP&Design, Computer Sweden, Corporate Computing, MacWorld, Maxi Data, MikroDatorn, Natverk & Kommunikation, PC/Aktiv, PC World, Windows World; **SWITZERLAND:** Computerworld Schweiz, Macworld Schweiz, PCtip; **TAIWAN:** Computerworld Taiwan, Macworld Taiwan, PC World Taiwan, Publish Taiwan, Windows World; **THAILAND:** Thai Computerworld, Publish in Asia; **TURKEY:** Computerworld Monitör, MACWORLD Turkiye, PC WORLD Turkiye; **UKRAINE:** Computerworld Kiev, Computers & Software Magazine, PC World Ukraine; **UNITED KINGDOM:** Acorn User, Amiga Action, Amiga Computing, Amiga, Appletalk, CD Powerplay, CD-ROM Now, Computing, Connexion, GamePro, Lotus Magazine, Macaction, Macworld, Open Computing, Parents and Computers, PC Home, PC Works, The WEB; **UNITED STATES:** Cable in the Classroom, CD Review, CIO Magazine, Computerworld, Computerworld Client/Server Journal, Digital Video Magazine, DOS World, Electronic, InfoWorld, I-Way, Macworld, Maximize, MULTIMEDIA WORLD, Network World, PC World, PUBLISH, SWATPro Magazine, Video Event, WebMaster; **URUGUAY:** PC World Uruguay; **VENEZUELA:** Computerworld Venezuela, GamePro, PC World Venezuela; and **VIETNAM:** PC World Vietnam   10/17/95a

Authors' Dedication

This book is dedicated with love and respect to our parents, with whom we first negotiated. They showed us the ropes of life, showed us how those ropes can protect and hold, and showed us how they can also give you rope burns.

Dr. William and Norma Schwied — thanks for being our cheerleaders.

Wyman Donaldson and Ernestine Donaldson — wish you were here to see this.

Speeches, Seminars, and Consulting

Mimi Donaldson is among the most sought-after presenters on the speaking circuit, and offers in-house training courses, workshops, and keynote presentations, including:

- The Art of Powerspeak
- Negotiating with Men and Women: Can We Talk?
- Gender on the Job: Preventing Sexual Harassment
- All Stressed Up and No Place to Blow
- Your Time Is Yours: Effective Time Management
- Empowering Your Team: From Vision to Reality
- Four Steps to Managing Anyone
- At Your Service: Gaining the Competitive Edge in Customer Relations
- Telephone Techniques
- Effective Presentations: How to Manage the Butterflies
- Writing for Results: Effective Business Writing
- Assertive Communication
- Managing Conflict

Mimi and Michael conduct negotiating seminars separately and together for in-house training, conferences, and conventions. For more information, contact:

Mimi Donaldson
9016 Wilshire Blvd., Suite 327
Beverly Hills, CA 90211
Phone: (310) 273-2633
Fax: (310) 275-8854
E-mail: MikelMimi@aol.com

Publisher's Acknowledgments

We're proud of this book; please send us your comments about it by using the Reader Response Card at the back of the book or by e-mailing us at feedback/dummies@idgbooks.com. Some of the people who helped bring this book to market include the following:

Acquisitions, Development, & Editorial

Project Editor: Shannon Ross

Acquisitions Editor: Kathleen A. Welton, Vice President and Publisher

Permissions Editor: Joyce Pepple

Copy Editor: Susan Diane Smith

Technical Reviewer: Melissa Thomas Hunt

Editorial Manager: Kristin A. Cocks

Editorial Assistants: Constance Carlisle, Chris H. Collins, Ann Miller

Production

Project Coordinator: Cindy L. Phipps

Layout and Graphics: Brett Black, Cameron Booker, Linda M. Boyer, Todd Klemme, Jane E. Martin, M. Anne Sipahimalani, Kate Snell

Proofreaders: Kathleen Prata, Joel Draper, Christine Meloy Beck, Michael Bolinger, Nancy Price, Dwight Ramsey, Robert Springer, Carrie Voorhis, Karen York

Indexer: Sherry Massey

Special Help

Jamie Klobuchar, Mary Bednarek, Stephanie Koutek

General & Administrative

IDG Books Worldwide, Inc.: John Kilcullen, President & CEO; Steven Berkowitz, COO & Publisher

Dummies, Inc.: Milissa Koloski, Executive Vice President & Publisher

Dummies Technology Press & Dummies Editorial: Diane Graves Steele, Associate Publisher; Judith A. Taylor, Brand Manager; Myra Immell, Editorial Director

Dummies Trade Press: Kathleen A. Welton, Vice President & Publisher; Stacy S. Collins, Brand Manager

IDG Books Production for Dummies Press: Beth Jenkins, Production Director; Cindy L. Phipps, Supervisor of Project Coordination; Kathie S. Schnorr, Supervisor of Page Layout; Shelley Lea, Supervisor of Graphics and Design

Dummies Packaging & Book Design: Erin McDermit, Packaging Coordinator; Kavish+Kavish, Cover Design

◆

The publisher would like to give special thanks to Patrick J. McGovern, without whom this book would not have been possible.

◆

Authors' Acknowledgments

We gratefully acknowledge the contributions of so many beloved people whose talent and willingness to help were indispensable:

- Michael's daughters, Michelle (and Ray) Rapko, Amy Donaldson, and Wendy Donaldson, who have taught us more than we ever wanted to know about negotiating with children

- Our siblings, Debbie (and Randy) Riley, Sally (and Bart) Tompkins, Dr. Ellis (and Shelley) Schwied, and Anne Laidlaw, for early training and continued support

- Betty White, whose genuine enthusiasm encouraged us from the earliest stages to the quote on the back cover, and who devoted her time in spite of a heavy acting, writing, and animal-care schedule

- Michael's uncle, Jim Greenwood; Peter Hay; Greg Goodell; and Mark Lee, professional writers all, who read and carefully commented on the earliest incarnation; and Carole Mann, who agented the book for over a year

- An army of typists, proofers, and commenters lead by long-time, loyal assistant, Rebecca Shearer

- The dozens and dozens of people who provided quotes, quips, information, and insights that enrich the book; including such professional writers as Howard Rodman, Melissa Peteron, and Phil Proctor — your donated time is particularly appreciated

- Our clients, with whom and for whom we hone our skills every day

- And — from beginning to end — the wonderful, supportive, and flexible staff at IDG Books Worldwide: Kathy Welton, who first brought us into the fold and marshalled the forces; Shannon Ross, our fabulous editor, who shaped the book; and Stacy Collins, Kathy Day, Jamie Klobuchar, Mimi Sells, and all the wonderful people in marketing, who delivered this book from the presses to you

Contents at a Glance

Cartoons at a Glance

By Rich Tennant • *Fax:* 508-546-7747 • *E-mail:* the5wave@tiac.net

Table of Contents

· ·

Foreword

*W*hen I was asked to write the foreword to this engaging book on negotiating, I responded quickly, having already read some early chapters. I have known Michael Donaldson since our days in law school together. I have grown to know Mimi more fully through these writings. We share fundamental values about our human community and agree about how honest negotiation can help us realize those values.

Now that I've reviewed the final text, it is gratifyingly obvious that this is not merely a book about techniques. It is not a book about cheap tricks. As far as I know, it is the only book on negotiating that begins with a chapter on creating a personal or business mission statement that explores and then incorporates your values and beliefs. I strongly agree that people must always negotiate from an informed, deeply held belief system.

This is also the only book on negotiating I have seen that has an entire chapter on listening to one's inner voice. You must learn to hear what your heart and your gut tell you before you can best use the other insights of this book. No practical guide can overrule your inner sense of what is right and wrong.

I am no stranger to high stakes, complicated negotiations. My own background as the Attorney General of the State of Oregon includes some hefty negotiations. I was one of three chief negotiators representing all 50 states in a case involving some extraordinarily complicated issues of oil pricing. The case resulted in a settlement exceeding 4 billion dollars. At the time, it was the largest settlement in American legal history. That negotiation took place in some 15 different locations over a period of four years and involved dozens of parties.

From this and other experiences, I know that superficial technique can be no substitute for beginning with an informed, deeply held belief system. The reason I like this book is that it makes clear how every negotiation is premised on alignments of fundamental values. We must understand ourselves and what we wish to accomplish and then develop these values and feelings with those who might seem, on the surface, to be our adversaries. In this book, you will discover how we all may be more effective in resolving the big and little negotiations that our turbulent existence shows us every day.

Dave Frohnmayer
President, University of Oregon
Attorney General, emeritus — State of Oregon (1981–1991)

David Frohnmayer was President of the National Association of Attorneys General (1987–88). He received that association's Wyman award in 1987 saluting the nation's most outstanding attorney general. He was one of the three chief state negotiators in the Stripper Well litigation that led to what was then the largest civil settlement in the history of American law. He was the lead counsel for the states when the settlement was argued in court.

Introduction

Welcome to *Negotiating For Dummies* — a new way to get what you want in life.

You negotiate all day long, not just on the job but in every situation you encounter — with your boss or your employees, with your vendors or your clients, with your spouse or your kids, even with the serviceperson who comes to your house but doesn't repair that refrigerator after all. All these relationships call for constant negotiation.

A *negotiation* is any communication in which you are attempting to achieve the approval, acquiescence, or action of someone else. Most people tend to think of negotiation in the business context or in connection with major purchases such as a home or a car. But you probably spend more of your energy in one-minute life negotiations such as, "Dad, can I borrow the car?" or "Honey, will you please put the seat down?" The lessons in this book apply to both the once-in-a-lifetime, million-dollar deals and the everyday, one-minute life negotiations.

The Big Six

The skills you need to be a successful negotiator in your everyday life are the same skills required for major international and industrial negotiation. Sure, you can refine these skills with additional techniques and strategies, and you enhance them with your own personal style and personality. But only these six skills are *essential:*

- ✔ Thorough preparation
- ✔ The ability to set limits and goals
- ✔ Keeping your emotional distance
- ✔ Good listening skills
- ✔ Clarity of communication
- ✔ Knowing how to close a deal

These six skills are so important, we believe that they should be on a chart on everybody's wall, just as the elements that make up the Earth hang in every chemistry lab. In fact, we list them on the tear-out Cheat Sheet in the front of this book, so you can grab some tape and begin the trend right now.

This book devotes a great deal of real estate to each of the six skills. Because the six basic negotiating skills apply to all areas of life, *Negotiating For Dummies* can empower you to get more happiness and success out of your life right now by helping you gain

- ✔ More respect
- ✔ More money
- ✔ More results from employees, coworkers, and bosses
- ✔ More successful agreements with your friends and family
- ✔ More control in your negotiations
- ✔ More satisfaction for both parties as a result of your negotiations

Where We're Coming From

We share a common approach to negotiating even though our backgrounds are different. We believe in building long-term relationships that can grow to yield greater satisfaction with each passing year. During the course of such relationships, both parties must get the core of what they want at a cost they are willing to pay. If one party is suffering in silence, the relationship is sure to end — in a loud explosion or with nary a whimper, it will end.

Your personal integrity is at the core of every negotiation. You must take great care to be ethical in your dealings with everybody you meet. We practiced these principles before we met, and we continue to apply them to every deal we enter. Your principles should be at the core of every business transaction you make.

When we met, our careers did not overlap. As our personal lives grew together, so did our professional lives. We began writing and speaking on our shared interest: negotiating.

Building a career in negotiation

I have always been interested in the elements of successful persuasion, even before I thought of organizing all the information under the umbrella of negotiating. In college, I went to hear every notable speaker who came to campus, from the conservative Reverend Billy Graham to socialist speakers trying to lean the campus to the left. As editor of the school's literary magazine, I got to interview most of those individuals.

Right after graduation, I became a U.S. Marine Corps officer with my own reconnaissance platoon. I began studying the elements of leadership because I knew that my leadership abilities may mean someone's life someday — maybe mine. You probably don't think giving orders in the Marine Corps has anything to do with negotiation. Marine Corps officers do operate under many pre-set limits. But I found that the better the preparation (mostly in the form of good training) and the clearer the orders, the better the troops followed. Our little platoon was selected to be the first Marine ground combat unit in Vietnam. We shared our missions with a group of Navy Seals. Careful negotiations within our unit and with the Seals resulted in many successful missions.

After building a successful law practice in the city of Torrance in the southwest quadrant of Los Angeles County, I decided that I was going to do what I wanted to do. I moved to another part of the city and hung a shingle in what was probably the most challenging facet of law — entertainment law — in what was probably the least compassionate environment — Hollywood! I didn't have a single entertainment client; all I had was my skill in negotiating. At the time, very little was written on the subject. No courses on negotiation were offered at any college I attended. I continued my self-study of the field. My knowledge paid off on my first (and, at that time, only) entertainment client, and he recommended me to another person, and so on, and so on.

Since then, I have enjoyed great success. I have negotiated for and against some of the biggest names in Hollywood and against every single studio in town (in all their incarnations). I negotiated every production deal for Michael Landon during the most productive years of his life. I still negotiate the use of names and likenesses of such Hollywood greats as Donna Reed and Elizabeth Montgomery. Always, in Hollywood, the power is with the studios.

For examples in this book, I draw primarily from my law practice as a full-time negotiator in the entertainment industry where I represent actors, writers, directors, and independent producers in their negotiations with studios, financiers, and each other. In the text, I also use examples from my family life as the father of three teenagers and the husband of Mimi, who is one of the master negotiators of all time.

Giving people tools to enhance their lives

My business is management consulting and keynote speaking to Fortune 500 companies. My courses include "Managing for Results," "Four Steps to Managing Anyone," "Team Building," "Stress Management," "Presentation Skills," "Time Management," "Customer Service," and "Conflict Resolution." For over 20 years, I have been teaching these courses to people across the country to enhance their personal effectiveness in every area of their lives.

Good working relationships involve negotiating with employees, clients, vendors, and customers. The ever-challenging task of managing people entails delegating tasks, which means empowering people to get results for which you are ultimately responsible. Managers engage in these negotiations every day. All of us must negotiate in one way or another.

Another area of my expertise is gender differences. In courses such as, "Men & Women: Can We Talk?" and "Gender on the Job: Preventing Sexual Harassment," I give people tools to communicate and negotiate with the opposite sex at home and at work. In addition to teaching courses, I give speeches on these techniques to national meetings and conferences to audiences of thousands.

When I started teaching "The Art of Power-speak" and "Assertive Communication" in the early '80s, women wanted to learn how to speak the language of power in the workplace — language that had been, up to that point, pretty much men's domain. Now, with women gaining in power and position, the language of power is no longer gender based. Role models are no longer just male; they are also female.

I have always taught men and women to negotiate fairly and appropriately. You can get what you need and want and build relationships in the process. You may have to risk upsetting someone for the moment. You may have to risk not being liked by everyone all the time. That comes with the territory of achieving results. You always have to choose between comfortable safety and risking discomfort to go for what you want. I use these principles as the basis of my courses in negotiation.

When I met Michael and watched him bargaining in a little shop, I realized I was in the presence of a master. I resonated with his energetic integrity. His eyes were twinkling, and so were the eyes of his counterpart in the negotiation.

My work has been enhanced by Michael's approach to negotiating. More importantly, the application in my personal life has been very positive. As someone who came to marriage late in life, I can attest to the fact that the approach works at home as well. Together, we applied negotiating techniques to turn his daughter Wendy into an "A" student from a decidedly nonacademic type. We used the same clear methods for establishing curfew, car use, and household responsibilities.

Who Needs to Read This Book?

Everyone.

Face it, you negotiate all day long, and you could do a much better job of it. No matter how you perceive your skills today, they can be stronger tomorrow. And your progress can start with this book.

Many people assume that they know a great deal about negotiating because they have done it so often, but these same people have never given a moment's thought to the fundamentals of successful negotiating. Worse, many people believe that their lawyers are knowledgeable about negotiating simply because they are lawyers! The sad truth is that most people who negotiate for a living are untrained for that part of their endeavor.

Those people who do want to understand more about the mechanics of negotiating often decide to take a course, buy a book, or read an article. But all too often, the course, the book, or the article assumes that they already know the fundamentals. This book does not assume anything. We dissect the basic structure of every negotiation. If it relates to negotiating, it's in here somewhere. If you still have a question after searching the entire book, fill out the reader response card at the back of the book, tell us your question, and we'll get back to you.

The mission of this book is to help you to negotiate from strength. Understanding the structure of every negotiation in which you are involved transforms you into a confident and successful negotiator. After you have mastered the six basic skills of negotiating and achieved this position of strength, every tough situation you encounter becomes easier to analyze and conquer.

This book is for you whether you are

- ✔ Beginning a career or just looking to brush up your skills

- ✔ A pushover who never seems to get your way or a master negotiator — widely admired but constantly striving to improve

- ✔ Unemployed and want a job or employed and want a raise

- ✔ A teacher searching for a way to get your students to do what you want them to do, or a parent wanting to talk more convincingly with your children

- ✔ Going for a specific win or an improvement in your overall negotiating skills

Students who have attended our seminars tell us that they use our material to get raises, to get promotions, and to close deals. They tell us how they use the course materials to improve the quality of their office life by approaching coworkers using negotiating techniques. One student wrote: "I don't have to yell anymore."

How to Use This Book

This book is not about tricks or one-upsmanship. This book answers your questions and gives you guidance by breaking negotiations down into their basic elements. Call these elements skills, steps, basics, or whatever you like — each has the potential to become your personal negotiating power tool.

We follow the theories of a championship sports camp. Think of the greatest tennis player you have seen in your life. The strokes that this player uses are the same strokes every beginning player learns: the serve, forehand, backhand, overhand, and volley. The difference between the expert and the novice is that the expert has used the basic strokes over and over — at the net, the midcourt, and the baseline — with a friend or coach providing guidance.

Think of this book as your friend and coach, someone to go to when you have a question about negotiating. Just like a tennis lesson, this book identifies each basic skill and then demonstrates its use in every situation. If you practice these skills enough, you can become a world-class negotiator, turning the basic strokes of a negotiation into winning power strokes.

This book divides the negotiation process into the six basic elements and deals with each one in a separate part. After surveying the book, you can start on whatever part you want. You probably won't go immediately to the part that discusses the skill that you need to work on the most. That's okay. Improve on any skill, and you become a better negotiator.

The Part of Tens deals with overall negotiating skills. You can work on specific skills in the first six parts of the book or on your overall technique in The Part of Tens. Every page contains information that can help you. Work at your own pace but keep going. Even five minutes a day makes a difference. Improving your negotiating skills can be fun, and it doesn't take long to notice the improvement.

Enjoy the games, books, and movies mentioned throughout the book. In the weekend seminars that we occasionally teach at a UCLA extension, these materials generate genuine fun and lots of progress. Involve your entire family in your growth as you develop the practical skills that are at the core of every master negotiator's success.

How This Book Is Organized

This book tackles a different negotiating skill in each part. We analyze and evaluate each skill and provide many different ways to use it. The final part includes top-ten lists to improve your overall negotiating style.

Part I: Follow the Scout Motto: Be Prepared

Long before a negotiation begins, one of life's most important questions faces you: Why am I here? Do I really want to enter this negotiation? What are my choices? Too many people let themselves be tossed around by life itself. Take control. Your first negotiation is with yourself.

Know yourself and know why you are involved in a negotiation. Keep the big picture in mind every step of the way. Assess your personal power and the power of your position. Then do the same process for your counterpart in the negotiation.

This part is all about preparing yourself for a negotiation — in general and in particular — and why preparation is the key to real power in any negotiation. Chapter 2 covers the most common mistake people make when preparing for a negotiation and how to avoid that mistake.

Part II: Drawing Lines and Setting Goals

Just before the actual negotiation begins is the time to set your goals and define your limits. Only when you've laid out your goals and limits can you prepare an opening offer. Your goals and limits carry you right to the end of the negotiation, enabling you to decide when to close a deal and when to walk away. Probably the toughest to master, the essential skill of setting limits — if used regularly — empowers you to change every aspect of your life. The very process of setting limits gives you power in a negotiation, because the process forces you to focus on your alternatives if a negotiated agreement is not reached.

Part III: Maintaining Emotional Distance

Ever notice how world-class negotiators always appear calm and focused? This part tells you how to remain dispassionate throughout even the most heated negotiation. Turn here to find out how emotions can influence and upset a negotiation; then discover how to curtail your emotions using your pause button. Like the pause button on your VCR, this essential skill enables you to freeze-frame the negotiation and take a break — a great way to keep your emotional distance.

Discover how to push the pause button at every critical juncture during the negotiation to eliminate buyer's remorse, prevent emotional upset, evaluate your progress, and decide whether to make the deal or to walk away.

Part IV: Do You Hear What I Hear?

This part covers the most underrated skill of all — listening. Most beginners want to rush by this essential skill. They seriously underestimate its importance and submit to the many barriers to productive listening. The experienced negotiator often gains control of the negotiation through listening. In fact, studies show that successful negotiators spend more time listening than talking. If a counterpart doesn't open up, effective negotiators tickle out the truth with well-asked questions.

Part V: Telling It Like It Is

In this part, we flip the coin to look at the other side of effective communication: speaking. Because everybody talks so much each day, becoming sloppy with this essential skill is easy. Turn to this part if you want to make each word count and make sure that people hear you every time you speak.

Part VI: Closing the Deal

This is the glory moment when it all comes together and you bring closure to the negotiation. You either close the deal or choose to end the discussion. Either way, a successful closure is the ultimate goal in every negotiation. Just before you bring closure, step back and be sure that you have a win-win situation. Closure is also a separate skill that you must develop if you are to become successful in every negotiation you undertake.

At this point in the book, we discuss all those mishaps that can keep a deal from closing. This part discusses those situations in which you feel you have done everything right, and yet the deal still won't close. First you must identify the glitch, and then you can get past it.

We also take a look at the people who keep negotiations from closing. They are out there. They are frustrating. Find out how to identify and overcome them — without significant battle scars.

Part VII: The Part of Tens

These short chapters cover matters that span the entire negotiation process. The parts leading up to The Part of Tens burrow into the individual phases of a negotiation. The chapters in this part cover ways to strengthen your overall negotiating skills. Use this section even as you dip into the other parts.

The Part of Tens looks at the negotiating process as a whole. Some lists enable you to get your whole family involved in an exciting way, such as the list of good movies to watch. You and your friends or family can begin to look at the world through the eyes of a negotiator. Honing negotiating skills can become a family affair.

Icons in This Book

Check out the margins of this book and you find lots of little pictures. Cute, aren't they? These are *icons* to guide you to the information you crave. Looking for help negotiating with members of the opposite sex? In need of negotiation skills in the workplace or on the home front? Just scan the pages for the appropriate icons.

This icon points out fun activities for the whole family. Gather your friends, your kids, your parents, or your significant other and improve your negotiating skills with one of these games, movies, or books.

The most emotional and, sometimes, the most challenging negotiations you face in life are on the home front. Find helpful tips for negotiating effectively with parents, children, or spouses wherever you see this icon.

Whether you're an engineer, a production manager, or a receptionist, negotiating is a part of your job. Follow this icon to get an inside edge on professional negotiations.

This icon marks the dirty tricks sharks try to play on you. Don't fall prey to these pitfalls — and avoid using these nasty tactics yourself.

This icon marks a story from inside Hollywood or from our personal lives to illustrate an important point. We both like telling stories to get a point across.

You could find yourself negotiating with someone from another culture just about anywhere — even your own office. Whether you're planning a vacation to a foreign shore or just want to be prepared for a global economy, these icons can point you to the multicultural information you need.

Yes, men and women are different. *Vive la différence!* But don't let the differences frustrate a negotiation. With the information accompanying this icon, we demystify your male-female communication conflicts.

Just looking for the bottom line? This icon emphasizes information that you should absolutely, positively keep in mind at all times if you want to be a successful negotiator.

This icon denotes honest tricks of the trade, shortcuts, and loopholes. We've stumbled across plenty of tips that you may want to have at your fingertips. Look for these icons to save time, money, and face in your next negotiation.

This icon points out those specific places in a negotiation when you should get out a pen and paper and write information down. It's time to take notes.

Where to Go from Here

Look through the book to get an overview of the six essential skills you need in every negotiation. Then find which part or chapter turns you on. That is the best place to begin.

Most people won't start in the area in which they need the most help. They usually choose their favorite area — the area about which they are confident. That's okay. Even your strongest area can get stronger. Then, as you shift your focus to your weaker areas, you enjoy the greatest amount of progress.

The most important point to consider right now is that you're already headed toward the winner's circle. The most successful people in life are those who continue to grow. The fact you have this book in your hand now puts you into that realm. It's not how much you know that counts, but how much you are willing to add after you "know it all."

Part I
Follow the Scout Motto: Be Prepared

"Sorry, Mr. and Mrs. Binney. As your accountant, I wasn't prepared for this kind of negotiation."

In this part . . .

1 f you want to negotiate successfully, you must be prepared. This part explains that preparation doesn't just mean reading up on your subject matter but also understanding the person with whom you'll be negotiating, and being in touch with your own strengths and limitations. The last chapter in this part deals with preparing for that actual first negotiating session — time, place, seating arrangements, the whole nine yards — including tips for negotiating with people from other cultures.

Chapter 1
Negotiating for Life

● ●

In This Chapter

▶ Creating your vision

▶ Identifying your own values

▶ Choosing the path to your purpose

▶ Making an action plan

● ●

*N*egotiating is not a skill to take out once in a while when you have to make a deal. Negotiating is a way to get what you want out of life. Many people blame a lack of negotiating skills for not getting what they want. That is only part of the answer. People must also do some long-range thinking about their own lives. Often, people are unhappy about the results of specific negotiations, when the real problem is that they should not be in those negotiations in the first place.

To use your negotiating skills most effectively, you require a *master plan* — that is, a strategy for achieving your hopes and dreams. Everyone should have a master plan; it gives you a choice about where you are on the train of life. You can either sit up in the engine driving the train, or you can hang on for dear life off the back of the caboose.

Several steps, large and small, can help you take charge of *all* the negotiations you face in your life. Even if you currently think that you could never take control of certain areas of your life, we challenge you to entertain the possibility that you can. Consider actors, who do a great deal of waiting (and not just tables). Think of some employees who regard their roles as reactive and not proactive, whose job descriptions entail responding to someone else's needs. The fact that your dreams or your paycheck seem to hinge on forces beyond your control shouldn't stop you from creating a master plan for your life.

Create Your Vision

Most corporations and businesses have a mission or vision statement. Employers often distribute this statement to employees at every level, post it on a prominent wall, and print it in various company publications. Every employee is expected to know this statement. But ask those same employees whether they have a vision statement for their own lives and careers, and you usually get a blank look.

If you want to have the best personal life and the most successful career you can have, you need a plan. Even a little planning is more than most people do, so making a small effort now puts you far ahead of the pack.

The first step in creating a master plan for yourself is to identify your vision. A *vision* is an image of a desired future. The word vision is from the Latin *videre,* meaning to see. You should state your vision by describing, in present tense, a picture of the future you see for yourself. Your vision should be as rich in detail and as visual as possible. The description must be clear, understandable, and descriptive. Most important, your vision needs to motivate you. You count on your vision to give your life shape and direction. Sample vision statements follw:

- ✔ **Nordstrom:** "To become America's store of choice through the commitment of each employee to provide customers the very best in quality, value, selection, and service."

- ✔ **Microsoft:** "Someday we'll see a computer on every desk and in every home."

- ✔ **Michael's law office:** "To help my clients realize their dreams."

- ✔ **Mimi's business:** "To assist people to realize and achieve their full human potential."

- ✔ **Randy Riley:** "To grow and help other people grow enthusiastically."

Who is Randy Riley and why is his vision statement in this book? He is our brother-in-law and the only person we know (besides ourselves) who writes out his personal mission statement each January. Maybe that's why, at just over 40, Randy manages 25 people selling insurance out of his office, has a huge home in Boulder, Colorado, and owns more toys than any other grown man on Earth.

We, too, have taken care to go through the process of evaluating our mission statements each year. In fact, this book is a direct result of our annual examination of where we are and where we want to be. In the past, we assessed our visions verbally — with each other — usually on a Sunday in the backyard sometime after Thanksgiving. This year, we took a tip from Randy and wrote our vision statements down. Keeping a written record creates better accountability.

Your vision is a long-term, ongoing, open-ended process. When you read your vision statement, it motivates you to passionately seek to achieve your goals.

Preparing to create your vision

You don't have to *know* what your vision is in order to do the next exercise. Write the answers to these questions without thinking too much first. Just let your pen go. Allow your thoughts to flow freely.

What do you want to be when you grow up?

_____

_____

What do you do well?

_____

_____

What is your unique contribution to the world around you? What positive things have other people said about you? What have they thanked you for?

_____

_____

How do your answers to the preceding questions translate in the marketplace?

_____

_____

What would your ideal day look like if you could structure it your way?

_____

_____

To what are you willing to commit yourself?

_____

_____

The preceding question leads you to your vision statement. To answer this question, you should be very clear about the concept of *commitment*.

Making a commitment

Sure, you have an idea of what a *commitment* is: a binding obligation, a pledge, or a promise. But do you really know how to make and keep a commitment?

In our experience, people *want* to commit, but they lack the stuff to carry through with that desire. For example, people who say they want to be thin may really *want* to be thin. However, they don't exercise, and they keep eating too much of the wrong things. They don't want to be thin badly enough to commit to the steps they need to follow to *get* thin. The truth is, they *wish* that they wanted to be thin badly enough to *commit* to it. The first step is to commit. You must be so committed to your vision that you will do the hard work necessary to get where you want to go.

Upping the stakes

Here's my definition of commitment:

> If you don't achieve your objective, someone will cut off the index finger of your writing hand below the second knuckle.

This definition, which sounds harsh, grew out of a discussion with a resistant participant in a team-building seminar. She insisted she had done *all* the right things, and the "other guy" was *still* late on a report due to her every Thursday by 5:00. The "other guy," in this case, was a coworker in another department of her company, and she depended on his information.

I said to her "What do you do at 5:01 on Thursday when you don't get the report?" She said, "Well, I call him Friday morning and. . . ."

I interrupted, "Friday? What about Thursday? You needed it Thursday!" Just as I suspected, she called Friday to chastise him for not turning in the report. She was one of those people who prefers to have reasons for *not* getting a job done than to do whatever it takes to get it done.

I was so frustrated by her defeatist attitude that I spontaneously shot her this question: "What if the index finger of your right hand will be cut off

at 5:01 on Thursday if you don't have the report from him?" Her entire demeanor changed. She thought for a moment and said "Well, I guess if it were *that* serious, I might tell him that the report was due Wednesday."

The other participants vocalized approval, and a couple of them applauded. Then she started really getting into the exercise. She said, "Not only would I tell him it was due Wednesday, but I would probably be a lot nicer to him."

The class exploded in approval. One man raised his hand and said, "Yeah, you would probably want to know who was in charge of the material for his report in case he died before 5:00 on Thursday." Another person said "I would visit his office, ask about his kids, and make sure that the material for my report is in a fireproof filing cabinet."

The class was beginning to get the meaning of *commitment*. If the stakes are high enough, you change your behavior, even if it means taking extra steps — that's commitment. Feedback after the seminar indicated that, even with the people who seem most impossible, you can get what you want if you are committed to getting results.

Look at what you wrote in the previous exercise (in the section called, "Preparing to create your vision"). Now write out the purpose you see for your life. This is your vision statement. Make sure that what you write inspires you.

_____

_____

Now evaluate your vision statement.

What are the key words for you? _____

_____

Do you identify with and own this statement? If not, change it._____

_____

How does it strike your senses? If it's not quite bulls-eye, change it._____

_____

Keep adjusting your vision statement until you are satisfied. Revisit this chapter in one year. How has your vision changed? _____

_____

Planning your life — together

To be a successful negotiator at home, you must go through the same process as if you were negotiating in business. Writing visions, values, and goals for your family may not seem as natural as preparing the same statements for your business. But if you don't write these things out (or if you aren't specific enough when you do), you are setting yourself and others up for disappointment and frustration.

Visions with spouses or significant others

In a romantic relationship, your vision may be that both partners are fulfilled, that both are basically satisfied with the relationship, that both feel that they have room to grow and change, and that both admire and respect themselves and each other.

Your vision with your spouse or significant other may include a better future lifestyle, such as a bigger house or more spending money, and you may decide to work toward being able to afford that goal.

Visions for your children

Your vision for your children shouldn't include any specific profession — that's for them to decide. But you should have some basic vision for your children, such as to see them grow into good human beings: happy, fulfilled, and contributing to humanity.

Identify Your Own Values

Your *values* are the principles and standards you live by. They define how you regard others, and how you expect to behave toward the people with whom you interact. Figuratively speaking, values define both where you want to go and how you expect to travel.

Values also define your *limits:* the boundaries of behavior you will not cross. The clearer you are with your values, the more you understand what it is you cherish. Then, making choices about your goals becomes easier. To be a master negotiator, you must be able to look into your own eyes in the mirror *every* morning and know you are living up to your own standards. We discuss more about the relationships of values, goals, and limits in Chapter 5.

Negotiating a Family Mission Statement

At a family meeting, list:

- ✔ Activities we like to do
- ✔ Traits we want our family to have
- ✔ How we want our family and our world to behave

Then write your purpose. Here's ours

> "Our purpose is to love each other, believe in each other, and share our lives through reading, sports, family meetings, and other activities that contribute to our own and the world's caring, freedom, and opportunity."

Planning ahead, before you are in the middle of a stressful decision, is critical to keeping your head (and sticking to your values) in a negotiation. That's why we recommend writing your values down now. The values on your list are the stars to steer your ship by. We find it helpful to list our values in order of importance, because there are times in life when you have to choose between your values.

We only include the following list to demonstrate how to record values, not to imply that ours are any better than anyone else's. Your values must come from within you. Your list may not look very much like ours. The important thing is to think about the values that are constant for you as the vision you have for your life evolves. Here is our value list with a little editorial comment we find necessary for those values to have meaning in our lives:

- ✔ **Love:** We are committed to the health and well-being of our relationship.
- ✔ **Trust:** We care about how our actions affect each other, and we would not deliberately hurt each other.
- ✔ **Respect:** We consider ourselves and each other worthy, and it's okay for the other person to have thoughts, feelings, and opinions different from our own.
- ✔ **Appreciation:** We do not hold back appreciation for the other.
- ✔ **Affection:** We hug and kiss at least twice a day, every day.
- ✔ **Financial independence:** Although the joining of monies may change closer to retirement, we value our respective abilities to be totally financially independent of each other or anyone else.
- ✔ **Integrity:** We are honest (we do not lie, cheat, or steal) in dealing with each other and other people.
- ✔ **Contribution:** We lead *useful* lives that contribute to the health and well-being of others.
- ✔ **Responsibility:** When we unwittingly cause someone pain, we recognize it, admit it, and make amends.
- ✔ **Growth:** We are dedicated to self-growth and awareness. We know that we came into the relationship with our own baggage, and we don't argue from the point of view that one of us is a finished product and the other person is not.

Interestingly, even values you hold deeply must still be nurtured. Realize that merely holding values is not enough. You have to put some energy into being sure that you both adhere to them.

List ten values *you* live by. Don't worry about the order at first; just write them down. You can prioritize later.

1. _____

2. _____

3. _____

4. _____

5. _____

6. _____

7. _____

8. _____

9. _____

10. _____

One of the most enjoyable things about traveling is noticing how values change around the world and how they impact negotiations in various countries. We were on a train going from Mexico City to the Mayan ruins near Merida. The train made an unscheduled stop. After half an hour, we learned that the engineer had stopped to take care of some family business. Nobody thought that was inappropriate. Everyone just waited patiently. Family values override just about all other considerations in Mexico. Understanding this value when you negotiate in Mexico may prevent you from feeling snubbed. The deal isn't falling apart — it's just that the kids need to be picked up.

Even within the same family, differences in values exist — even if those differences only lie in how the values are defined. Your child's list of values will not look exactly like your own. Teach your children which values are *not* negotiable. Here are some examples of values that you may decide are set in stone:

- ✔ **Education:** When college attendance is expected from early childhood, the likelihood of a child receiving a college degree is greater.

- ✔ **Health and safety:** For example, being strapped into the car seat is not negotiable for a two-year-old.

- ✔ **Honesty:** Both our mothers stressed telling the truth. We passed on the same lessons.

- ✔ **Responsibility:** This means owning up to mistakes and making amends when necessary.

A big part of negotiating with children is providing guidance; that is, parenting. Many children are given *way* too much responsibility for negotiating before they can even pronounce the word.

Decide How You Are Going to Get There

Okay, having a vision and knowing your own values is great, but you need to know how you're going to get where you want to go. You have to set a path for yourself so that you can eventually live in that picture you have in your head.

Note that values even come into play in the business world. Big and small companies must be specific when translating their missions into action. Think of the *values* (those things that are treated with importance and respect) affirmed by McDonalds. This chain's clean, well-lighted restaurants have brought it success. Consider Blockbuster Video stores. Unlike many, if not most, video stores, Blockbuster doesn't have an adult-movie section. That feature has made Blockbuster a safe place for parents to send their kids to pick up videos. Granted, Blockbuster isn't the only company that refuses to carry these materials, but this policy is an example of the interplay between the corporation's vision, values, and action plan.

In this section, we are talking about making a life plan. See Chapter 5 for a detailed discussion of setting goals for a specific negotiation.

The five-year plan

To negotiate effectively, you need to know why you are engaged in the negotiation in the first place. During the Cold War years, many Americans scoffed at the Soviets for developing five-year plans, complete with production quotas for every individual company, every industry, and every segment of the economy. We now know that five-year plans are an excellent tool for your personal life.

Maybe five years from now you won't achieve everything you planned for, but if you don't give any thought to what you want to accomplish over the next five years, you don't stand a chance of attaining much of anything. Most people who aren't happy with their lives and what they accomplished during the last five or ten years never bothered to look forward and develop a plan for that time period. Don't let that happen to you. Make a five-year plan and then make sure that your negotiations contribute to achieving that plan.

Close your eyes and picture your ideal personal and business life for the next five years. Try for a picture that includes both the personal and professional aspects of life. Think about ways in which you hope to have helped others, how you would like to have impacted your community, what you and your family want to be doing, what business you will be in, how successful you will be, where you will be living, what car you want to be driving, and what your yearly income would be. Imagine how your family will contribute to society and to each other. Use the space below to describe your vision.

_____

_____

_____

_____

The larger context decides specifics

We were teaching a negotiation course at Sheila Cluff's resort, The Palms, located in Palm Springs. We had just added the encouragement about making a five-year plan to the introduction of the course. We felt disheartened as a hand shot up, because the questioner had an annoyed look on her face. "I came here because I wanted to negotiate the purchase of my next car. I've been unhappy with my last two purchases. Will you be addressing *practical* things like that?"

"We just did," was our immediate response. The woman was nonplussed. "I'm sorry, I guess I missed it," she said. Suspecting she hadn't missed a word, we asked her what kind of car she was thinking of getting.

"I'm not sure," was her predictable reply. We asked her a series of questions about her life and where it was going, such as how soon she was planning to retire, whether she was staying at her present job, how far she drives to work, and what community activities she was involved in.

The answers defined the cars that would fit her needs within four or five models, two or three years of manufacture, and even the fact that she needed a subdued color. She became very excited and felt that she had already saved weeks of shopping and agonizing. Our point about reflecting on your own life before you enter any specific negotiation was so well made by this exchange that some of those in the audience thought we had planted the woman in the audience.

Randy Riley, our friend and relative who restates his vision every January, also develops an action plan every year. This guy spends a great deal of time planning his life. And the effort pays off. He doesn't always achieve his goals, but he sets them, he holds himself accountable, and he keeps trying. The consequence is that his financial goals are already basically achieved. Sometimes, he works only four days a week, meaning that he gets to spend more time with his three boys and lovely wife than most men spend with their families. And he gets recognized at his company's national meetings for outstanding achievement.

Think big

Step one in achieving great results is to think big. In every aspect of a specific negotiation and in planning your life, think big. You can always scale back later. This is your life. When the next year goes by, it will be gone. You don't get to do it over again. So take off the ball and chain; don't let your life be shackled by small thoughts. You can never get more out of life than you choose to.

Think bold

In addition to thinking big, you need to think bold. When your vision seems very distant — when the road seems all uphill — you have to be very creative. Try tackling the problem in a different way to reach a solution. The *problem* of figuring out how to make your vision become a reality is really an *opportunity.*

Many fun puzzles and riddles have been developed to demonstrate the same thing: To solve life's knottiest problems, you have to think outside of the box. One of our favorite puzzles is to place nine dots on a sheet of paper (three rows of three dots). Without lifting your pencil, draw four straight, connected lines through all nine dots. Go through each dot only once. Keep at it. If you get frustrated, relax and let your imagination flow. Think outside of the box. Play with it. The answer is on the next page.

Think in sound bites

We used to discourage students from using catch words and phrases during life planning. We thought that a life plan ought to be more tailored and personal. Over the years, we have learned individually and together that some phrases act as strong guideposts. They are particularly helpful in getting some complicated concepts across to others in seminars and lectures. We list a few of our favorite tips for life planning. We like to offer these phrases after people have established their mission statements, and before action plans are designed.

- ✔ **The tyranny of "or":** As people make life plans, they often ask themselves whether they want This *or* That. Try to use the word *and*. The word *or* is limiting. The word *and* is expansive. Frequently, finances require that people choose between desired purchases. When you make a life plan, however, include everything you want in life. You only get one chance to live this life. Live it free of the tyranny of or.

- ✔ **The banishment of "just":** Whatever you do in life, do it well and with pride. Never again say, "I am just a housewife" or "I am just a baker" or "I am just. . . ." *Just,* as an adjective to describe one's life work, should be banished from the kingdom. After you have established your vision, never diminish it with a *just.*

- ✔ **The law of parsimony:** You have limited time in your life. You can't help everybody. Only help the people who can *use* your help. Those are not necessarily people who *need* your help. Needy people, who would love to distract you from your life purpose, pop up all the time. Your job is to keep a steely eye on those goals you want to achieve for yourself and your family.

Putting it into action

After you are clear about your vision and on the path to that vision, the next step is to create your action plan. Your action plan includes the specific tasks you need to do, whom you need to help you do them, and when you need to get each step done. Action plans make you more efficient and effective. They enable you to anticipate needs, potential problems, and the time necessary for each step. The process of creating an action plan brings to light any potential obstacles that you may encounter in completing the steps. Then you can be clear about what you need to do to overcome these obstacles.

Married priorities

Our first priority as a married couple is time alone with each other, because it seems we never have enough. What you lack, you most desire. When it comes to sharing our time with other people, there are priorities we can list: beloved friends and family, theater, movies, and so on.

If the activity in question is not strictly for pleasure, we ask ourselves this question to decide whether we should go: "Is it good for business?"

Our vision, values, and agreed-upon goals help us to be clear. Because we are both entrepreneurs, we invest our time in growing and improving our businesses. Sometimes, our leisure preferences and professional goals coincide. For example, we go to opening nights at Los Angeles's most prominent theaters, the Mark Taper Forum and the Ahmanson, because we love theater *and* because both theaters are clients of Michael's.

Here's how we recommend that you create your action plan:

1. **Prioritize each of your goals.**

2. **List the action steps required for you to accomplish each goal.**

3. **Identify people you need to support you to achieve each action step.**

4. **Identify potential obstacles to each of the action steps.**

5. **Estimate the completion date for each of the action steps.**

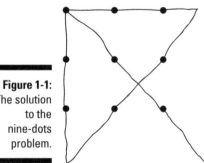

Figure 1-1:
The solution to the nine-dots problem.

Looking at Figure 1-1, you can easily see why solving this puzzle is called "thinking outside the box." Now when someone tells you to think "outside the box" or "beyond the nine dots," you'll know where the phrase comes from. Take the exercise one step further. How could you cover all nine dots with a single straight line?

Answer: Use a paintbrush!

Chapter 2
Preparing for Success

. . . .

In This Chapter
▶ Preparing for a negotiation
▶ Developing a negotiation checklist
▶ Getting ready to negotiate in another culture

. . . .

*P*reparing may be the most critical of the six basic negotiating skills. Perhaps a better title for this chapter would be "Prepare, Prepare, Prepare." That's how important this skill is.

Good preparation forms a solid negotiating foundation, giving you the confidence you need to negotiate successfully. If you prepare adequately, you approach the negotiation from a position of strength. Armed with facts and background information, you can correct any perceptions that you are weak.

The act of preparing continues throughout a negotiation and, indeed, throughout your life. If you listen well during a negotiation, you uncover additional information that may not have been available from any other source. What's more, if you confront the same subject matter in future business transactions, the benefits of this preparation can continue long after that particular negotiation is over.

Most people take the path of least resistance. Preparation is one of the first places that busy people cut corners. Therefore, you can give yourself an enormous advantage just by taking the time and expending the effort to prepare properly for a negotiation.

Pop quiz: How prepared are you?

Here's a little quiz to find out how well you tend to prepare for a negotiation:

✔ In preparing for a negotiation, do you often consult an outside source for information?

✔ List five resources, other than your personal knowledge and intuition, (books, people, or periodicals) that you used during the last year in preparing for a negotiation — any negotiation.

✔ Name the five most widely recognized sources of authoritative information in your profession.

✔ Of these five resources, how many are in your personal library or your office library?

✔ Think of your last negotiation. Try to recall five pieces of information that you learned during the course of the discussion. Could you have obtained that information before the negotiation ever started?

As you answer these questions, you can decide for yourself how prepared you have been in the past. No matter how good you are at preparing, you can become better. Time spent on preparation pays off in handsome dividends.

The One with the Most Knowledge Wins

Some people think that power comes from size, gruffness, or clout; but the easiest and most effective single thing you can do to increase your power is to prepare. You may be facing the greatest negotiator in the world, but if you are prepared, and the greatest negotiator isn't, you have the upper hand.

Yet people routinely shortchange themselves when it comes to preparation. Even experienced negotiators often sacrifice solid preparation on the altar of self-confidence or a crushing time schedule. Some negotiators don't fully appreciate the value of spending the extra time and effort on thorough preparation. To others, preparing just feels like drudge work.

Preparation doesn't have to be dull. Preparing for a negotiation can trigger the same type of excitement experienced when preparing for a military scouting mission. Your palms may not sweat, but the rush is similar. You are about to head into the unknown. The outcome is uncertain. Pulling together data is like girding your loins, checking your ammo, becoming secure, and getting ready. Prepare as though you are going into battle.

Playing Detective

You should know about all aspects of a negotiation before you begin. Identify the items that are most important for your next negotiation and get to work. The task breaks down into two major categories:

✔ **The issue under negotiation:** When you begin the actual dialogue, make sure that you know more about the subject matter than does the person with whom you are negotiating.

✔ **The person with whom you are negotiating:** Learn as much as possible about your counterpart and what that individual wants out of the negotiation. Leave no unanswered questions about your counterpart or your counterpart's client.

AT WORK

Mi Says • Mimi Says • Mimi Says • Mimi Says • Mimi Says • Mimi Says • Mimi Says • Mimi Says • Mimi Says • Mimi Says • Mimi Says

Firsthand knowledge is best

I learned early on in my consulting career not to assume that I knew what specific problems managers were encountering unless I visited the worksite myself. A production manager on the F-18 assembly line taught me this lesson. I was waxing eloquent about management theory based on praising employees to maintain good performance when I was interrupted with this inquiry, "Hey, you ever bucked a rivet?" I said, "No, what's a rivet?" The six other male managers in the class laughed, and I realized the real question was: Did I know what he was up against in that particular situation?

He explained what "bucking a rivet" meant. The process involves using a very heavy piece of hydraulic machinery, like an electric screwdriver, to drive a small screw-like piece of steel into the fuselage of a jet fighter. Hundreds of these things are riveted into each piece of steel. The riveter makes a horrible sound (many workers wear earplugs) and is extremely heavy. I said, "Well, I've never bucked a rivet, but I probably should." They all chuckled, and one

said, "Be at my station tomorrow at 6:00 a.m. in pants and soft-soled shoes. We'll issue you a hard hat and safety glasses."

It was a dare. I am 5 feet short and weigh not much over a hundred pounds. No manager had ever asked me to do this. That afternoon, I had to take the issue up two levels to the vice president of human resources to get the go-ahead. The next morning, I learned a great deal about the people this man supervised. I never would have dreamed of the things that motivated them; a short 15-minute break meant a great deal, as well as strong coffee and the availability of a certain kind of jelly-filled donut.

Since that time, at the beginning of my training career, I try *never* to teach about an environment I haven't physically seen, about people I have never spoken to directly. In my business, this principle is called *needs analysis*.

The very few times I tried to conduct management training about an unfamiliar environment, I was at a definite disadvantage.

Mimi Says • Mimi Says • Mimi Says • Mimi Says • Mimi Says • Mimi Says • Mimi Says • Mimi Says • Mimi Says • Mimi Says • Mimi Says

Part II of this book explains how to decide what you want out of a negotiation and how to organize your hopes, dreams, and aspirations with regard to any given negotiation. But before you move on to that step, gather the information mentioned in the preceding two categories. Remember: The negotiator with the most information wins!

Solving the mystery of value

Some types of preparation seem almost instinctive to many people. Every family seems to have a designated researcher. In our family, it's Debbie from Denver. Before we rendezvous for a vacation, Debbie prices out every hotel in the area and gathers information on restaurants. She is amazing. She actually enjoys making all those calls and being the repository for all there is to know about the area we are visiting, the room availability, and the reasonable cost of just about everything.

For others, the exercise is not so instinctive. If preparation know-how doesn't come naturally to you, try to make a game of it. If you are entering a negotiation to buy or sell a product or service, pretend that you're solving a mystery — the mystery of value. What is the product or service worth? Forget about the asking price — what is it *really* worth?

Begin with these two important facts:

- ✔ Value is always in the eye of the beholder. When you finish with your research, only you can conclude the ultimate value a service or product holds for you. You are the one who will be spending (or receiving) your money. You must decide.

- ✔ From diamonds to dime stores, experts compile price surveys and put out a report on the item's value; this publication is how insiders know what's going on in the world. Whether you are buying a hotel or a holiday in a hotel, you can find insider information on the value of the purchase.

Don't forget that values change over time. One important thing for you to decide, if you are a purchaser, is how long you're going to keep the item you are buying. The longer you plan to keep your purchase, the longer it needs to hold its value. Information about normal depreciation is as available as information on current value — usually in the same place. Knowing the rate of depreciation for an item is certainly just as important as knowing its current value.

As you gather information, be sure to keep good notes. You can't expect to keep all the facts you gather in your head. Good notes are easy to make as you go and can be invaluable as negotiations progress. Usually, one or two kinds of negotiation recur in your business. For those recurring negotiations, you may want to keep a separate notebook with the information you gather.

For example, if you are a service provider or a consultant, your time is your inventory. You may have a set fee (or fee range) depending on how much time you spend and how far away the contract takes you from your home base. (*Remember:* You usually can't charge for jet lag recovery time, but you expend your time nevertheless.) Keeping accurate notes can help you determine whether your fee structure is adequate or you need to demand more during future negotiations.

Consult Consumer Reports

Consumer Reports is an old stand-by. Don't overlook this valuable source of information when you buy any kind of consumer goods. From microwaves to mortgages, *Consumer Reports* has tested, rated, valued, and devalued a wide range of products and services. Why reinvent the wheel?

You can now order specific articles from *Consumer Reports* through a completely automated service called Facts by Fax. You no longer have to rummage through back issues of the magazines; just call 1-800-999-2793. After you get into the system, the service is very efficient. You can order specific reports, give your credit card information, and provide your faxing information — all without ever talking to a human being.

Browse online services

The Internet is a giant warehouse of information on any topic you can imagine. If you have access to the World Wide Web, we recommend browsing for information before you begin any critical negotiation. Chapter 23 discusses some Internet resources for negotiating in general, as well as some search tools to help you get to the specific information you need. You can also buy a directory of Internet locations, similar to a telephone book.

A great deal of the information on the Web is glorified advertisement put up by companies trying to sell you something. Don't assume that the material you find is objective just because it's on your computer. Dig deep into the pages to see whether the material is created by an objective resource or someone with a financial interest.

Visit the library

What a concept. The library is one of the most underused negotiating resources in your community. Reintroducing yourself to this great institution can be a blast. The library has all sorts of resources you can use to find the value of various goods or services.

When you go to the library, don't be afraid to ask for help. Most city libraries designate a staff person to assist in research. In our experience, we have found librarians to be among the most helpful people in the world.

Shop the competition

Don't hesitate to do your own research. Rather than read about value, pound the pavement for the information. A firsthand look can be a real eye-opener. Suppose that you're planning to purchase an apartment building. You may want to play the role of a prospective renter before ever offering to become an owner of the entire building. Walk through the neighborhood, visiting other apartment buildings. In an hour, you can become the world's leading expert on the price and availability of apartments in that block or two. Talk with tenants in the building you are planning to buy. That approach always produces more reliable information than talking with the owner or the owner's representative.

Whether you are buying or selling, a shopping trip is one of the best ways to educate yourself about price, availability, and quality considerations. We're not talking about buying — just shopping. Frankly, this is the only kind of shopping we really enjoy. The more we know, the better we feel.

Don't forget to make notes during your shopping expedition. You will be gathering a great deal of new information. You may remember most of it; but without good notes, you will not remember where you got the different pieces of information.

Ask questions

Even after a negotiation gets under way, you can continue your preparation by asking your counterpart questions. Some people are reluctant to ask questions because they are afraid of appearing dumb. This is false pride at its most expensive. You are flying blind without accurate information. You can't worsen your position by requesting information from your counterpart. Your job is to get a good outcome — not to impress the seller. If you have unanswered questions, ask.

Keep in mind that the answer you receive during a negotiation may or may not be accurate. Always accept it with respect . . . and then check it out for yourself. You have an obligation to be sure that any information you are relying on is, indeed, reliable.

What if you are out of your element? Don't try to hide your lack of expertise. If you are dealing with someone who is really knowledgeable in a field, and you are not so experienced, honesty — once again — turns out to be the best policy. Eventually, the differential will surface. It's better to reveal your inexperience yourself, and then you can ask all the questions necessary and request additional time to research the topic.

Remember, you don't have to make a deal until you are ready. Closing a deal is a voluntary act. Get your information from anyone you can — including the opposition. The more your counterpart wants to reach an agreement, the more quickly you will receive the data you need to make your decision.

Read insider reports

Take time to find out what the people in the business pay for the goods or services you want to buy or sell. This strategy can save you a fortune over the course of your life. Don't rely on what friends tell you, although they may provide good hints and direction. Go to the people who tell the merchants what to charge. Go to the source the insiders use.

No matter what the subject, someone has devoted a lifetime of work to evaluating and commenting on it. This is just a fact of modern life. Nothing is too arcane to study, dissect, catalog, and chronicle. Often, you find out about these insider reports from someone trying to convince you of just what a great deal you are getting.

- For automobile dealers, the bible is called the *Kelley Blue Book Auto Market Report.*
- Prices of gold and other basic metals are printed in the Sunday paper.
- The cost of money for almost anything (home mortgages and interest paid on savings accounts or car loans) is printed regularly in *The Wall Street Journal.*

INSIDE SCOOP

Michael Says • Michael Says • Michael Says • Michael Says • Michael Says • Michael Says • Michael Says • Michael Says • Michael Says

Finding the best deal

As I was shopping for Mimi's engagement ring, one anxious merchant whipped out a sheet of paper and waved it in my face. "See, you are getting such a good deal. Don't you want me to make any money?"

Bingo. Lights went off in my head. This must be the information I had been looking for — the report that the diamond trade relies on. (I had actually asked one merchant in the jewelry mart for such a report, and he looked at me as though I were crazy.) "Ah, you must be right," I said, reaching for the paper. "Show me how to use it," I asked innocently.

Although this particular merchant was trying to flimflam me, I was learning valuable information. The top of the sheet had the most important

information: *Rapaport Diamond Report* and a New York address. The organization of the information by size and quality of the diamond was self-explanatory.

I spent the next hour talking to merchants. When I began our conversations with some background knowledge (gained from the insider report) and a willingness to learn more, merchants treated me with more respect and offered more information about the diamonds. Eventually, I purchased an unmounted stone for cash (subject to a formal appraisal). I then had the stone mounted by a local merchant in the neighborhood. I was able to buy Mimi a substantially larger and better quality diamond for my budget than if I had gone blindly into a fancy jewelry store in Beverly Hills.

Michael Says • Michael Says • Michael Says • Michael Says • Michael Says • Michael Says • Michael Says • Michael Says • Michael Says

Stay informed

Prepare yourself on an ongoing basis for the most common negotiations in your life. If you sell boats for a living, you should know more about the kind of boats you sell than anybody else in the world. Attend boat shows open to the general public as well as seminars for the professional salesperson. Seek out the designers and manufacturers of your boats for detailed information. Talk with your coworkers over the watercooler. Take advantage of all these varied resources.

The quality of the advice and information you receive varies widely. Decide what to keep in your treasure box of information and what to reject, but keep exposing yourself to anything and everything that can increase your stockpile of information. You never know when some bit of trivia can become your secret weapon in a negotiation.

Researching your opponent

Even experienced negotiators who focus on preparation as a separate step almost always shortchange themselves in one area: They fail to gather enough information about the individual with whom they are negotiating. This person may be a spouse, a valued employee, or a vendor. There really isn't one word to describe that person; *opponent* isn't appropriate for many situations. Whatever you call this person, and we use several different labels in this book, find out all you can about that individual.

No boxer or wrestler would dream of beginning a match without studying the opponent's techniques, strengths, weaknesses, and idiosyncrasies. Such athletes carefully study scouting reports and films. They stage mock matches with partners mimicking the style of the opponent. Do yourself a favor by doing the same thing when you enter an important negotiation. Study the opposition.

Failing to learn enough about the person with whom you are negotiating is the most common mistake made in the preparation phase of a negotiation. In fact, people repeat that oversight everyday all across the country when making the largest purchase of their lives: the purchase of their own family home.

Don't buy houses from strangers

If you plan to buy a house, you probably have a checklist of requirements, such as the maximum down payment and monthly mortgage you can afford. Some Realtors even provide a form answering the most common questions about a house, including total purchase price, number of rooms, total square footage, age of the home, type of heating and cooling, siding material, and so on.

When you finally locate a house that meets all your specifications, you typically find out the asking price of the house. You may even ask about past offers or inquire how *soft* (how flexible) the price really is. If you're a more sophisticated buyer, you may obtain actual sales prices in the neighborhood for the previous six to twelve months.

With all this information, you should be ready to make an offer, right? Wrong. You still need to find out about the seller! The seller and, more accurately, the seller's situation are important ingredients in an accurate assessment of the marketplace. Find out why the seller is selling!

Make a conscious effort to answer these questions:

- ✔ What financial and other pressures is the seller under? (For example: Is a divorce involved? Is a change of job or city involved? When must the seller move? Has the seller already bought another house?)

- ✔ How long has the house been on the market? And how does that compare to the average time on the market for houses in the same area?

- ✔ When and for how much did the seller originally buy the house?

- ✔ What changes has the seller made to the house, and were those changes contracted out or performed by the owner?

You can best glean most of the answers through casual chatting with the sellers themselves, their real estate agent, or even outside sources. To obtain this information, begin by putting people at ease. Don't start with direct questioning like a prosecutor. That approach can turn people off. Lean against the fence and have a friendly, get-to-know-you kind of conversation.

We use the example of buying a house in our negotiating seminars for two reasons:

- ✔ A home is the most important purchase most people ever make.

- ✔ Realtors often act as professional gatekeepers — with a vengeance. Therefore, gathering information about the owner can be difficult.

You can always make direct contact with a seller. The owner of a piece of real-estate property is a matter of public record. If necessary, you can always go to the place where deeds are recorded, look up the identity of the owner, and call the person yourself.

Getting to know the seller pays off

My first wife's father was a real estate appraiser, so I invited him along to look at the house of my dreams. I had never bought a house before, and I was hoping he would be able tell me exactly what this one was worth.

Soon after my father-in-law arrived, I noticed that he was nowhere to be found. The rest of us continued the walk through the small, early California home. Thick adobe walls made the house cool on that hot summer day. Tasteful decorating gave it a soothing, peaceful feel. But where in the world was my father-in-law? We finished the tour and went out in the front yard. Still no father-in-law. His wife kept insisting that he was around, not to worry. Finally, he emerged from the neighbor's yard!

"Okay, let's go," he said.

My heart sank. He didn't even look at the house! We piled in the car. He then taught me the value of maximum information about the person with whom you are negotiating.

He told me about his chat with the neighbor. He learned that the wife, whom the rest of us had met on the house tour, did not want to sell. Her husband had moved almost a year before to take a job his psychic advisor said was right for him. Her psychic advisor told her to stay put. So she stayed behind, vowing not to sell the house to anybody until the right couple — one who really loved her house — came along! To keep the house out of the hands of just anybody, she kept the price high and made it difficult to see inside the house.

We had our work cut out for us, especially because the Realtor who accompanied us kept repeating her golden rule: Never let the seller know that you like the house.

My then-wife and I went back that night alone and told the lady that we adored her house; we really wanted it, but we simply could not afford her asking price — all true. We talked long into the evening about all the wonders of this cozy two-bedroom home that had been so lovingly cared for: The private garden, the spare room on the back lot. We talked of our first child, who would be born in the home. We never mentioned price again.

The next morning, we received a call from a surprised real estate agent who said we could buy the house. I protested that we had not put in an offer. We had not even discussed price or terms other than to confess our impecunious position.

"Never mind," said the agent. "We'll settle all that today. She wants to sit with you and agree on a fair price and then figure out how you can have the house. She will loan you the money you need on whatever terms work for you."

After we closed the transaction (on unbelievably favorable terms), the seller thanked us for bringing peace and tranquillity back into her life. Her husband had been losing patience with her. People were not even looking at the house anymore. She needed a way out of her self-made dilemma. We had given her a solution and made her happy.

I have since made many good purchases in real estate. I always take a little extra time to learn about the seller. I won't put an offer on the table without doing so. Depending on a variety of factors, I sometimes walk away. After I learned this valuable lesson, I never again bought a piece of real estate without substantial information about the seller.

Knowing the other party is preferable in a transaction in which money is exchanged for ownership of something tangible. However, you can always have the house (or car, painting, lawn mower, and so on) inspected by an expert. Then you have a pretty good idea of what you are getting. Knowing the owner is important but not essential.

The importance of knowing about your counterpart becomes crucial if the issue under negotiation is intangible. Services or intangibles such as the right to do something (cross land, publish a book, distribute a movie) require complete knowledge about the reliability, honesty, and ability of the other party. In order to work, long-term contracts and intangibles rely heavily on the other party. You simply must gather as much information as possible about your counterpart.

Don't undervalue information

Is all this gathering of information really necessary? If you are intent on collecting enough information, you are bound to gather some unnecessary scraps. However, having too much information is better than not enough.

What do you do with all that data? You use the relevant information to build a model of what the upcoming negotiation is going to look like. We draw an illustration similar to Figure 2-1 during our negotiating seminars. You can see graphically why information is critical and how the entire negotiation is shaped by your perception of your own position and the other party's.

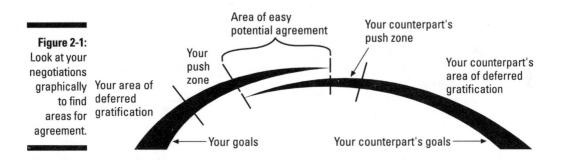

Figure 2-1:
Look at your negotiations graphically to find areas for agreement.

Note the large center portion of Figure 2-1 in which the agreement will most likely occur. This area represents the terms with the most potential for resolution; the parties can probably reach an easy compromise on these issues.

The areas to the upper left and upper right represent points of contention that require you or your counterpart to compromise more than is desirable in order to reach an agreement. We call these areas the *push zones.*

The area on the lower left represents goals that you may not be able to achieve during this negotiation. The area on the lower right indicates the goals that your counterpart may not be able to attain during the current negotiation. You and your counterpart may have to defer demands for these terms to future negotiations.

Taking gender into account

Most women in corporate America spend a great deal of time preparing for any given negotiation. This tendency is frequently cited as a good quality of women executives. But women need to prepare themselves in a special way for negotiations with men. They cannot talk to men in the same way they talk to women. Women must ignore two common myths to become good at negotiating with men.

✔ **Myth Number 1:** Men already respect you. Wrong. Women may already respect you coming in the door. They probably read your brochure and have specific questions outlined. But many men are going to make you earn their respect right at the negotiating table. Never assume that your credentials precede you and that your background, education, and brilliant maneuvers in your industry establish you before you walk in the door. Picture in your mind the male negotiator behind a big desk, clean surface, his eyes glittering, his arms outstretched, hands placed firmly on his desk, saying "So! Tell me why you should get my business!" He wants to play, and the game starts now. Every sentence out of your mouth must sell yourself or your company, in some way building your credibility and respect in his eyes. This self-promotion may sound like bragging. Even if it is, it's okay. Successful women long ago got over feeling offended at being called "pushy."

✔ **Myth Number 2:** Men are complex creatures. They are not. Men are very direct. They mean what they say, and they say what they mean with very few hidden meanings. Plan your communications with men to be short and to the point. Give them bullets and a one-paragraph summary of your conclusions. Most busy female executives prefer the precise, to-the-point style as well. But whereas women may engage in a side conversation and segue right back to business without missing a beat, men mostly talk about one subject at a time and don't switch back and forth.

Identifying the Right Person

You can't very well research the person with whom you'll be negotiating if you don't know who that person is. Finding out exactly which individual you're going to be negotiating with is critical to proper preparation. Sometimes you can choose the person, and sometimes you can't

Often, you are approaching an organization from the outside. Research the organization and make your initial contact as high up the organizational ladder as possible. It never hurts to have the boss's boss send a memo down the line asking for someone to give you an audience. The person you deal with won't know that you got the letter from cold calling and should treat you with the respect due someone who came in through the boss. Be sure to read the section in Chapter 14 about getting past the gatekeepers.

Working with what you get

Many times, you don't get to designate the person with whom you negotiate. More often than not, you end up negotiating with an assigned person.

Some people try to negotiate with someone higher up the corporate ladder than their assigned negotiator. That tactic usually backfires, because it violates the corporate culture within which the deal is being made. Besides, sometimes negotiating with a higher authority is downright impossible. You can't very well say, "Send me a sales rep I know" or "Hire a different Realtor if you want to sell me your house."

Be sure that the designated negotiator is enthusiastic about the final agreement and believes that the deal is good for his company or client. Turn that person into an ambassador for the agreement by negotiating hard, but in a friendly manner. Never lose your cool. After you reach an agreement, the person you are negotiating with has to sell the final result to his company or client. That person must feel positive about the outcome.

Choosing the person you negotiate with

In some situations, you really do have some control over which person you negotiate with. For example, if you're going to negotiate strenuously for a particular item in a small shop, you want to negotiate with the shop owner, not a summer clerk. (Of course, you should state this request gently so that you don't insult the summer help.)

If you don't know whether or not you're talking to the best person for the negotiation at hand, start with a friendly conversation. In the course of finding out how long the person has been on the job and what that person's previous experience was, you can make a pretty good assessment of how much authority — and flexibility — the person has. People who are new to an organization tend to have less authority and less flexibility than people who have been with an organization longer. If someone has been repeatedly passed over for promotions, you know that you're dealing with a person who may have frustrations and a lack of loyalty to the company.

There's no magic to finding a sympathetic ear

Consider the case of David Copperfield. The year was 1984. He was in the process of masterminding the largest illusion in the history of magic: He was going to make the Statue of Liberty disappear on national television.

The importance of the event to David and to his career was immediately apparent. Unfortunately, the Director of the Statue of Liberty hated anything that smacked of a commercial use of the monument. He told David that he would not permit him on the island to perform the illusion.

After David called me in to help, I did some research and discovered that the director's reluctance was a routine problem with this particular national monument. I knew that established guidelines and fees exist for using all national monuments in film and television projects. The solution was simply to identify a receptive individual who was senior enough to make a decision stick.

Fortunately, the Secretary of the Interior thought that Copperfield's proposal was a smashing idea, and he authorized the event. The illusion was one of the most impressive of Copperfield's distinguished career.

The trick to contacting people who seem to reside across a great gulf from you (either socially, geographically, or politically) is to start with the person you want to meet, not with your own circle of friends. Beginning with your friends if you want to meet the Pope or the President can seem like a daunting task — unless one of your friends happens to have an in at the Vatican or the White House. Barring such a lucky connection, begin instead with the person you want to contact and work backwards toward yourself.

Getting through to the Secretary of the Interior may seem like a magical feat on the order of some of David Copperfield's illusions. From an ego point of view, I may enjoy leaving that impression. However, the truth is that it was the natural result of lots of old-fashioned hard work.

Obtaining an organizational chart of the Department of Interior and the Parks Department required a simple call to my local Congressperson's office. The chart showed who reported to whom all the way up to the Cabinet level.

My next step was to discover the decision-maker's willingness to override the Director of the Statue of Liberty Monument. So I needed a preliminary, delicate conversation before I ever put the question of David's request on the table. I felt that this dictated my personal contact rather than an intermediary. In other words, I was not able to use any political friend to intercede. I had to make the call personally.

The task was simply to make a series of tedious phone calls. I started each call by identifying myself. Then I explained who David was and what he wanted to accomplish. These were all cold calls; I talked to whoever answered the phone.

I decided to start at the top and work down. By cold calling first the White House and then the Department of Interior, and shmoozing with staff members over two weeks, I learned a great deal about the viewing tastes of various officials, including the President and his wife.

Finally, a staff member of the Secretary of the Interior responded so enthusiastically that I was able to obtain a general letter of endorsement over the Secretary's signature without ever speaking directly with the Secretary himself. After that, getting permission for the illusion was merely a matter of processing the paperwork through regular channels.

How do you get to the head honcho? For starters, watch John Guare's play (or the wonderful movie it was made into, starring Stockard Channing and Will Smith) called *Six Degrees of Separation*. It's based on the true story of a street hustler who successfully convinced several members of the upper crust of New York City that he was both a school friend of one of their children and the son of Sidney Poitier. He obtained money, meals, housing, clothing, and enough information to move on to the next high-rise and repeat the scam. The victims were too embarrassed to report the matter until one couple went up to Sidney Poitier in an airport to tell him how much they enjoyed having his son at their home. They learned that Poitier has no son!

The title *Six Degrees of Separation* comes from the theory that only six people separate you from anybody else on Earth. It's a great concept; it also happens to be true. We're not suggesting that you go out and perform an elaborate hoax like the one in this play. But we are suggesting that the theory behind this story is correct — and, when it comes to negotiating, this principle can really work for you. Say you want to talk to the Minister of Commerce for Germany. The Six Degrees principle states that you know or can effectively contact someone who is the first person in a six-person chain that leads directly to the Minister.

Preparing for someone you know

When it comes to gathering information about the other party, every day is different. Don't assume that you can commence any negotiation without special preparation, no matter how well you know the person. When a seasoned purchasing agent sees a regular salesperson, the purchasing agent often opens the conversation by saying, "What's going on with you these days?"

Pleasantry or preparation?

A neighbor who's about to ask you to stop parking in front of her house begins by saying, "Hi. How is the family doing today?"

Pleasantry or preparation?

After the January 1994 earthquake in Los Angeles, even the least skilled negotiator first asked how the person on the other side had fared in the tumbler. No one pressed for resolution of matters until housing and offices returned to some normalcy.

Even if such questions have been a pleasantry for you in the past, start making them part of your preparation and treating the person according to the answer. I have actually put off a negotiation if the person sounded stressed out.

The Search for the Hidden Agenda

As you prepare for a negotiation, be alert to the fact that everything is not always as it seems. Maybe, besides buying what you have to sell, the buyer wants to establish a relationship with your company. Maybe the buyer wants to know how your business runs in order to enter the field as well. Maybe the buyer wants to teach another supplier a lesson. In the world of negotiating, these ulterior motives are called *hidden agendas.*

Hidden agendas are difficult to ferret out — that's why they're called hidden agendas! Without introducing paranoia into the process, be mindful of the possibility of hidden agendas. You rarely uncover them early in the process — or by asking directly. As part of your ongoing preparation, gather all the information you can about motive. The more you know about the other person's motive, the more you can create possibilities for yourself. Sometimes, you may even decide to walk away from a deal.

At work, the hidden agenda is sometimes hard to spot. On the surface, everyone should be working toward the same goal. The goals of the company are the goals of the individual: Better production, higher sales, or faster turnaround. But individuals within the company have personal goals in addition to the company goals. They want to get ahead within the company. Or they need peer approval. Or they desire neatness in the workspace. Their personal, secondary agenda is rarely stated. If it is, it is couched in the general statements about company goals. For example, someone wanting to get ahead in the company may volunteer to work overtime to get an important project done. Someone who needs to be liked may help a coworker attain a desired goal. These strategies aren't good or bad — just reality. The trick is to recognize these hidden agendas as early as possible so they can be considered for what they are.

Healthy families have little room for hidden agendas. However, children can often fall into *manipulative behavior* (which is just another label for working on a hidden agenda) when everybody else in the family is working on a family goal. Divorced parents often unwittingly promote manipulative behavior by being preoccupied with their own anger and hurt. For example, children of divorce often tell one parent that some activity is allowed at the other parent's house as a way to get permission at the moment. The child can count on the bad communications between the parents to prevent detection. The soaring divorce rate is probably giving rise to a generation of manipulators.

If you discover manipulative behavior in your own child, nipping it in the bud is important. This habit could plague your child throughout life.

A cousin to the hidden agenda is the *secondary reason* for being in the negotiation. Seldom does anyone have only one reason to be in a negotiation. For example, you are trying to sell your car because you want to drive a different (better or newer) car. But you also want to get the most money for your old car that you can. This is another, separate reason to sell your car.

If you make a good deal on your old car, you may be able to purchase the new car on desirable terms. The obvious example of this kind of three-way deal is the trade-in agreement offered at most car lots. You sell your old car to the dealer. The sale enables you to purchase a new car on acceptable terms. The dealer takes a profit on the sale of both cars.

The more you know about what is driving the deal from the other person's point of view, the more likely you are to come up with a solution that enables the deal to close to your benefit.

No hard-and-fast rules apply to every negotiation, except this principle:

> Keep your antenna out for all the information you can possibly gather about the people you negotiate with: Their motives, their hopes, and their needs.

It's ironic but true — you get more of what you want by being more attuned to what the other party wants.

Finding out what's on the test

For life's everyday negotiations, gathering information about your counterparts is key. To get what you need and want, you must learn their *hot buttons* — what turns them on and what turns them off. People won't be motivated to give you what you want unless something's in it for them. A key part of preparation is to find out what matters to your counterparts and how they can benefit from a negotiation.

Here's a little story I tell in class to explain how to motivate people. Once upon a time, you were in fifth grade, sitting at a little desk, listening to the teacher drone on and on, boring you to sleep. Suddenly, an obnoxious kid in the back row yelled out, "Hey, Teacher, is this gonna be on the test?"

You were so embarrassed to hear someone actually ask that question. Everyone avoided direct eye contact with the teacher. But you listened very carefully to the answer. If the answer was no, your reaction was probably to go back to sleep — it's not on the test. But if the teacher said, "Yes, this will be a very important part of the test," you straightened up, borrowed a pencil, and took notes — it's on the test!

Since those early school days, people do only what they perceive to be on the test. They do only that which promotes or satisfies their interests in some way. In school, the motivation was grades. Teachers got students to pay attention to what they were saying by putting it on the test. In adult life, the goal is money, happiness, or freedom from hassle.

Find out what motivates the person with whom you are negotiating. Then, during the negotiation, be sure that the other party understands how you can satisfy those needs. Put your priority on your counterpart's test.

Putting It in Writing

Make a mental checklist before commencing a negotiation. An even better idea is to write the checklist down. How elaborate or detailed your checklist is may change with the complexity of the negotiation, but the wisdom of writing it down does not. Even for a simple and straightforward negotiation, writing down the essential facts before you start negotiating is very helpful.

For example, if you are buying a used car, write down the value of the car you want most and your second choice (see "Solving the mystery of value" earlier in this chapter for a discussion of where to find this value). Also write down the asking price, time constraints, and some data on the seller's situation.

Even more important than writing down the information you gather about the subject of the negotiation is making notes each time you find out something about your counterpart. Lack of knowledge about the person with whom you are negotiating is the most common failure in preparation. The best way to avoid that pitfall is to retain whatever information you do have about the other party. Write it down. Save it. Add to it. This information is golden.

These days, you can let your computer do the remembering for you. Computers are great at remembering birthdays, the names of spouses and kids, and other information about the people involved in the negotiation. None of this information is irrelevant.

Why bother writing down the information you gather? Here are just a couple of good reasons:

- ✔ Research indicates that the very act of writing something down improves your chances of remembering the information, even if you throw the note away immediately!

- ✔ Writing down information gives you an easy retrieval system. If passion causes the seller to fudge the facts a bit, you don't need to challenge reality. You can merely say, "Let's check our notes." Read the original statements back. That approach is much less insulting than saying, "But you said. . . . " The latter frequently starts an argument that no one can win. The former generally settles or avoids an argument all together. Remember these words: "Gee, my notes reflect . . . but you said. . . . "

Think about your next business negotiation. Write down everything you know about the person with whom you are going to negotiate. This chapter includes an information checklist that shows how extensive the preparation about the person you are negotiating with can really be. Keep in mind that not all this information is necessary or even helpful in every negotiation, so tailor your information checklist for the specific situation.

Information Checklist

Fill out the following information about the person you plan to negotiate with:

Name:_____

Company:_____

What is your relationship to this negotiator?_____

How long with the organization?_____

Future plans with the company?_____

If planning to leave, when?_____ and to what sort of situation?_____

How qualified is this person for this negotiation?_____

What company policies exist with regard to this type of negotiation?

_____

How is the negotiator compensated? Is there an incentive program if money is

saved on this negotiation?_____

Is the compensation based on commission or straight salary?_____

What time constraints exist for the other side?_____

What other pressures originate from the negotiator's place of work?

_____

Who else must this person consult before a final decision can be rendered?

_____

Is there a cut-off to the negotiator's authority? That is, is there a point under which
the negotiator is authorized to close the deal and over which higher authority is
needed?_____

What is that point?_____

How is the negotiator for the other side perceived by superiors?_____

_____

What is the negotiator's attitude toward you?_____

    Your company?_____

    Your subject?_____

Who has made similar deals with this person in the past?_____

How can you contact that person?_____

What does that individual have to say about this negotiator?_____

_____

What is your overall assessment of this negotiator?_____

_____

Preparing to Negotiate across the Globe

If you are involved in an international negotiation, you must prepare for a whole host of issues. Most people have some advance notice if their business is heading in the direction of an international negotiation. If you have an inkling that international negotiations are in your future, start early to gather as much information about the culture, laws, and business practices of the nationality with whom you are negotiating.

The people who negotiate best in a culture other than their own have usually had the good fortune to live in that culture for a part of their lives. If they are really lucky, they were young at the time and could absorb the culture without judgment. If you weren't fortunate enough to have lived in the same culture as the person with whom you are negotiating, you have some extra prep work to do.

It's one thing to read a briefing paper about a culture that is different from your own. It's quite another thing to absorb that culture so that you can move comfortably with its rhythm and its rules. Learning to respect a culture takes even longer. When you respect the culture and truly understand its people's roots, you advance a long way toward effectively dealing with the individuals within that group.

How to speak like a native when you aren't

International negotiations require special preparation, but the tools are out there. Read books about the history, geography, customs, and religion of the people with whom you plan to negotiate. Such specialized knowledge makes your international negotiations much less frustrating and more fulfilling. If your negotiations take place on your counterpart's turf, the knowledge you gain in preparing for the negotiation adds immensely to your enjoyment of any free time you have on the trip.

The sources for your preparation are wide-ranging. Here are just a few:

- ✔ Talk to your friends and business associates who have experienced the culture. We always get a kick out of telling people about our international travels.

- ✔ Read the many books that are available and watch travel videos as well as movies that take place in that culture.

- ✔ The Internet can provide an electronic gateway to other cultures. You can chat with computer junkies from other countries or just visit international Web pages.

- ✔ Many large cities have cultural centers sponsored by the foreign government or expatriates from the country you want to visit.

- ✔ Ethnic restaurants can be another fun resource. Chat with the owners. You often find out a wealth of information about your counterpart's country while learning firsthand about that country's food.

Particularly, spend time acquainting yourself with the nature of foreign government involvement in your transaction. Corporate executives in the United States complain a great deal about business regulation. Many Americans think that their own federal, state, and local governments are too involved in supervising businesses. Americans often have a tough time with the even greater involvement of some foreign governments in individual business deals. Americans are surprised when they see an official — often a high-level member of a foreign government — right at the negotiating table on many deals which would be considered purely private in the United States.

The more you know about the level of government involvement, the less troublesome that involvement will be. You never help your cause by being judgmental about such things. Life is different in every country in the world. There is no abstract right or wrong, just different ways of doing things. Research these variations before you leave so that you can return home with more of what you want.

Michael Says • Michael Says • Michael Says • Michael Says • Michael Says • Michael Says • Michael Says • Michael Says • Michael Says

Negotiating for bananas

In the early '60s, I set out to see the world. I had just hitched a ride from Saudi Arabia to Tripoli, Libya. I entered the main market area in sandals, shorts, T-shirt, and day-pack. Although I was starving, I watched the locals make purchases before I jumped into the fray. The food stalls required a minimum of negotiation. After observing the price of bananas for locals, I politely offered the same. The merchant demanded ten times as much. When I protested, the merchant flew into a tirade. I didn't understand a word, and yet I understood the message. Hungry and tired, I reached into my pocket to offer double what the locals were paying. The response was contemptuous. A crowd was beginning to gather. The hostility was palpable. I paid full price and withdrew — to the airport. I stayed not one more hour in this beautiful, but frightening, city on the Mediterranean.

As I waited at the airport for a ride to New Delhi, I learned that anti-Americanism was rampant in Tripoli. The nation had just had an open and honest democratic election with a high turnout. A young firebrand by the name of Mu'ammar Gadhafi was overwhelmingly elected. This was not a place to wander around for pleasure. So much for not reading newspapers while on vacation.

Regarding the price differential that exists in many third world countries between the local price and the price for westerners, my view is quite different today. Most of these places have no airport tax. No tax is levied on hotel rooms as is in many cities in the United States. Instead, the visitor pays a sort of visitor's "tax" on a purchase-by-purchase basis. I still want to know what the locals pay. Acquiring this knowledge is part of preparing for the negotiation. I never again boorishly insisted that I pay exactly the local price. I accept a visitor's tax.

Michael Says • Michael Says • Michael Says • Michael Says • Michael Says • Michael Says • Michael Says • Michael Says • Michael Says

How to research the right culture, subculture, or individual

Before you dive into your cultural research, you must first be sure to identify exactly what culture you are dealing with. We cringe when anyone asks about negotiating in Asia, as though all of Asia is a single culture. The differences among Japan, China, and Korea are enormous. You can't lump them together if you are going to prepare effectively. The Muslims and Christians who live side by side in Malaysia have very different values, even though they have a great deal in common by virtue of being Malaysian.

Within cultures exist subcultures. The code of cab drivers seems to be the same all around the world. Rickshaw drivers in the Orient, jitney drivers in Manila, or taxi drivers anywhere all have a penchant for driving the stranger along the strangest (and longest) route and charging whatever the traffic will bear. If that happens to you, you are just paying the price for not preparing. If you ask a taxi driver at Los Angeles Airport to take you to our home in Benedict Canyon and say nothing more, you go by freeway and pay about $8 more than we do. We specify three surface streets that are more direct, cheaper, and more pleasant.

As you gather specifics about the culture of the person with whom you plan to negotiate, don't forget that you must also prepare information about the *individual* with whom you'll be negotiating. Although a vender at a roadside stand may know only her own culture's traditions, you can expect a highly experienced international negotiator like Sheik Zaki Yamani, the former Oil Minister of Saudi Arabia, to know *your* style and play to it.

But I'm Not Ready!

Never commence negotiations until you are ready — until after you prepare. This is not a rule; it's a fact of life. Neither side should start negotiating prematurely. You can stumble around on an impromptu basis, but you cannot negotiate effectively unless you prepare.

If someone tries to begin a negotiation at a time when you are not ready, just say, "I'm not ready to discuss this yet." Better yet, listen. Effective listening, especially at the commencement of a negotiation, is often merely an extension of preparation.

If you listen when the other person talks, you can't lose. If you are called upon to respond, merely admit that you are not ready to negotiate and set a time to return with a response. You may also ask whether the other person wants to tell you anything else so that you don't lose an opportunity to gather more data.

If someone asks you to commence negotiating before you have finished your preparation, ask for the precise data you are missing from your preparation. Good preparation can be as simple as listening. Listening is one good way to pick up needed information. Listening is also how you turn an ambush negotiation into a roaring success. (Part IV deals with the many aspects of listening during a negotiation.)

One way you know that you are asking for an essential piece of information is the intensity with which the other party refuses your request. If the response to one of your questions is: "Oh, I can't tell you that," you know that you have asked for an essential piece of information. Keep digging. Get the answer either from that person or from someone else but be assured that the answer is important to you if the other side is trying to keep it from you.

Admittedly, you can comfortably stall and use the preceding technique when you are negotiating on behalf of a client or company. The other party knows that you have to get instructions from your principals, that you are part of a team, and that you can't go off on your own tangent.

When you are negotiating on your own behalf, you sometimes get a derisive response to an avoidance technique: "What do you mean you don't know what you want to pay?" or "How long will it take you to do the job?" The implication is that if you are the right person, you would know this information. This situation calls for the absolute truth, calmly stated. Take a deep breath and say, "Oh, I could give you a quick answer right now, but I'm not going to. I want to be sure that I give you a number I can live with, and I want to check with my associate." State exactly what preparation is needed and how long you think it will take.

Being specific reassures the other side that you are not just playing some silly negotiating game. You must treat your need to prepare with dignity and respect in order to have the other side adopt the same attitude.

Once the other party fully understands and agrees with your need for a little more time, you can say, "However, if you have a figure in mind I'd like to hear it." If you rush this important question, your refusal will just look like a reluctance to put the first offer down. If they don't want to make such an offer, try to find out why. This information can give you an interesting insight into the other party. For example, you may learn that company policy prevents the other side from making an opening offer or that they are not ready to enter into discussion either. You may decide that the whole thing is a bluff — that they really want to do business with someone else, so they don't dare make a firm offer to you. The reasons for their reluctance can be as informative as the information itself.

Chapter 3

Planning the First Session

· ·

In This Chapter

▶ Setting the stage for productive negotiation

▶ Deciding who should attend

▶ Making an agenda

▶ Getting yourself psyched up

▶ Making a great first impression

· ·

*W*hatever the subject of your negotiation, you face some common issues in preparing for that first session. Even if you are prepared for the issue at hand, you still need to decide where and when to set the meeting, what to wear, and what to do if you're having a bad hair day. Stage fright sometimes sets in no matter how well prepared you are. This chapter helps you prepare for that first meeting so you can walk through the door with confidence.

Controlling Your Environment

People often spend very little time considering the best environment for negotiating, and they rely on rules that make arranging a time and place difficult. For example, when both sides consider it gospel to negotiate in their own office, getting things started is impossible.

If your position is low on the food chain and you feel you have no control over the details of the negotiating environment, giving this issue some consideration is even more important. For example, the location in which you negotiate for a raise may already be set, but read on. The material covered in this chapter helps make even your boss's office a more receptive negotiating environment.

Negotiating on your home turf

Your own office often provides a powerful advantage, because it's your *home turf.* You have all the data handy. You have supplemental staff, should you need their expertise. It is, after all, your operational base. Your comfort level is going to be at its highest in that environment.

The home turf is so important to the Grundig Pump Company of Fresno that they built a series of guest rooms right at their factory and hired a staff to look after visitors. You can see the plant, negotiate the deal, and never worry about accommodations, meals, or anything else while you are in town. Grundig set up an ideal negotiating environment. The visitor is freed from the shackles of travel arrangements and home office interruptions. This setup represents the epitome of the oft-stated rule "always negotiate on your home turf."

But be aware that the rule of negotiating on your home turf is not set in stone. The more time you spend on the other skills covered in this book, the less difference it makes whether you are in your office or someone else's. Sometimes, meeting in the other party's office is actually better for you. If your opponent in a negotiation always claims to be missing some document back at the office, meeting there could avoid that particular evasion. Sometimes bulky, hard-to-transport documents are critical to a negotiation. In that event, the best site for negotiation is wherever those documents happen to be.

The most important consideration is to be in a place, physically and mentally, where you can listen. Be an unrelenting control freak on this issue — both for your sake and that of the person with whom you are negotiating. If you cannot concentrate on what the other person is saying, you cannot negotiate. It's a physical impossibility.

The site of a meeting is a critical issue if you are involved in high-visibility negotiations between nations. In that context, the choice of location can often have widespread political implications with the voters back home. Appearances take on a political meaning of their own that have nothing to do with the negotiating environment. The opposing leaders must maintain an image of power at home, so the location of a negotiation can involve Byzantine discussions.

Seating with purpose

Seating arrangements are the subject of many jokes, and sometimes the importance of seating can be overemphasized — but not often. Definitely do not leave seating to chance, in spite of the number of people who seem willing to do so.

Here are some seating tips:

- ✔ Sit next to the person with whom you need to consult quickly and privately.

- ✔ Sit opposite the person with whom you have the most conflict. For example, if you are the leader of your negotiating team, sit opposite the leader of the other negotiating team. If you want to soften the confrontational effect, you can be off-center by a chair or two. Sometimes the shape of the table or room gives you the opportunity to be on adjacent sides with your opponent, rather than dead opposite.

- ✔ Consider who should be closest to the door, and who should be closest to the phone. If you expect to use the phone or to have people huddling outside the negotiating room, these positions can be positions of power. The person nearest the phone generally controls its use. The person nearest the door can control physical access to the room.

- ✔ Windows and the angle of the sun are important considerations, especially if the situation generates heat or glare.

In your boss's office, avoid the seat where you normally sit to take instruction. If your boss has a conversation area, try to move there for the discussion about your raise. Sofas are the great equalizers. If your boss is firmly planted behind the desk, do two things:

- ✔ Stay standing for the beginning of your presentation so that you are meeting at eye level.

- ✔ When sitting, move your chair to the side of the desk — or at least out of its regular position. You want to make the statement that this is a different conversation than the normal routine of your boss assigning you a task.

Making it easy to listen

When deciding where to negotiate, be sure that both sides can listen to everything that's said. If your negotiating environment includes constant interruptions or overwhelming noise, listening may not be possible, no matter how hard you try to do so.

Interestingly, every book about negotiating a better sex life (and such books are legion, they just don't use the word "negotiate") emphasizes this point. Making the atmosphere conducive to negotiating for sexual activity is always the subject of clear and extensive discourse in such a book. The authors of such books uniformly recommend a quiet atmosphere without distractions or interruptions. See Dr. Ruth Westheimer's *Sex For Dummies*.

Michael Says • Michael Says • Michael Says • Michael Says • Michael Says • Michael Says • Michael Says • Michael Says • Michael Says

Chickening out

My worst experience with a lousy negotiating environment was during the sale of the largest chicken ranch in California. My client, the potential buyer, invited me out to the ranch for the final negotiation. From the directions, I knew the place would be about as pastoral as it gets in Southern California. The ranch was built away from freeways, flyways, and functioning industrialism to encourage the chickens to maximize production.

The location exceeded my expectation for rural solitude. There was even a pleasant office, large enough to hold the entire group. Our host, however, thought that a nonstop walking session was the best venue for settling the deal. On the contrary, with the dust, the disorganized clumps of people traipsing around the property, and tens of thousands of chickens complaining nonstop about their cramped quarters, all he accomplished was to thoroughly confuse and wear out a previously receptive group of people.

Unfortunately, time to close the deal had almost run out, so another day of negotiating was difficult to organize. I tried to salvage the situation by suggesting that I host dinner. I asked for a quiet place, and I told everyone not to worry about the cost. I wanted this to be an enjoyable treat.

"Be sure to ask for a table where we can talk," I hollered after our host as he entered his office to call what he considered to be the perfect place.

At dinner, we could talk all right — to everybody from about ten miles around. This was the neighborhood watering hole. We were never alone. Everyone knew our host — a real disaster. The deal never closed. We never bought the ranch. To this day, I wonder whether the foxy owner really wanted to sell to my clients. Personally, I don't think he did — too many three-piece suits for his taste.

Michael Says • Michael Says • Michael Says • Michael Says • Michael Says • Michael Says • Michael Says • Michael Says • Michael Says

Many times, people choose a lunch meeting to discuss important matters. In our culture, meals are inherently social. That makes lunch meetings good for developing relationships, bringing people together, and getting to know one another. However, meals are generally not a good time to negotiate anything of any importance. First, many a trendy restaurant is synonymous with noise. Second, restaurants are rife with uncontrollable inquiries concerning your desires, the quality of service, and the ultimate aggravation concerning water replenishment, of all things.

Planning the environment far in advance

If your company is building a new space, get involved in planning the room where most of the negotiating occurs. Fight hard to make it the right size, near the restrooms, and near some break areas. Everyone has a tendency — during these days when money is hemorrhaging all over the place — to cut back on the negotiating space because "we don't use it that much," or "we can make do with less."

All this is true. However, if you consider how important selling is to your company, or negotiating major deals to your law firm, or closing a transaction to your bank or real estate business, you cannot overrate the value of this space. This location is the heart of your business. Maybe the executives can "do with less." Oops. Don't make that suggestion unless you happen to be one of the executives. Perhaps, with a good design, you can create additional space for negotiation by scaling down offices that aren't used much.

In Los Angeles, one of the best-planned rooms for negotiating is at the law firm of Gipson, Hoffman, and Pancione. This space has everything and is only steps away from the kitchen and bathrooms. Figure 3-1 shows a sketch of the space:

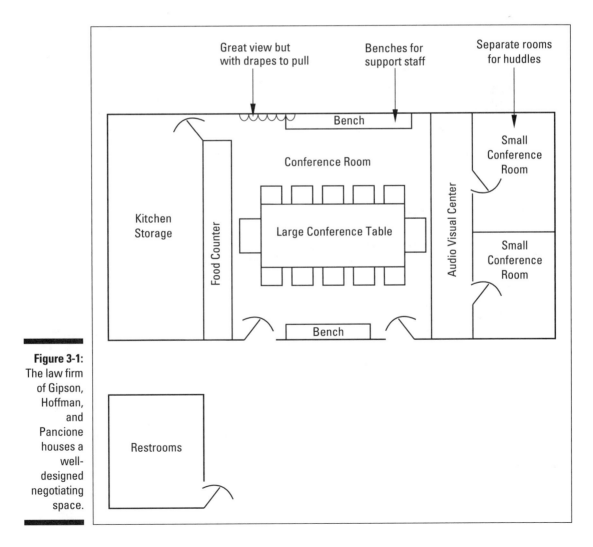

Figure 3-1:
The law firm of Gipson, Hoffman, and Pancione houses a well-designed negotiating space.

One of the best features of the floor plan in Figure 3-1 are the benches that line each wall. Designed for staff members, these benches are deep and comfortable. Many overworked young associates nap on them during long overnight sessions of preparing and proofing documents as a deal crawls toward its final moment. As fancy communication systems become the focus of planning the space, don't forget that human beings still have the same old needs to relieve, replenish, and rejuvenate their bodies.

Checking the Guest List

Who does or does not attend any given negotiation session can be the subject of some intense negotiations itself. For all the moaning about "one more meeting," some people get very bent out of shape if they are not included.

When you arrange a negotiating session, don't invite one more person than is necessary. (*Necessary,* in a negotiating session, means that the person has something essential to add to the dialogue that cannot be contributed by someone else.) Compensate for not being able to invite someone by sending that individual a memo. Paper is cheap. Extra voices at a negotiation session can be very expensive. Each person in attendance adds exponentially to the problem of control in communications. The chances of words being uttered when silence is needed rise sharply with each person added to a negotiating team.

Sometimes, you want to include a person with special expertise — an accountant, for example — in a single negotiating session, even though that person is not a part of the other sessions. Don't hesitate to bring in an expert to make a presentation and answer questions. However, it is most effective to have that person leave after all the information you want to share is on the table.

Research shows that female leaders tend to be more inclusive than males and more agreeable to group decision making and participatory management — a sort of "the more the merrier" approach. True, you don't want to leave anybody out. Nevertheless, when your purpose is to persuade another human being to do something specific, you don't want anyone there who doesn't contribute to that result.

In a family situation, calling a meeting can be very helpful in making decisions. Especially with kids (who often negotiate by manipulation), having everybody in the same room at the same time is a good idea. This arrangement avoids the message being modified as it's carried from Mom to Dad and back again.

If parents are divorced, having everyone in the same room is even more important. The opportunity for a child to embellish on a parent's word is even greater if the parents are living apart from one another. The parents and kids may want to meet with a professional counselor and discuss these concerns. Otherwise, the side issues between the adults may get in the way of helping the kids.

Setting an Agenda

Agendas are wonderful control devices. An agenda makes it more difficult for the other side to avoid addressing an uncomfortable issue. Creating the agenda is an advantage to you even if you are not in charge of the meeting. If you don't want to, or aren't ready to, discuss a certain topic, leave it off the agenda. Alternatively, you can include a related topic.

The written word has real power in our society. A written agenda in front of all the participants in a meeting has a power and an authority all its own. A plan also brings clarity to a meeting. By providing what amounts to an outline for the meeting, a written agenda inspires people to take notes on what is happening.

Creating the written agenda can be an art form unto itself. Here are some guidelines:

1. **Scrawl out all the things you want to talk about and everything you want to find out that you don't already know.**

2. **Check off the items you want on the written agenda.**

   Information you want to extract from the other side goes into your private notes, not on the written agenda that goes to everyone at the table.

3. **When you know what you want to talk about, determine the order.**

   Starting a session with things that are less emotional and easier to reach a consensus on is usually best.

4. **Make enough copies of the agenda for everyone at the meeting.**

   Make extra copies for people who wanted to attend but could not or were not included. Make extra copies for notetaking and filing.

In family meetings, agendas work the same way, except you need to involve everyone in the agenda-setting process. The first event in a family meeting would be to ask each child what he or she wants to talk about. You may add an item or two and then ask about the order in which to talk about things. This process can be helpful when emotional issues are involved. This approach lets everyone know right away that whatever they want to talk about will be dealt with in order and with due respect — after all, it's on the list!

The psychology of meeting planning could span volumes. The easiest shortcut is to set your agenda intuitively. Then close your eyes. Picture the table. Envision the faces. See the meeting start. Play it through in your mind. Create a comfortable rhythm to the meeting.

Remember that an agenda *suggests* the order in which issues will be discussed but does not dictate the order. If controversy arises on a particular point, an agenda makes it easy to move past the point and come back to the dispute later. An agenda also prevents such sensitive points from being permanently swept under the rug. Don't be upset if someone else reorganizes your perfect order, especially if you are not in charge of the meeting.

Don't underestimate the value of an agenda, both for creating control and ensuring that all the essential issues get addressed.

Leaving Enough Time

How much time to allocate for a negotiation session or for the entire negotiation is always a tricky matter, because you are not in control of the other side. If you want to have the negotiation over by a certain time, say so right up front. If a good reason exists for your desire, state that also. Leaving more time than you actually need for a negotiating session is always better than allocating too little time. You can always use the extra time for something else if you have over-estimated the time that a negotiating session will take.

Generally, an international deal takes longer to complete than the very same domestic deal. Be prepared to spend twice as long to complete such a deal. Several factors create a need for this extra time.

- ✔ Both sides proceed more cautiously as they assess the cultural differences between the parties.

- ✔ Language differences take time, even if both parties are speaking the same language but with different accents.

- ✔ Fatigue sometimes sets in when a host pushes a special event each evening — as is common when entertaining visitors from abroad.

Don't forget to take into account the different attitudes toward time around the world. The British have a very formal relationship with time. Everything from plays to trains must commence at the exact appointed time. Mexicans have a more casual relationship with time. Start times are more likely to be approximate.

Preparing Yourself

You are the most important single element in this negotiation. Even if you are the assistant to the assistant to the assistant, your performance at the negotiation is more important to you and your future than any room, agenda, or seating arrangement. Do not shortchange yourself. Take some time out of checking on all the arrangements to check on yourself. This concern for self is an important investment that pays off handsomely.

A is for Alert

To negotiate at your best, you must be well-rested and alert:

- ✔ You're more likely to be quick-witted and able to respond to questions or attacks.
- ✔ Your concentration and ability to listen are improved.
- ✔ You won't be rushing to tie things up so that you can get home or get to bed.

We instituted the Ten o'clock Rule for certain topics such as money issues or our children's discipline. These subjects tend to start arguments that are not quick to resolve. We now agree not to begin a conversation on anything on this short list of subjects after 10:00 p.m. We find we can always defer these discussions to the clear light of the next day. That way, we protect our time together and get a good night's sleep. Often, the issues don't seem so volatile the next day, anyway.

Your performance at any negotiation is aided by a good night's sleep. Sometimes, getting that sleep is easier said than done. If you find yourself thinking about a negotiation just when you want to go to sleep, try this trick: Pull out a pad and jot down your thoughts. Keep going until you have cleaned out your mind. Often, this exercise enables you to doze off and secure some much-needed sleep.

Dress for success

Two books have had considerable impact on what people wear in order to get power and respect. These books are geared toward the professional, but they have a much wider application if you read between the lines. The first book, *Dress for Success* by John T. Molloy, chauvinistically addressed only the males among us. The book's popularity led to a sequel, *The Woman's Dress for Success Book*. Both are valuable aids to rising young stars. The theory of both books is to look *at* the boss in order to look *like* the boss.

ael Says • Michael Says • Michael Says • Michael Says • Michael Says • Michael Says • Michael Says • Michael Says • Michael Says

Traveling smart

As a young man, I always took the red-eye to New York, and I set my first negotiation session for a 7:30 a.m. breakfast. I now prefer to have some time to go to my hotel, shower and freshen up, and gather my thoughts for a 9:00 a.m. meeting. I attribute that changing preference to wisdom, not age. If you can't get enough rest on an airplane to function well the next day, travel the day before. Don't be penny-wise and pound-foolish when it comes to long-distance travel.

When going to Europe to negotiate, I always insist on one and preferably two days to get over jet lag. For some reason, going to Asia is less stressful on my body, and I can be ready more quickly. If possible, I never change planes on a business trip.

Michael Says • Michael Says • Michael Says • Michael Says • Michael Says • Michael Says • Michael Says • Michael Says • Michael Says

The startling response to John T. Molloy's book was that, all through the '80s, droves of young female professionals began wearing dark blue suits, white silk blouses, and big, crimson bows at the neck. Perhaps they were helping themselves up the ladder of success, but the necessity (or perceived necessity) for ambitious young women to transform their appearance in order to break into the good old boys' club saddens us.

Our recommendation is less restrictive and simpler: Don't dress to distract. You are in a negotiation. You want people to listen and you need their eyes as well as their ears. Women, you pull the eye away from your face if you wear dangling earrings or expose any cleavage. Men, you improve no business environment anywhere with gold chains or a sport shirt open to reveal that remarkable chest. Although this attire may get you attention elsewhere, it doesn't contribute one bit to your negotiating position.

If a particular type of outfit works for you on vacation or at a party, more power to you. But don't confuse those casual social environments (which may very well include a bit of negotiating in the course of an evening) with the negotiating environment of the business world.

As you prepare yourself for your first negotiating session, we can give you no better overall advice than to *mirror your environment*. Respectfully absorb that which is around you. Sink into the surroundings. Become a part of them. Some negotiators even adapt to the pace of the speech. In New York, where people tend to talk fast, good negotiators speed up their pace a bit; in the South, where people tend to talk slowly, good negotiators slow it down a few notches. (Don't go so far as trying to take on the local accent unless you happen to be Meryl Streep.) Above all, know that good manners are different from place to place. When in Rome, do as the Romans do — out of respect for the Romans, not to one-up them.

Mimi Says • Mimi Says • Mimi Says • Mimi Says • Mimi Says • Mimi Says • Mimi Says • Mimi Says • Mimi Says • Mimi Says • Mimi Says

Dressing to build rapport

In business negotiations, you want the other parties to consider you to be a person they can connect with, someone who understands, someone who is *simpatico*. Part of appearing *simpatico* is dressing like the client dresses. When I worked in the aerospace industry in the early '80s, I wore conservative navy blue, gray, and black suits just like they wore. Even now, I call my navy blue suits my "financial industry suits," and my red suit with silver and gold thread design on the sleeves my "retail industry suit."

I wore a pants suit with artsy jewelry to the first negotiation meeting with an artsy, architectural firm in their beachfront, converted-garage office. And, sure enough, the firm's female owners were wearing pants and artsy jewelry. Wearing a business suit would have actually separated me from the client and maybe alienated me. Sometimes, a power suit is jeans and a sweater, if that's what your counterpart is wearing.

Mimi Says • Mimi Says • Mimi Says • Mimi Says • Mimi Says • Mimi Says • Mimi Says • Mimi Says • Mimi Says • Mimi Says • Mimi Says

Walking through the door

No matter how sleep-deprived, harried, or down-in-the-dumps you may be, always enter the negotiating room perky and assertive. Establish confidence and control from the opening moment. That moment sets a tone for the entire meeting. This fact is true even if you are not officially in charge of the meeting. These guidelines can vault the most junior person at a meeting to MVP status almost immediately.

Never forget the pleasantries. If the last negotiating session ended on a bad note, clear that away first. Otherwise, you run the risk that unrelated matters may ignite the controversy all over again. If you can resolve the situation up front, you can move forward unfettered. Ignoring such a situation just leaves the ill-will hovering over the negotiating table. The bad feelings creep into and influence every conversation. The negativity taints all the proceedings until it has been cleared away.

As your hand is on the door of the negotiating room or after you have dialed the phone number of your counterpart, put on your attitude. Take a beat and lift yourself up to the occasion. Grandmother was right — "Anything worth doing is worth doing well." Toss your head back — literally. Smile, inside and out. Focus on your immediate purposes. Have your right hand free to shake hands with whoever is there. If the meeting requires you to wear one of those awful name badges, be sure to write your name in large letters and place the badge high on your right side so that people can easily read it.

Improving your attitude just before the session begins can be one of the most valuable moments you spend in a negotiation.

Here are some guidelines for opening a meeting effectively:

- ✔ Make sure that all participants are present and ready to listen.
- ✔ State your purpose for having the meeting.
- ✔ State the items on the agenda and their time allotments.
- ✔ Make a clear request for agreement on the agenda and procedure.
- ✔ Acknowledge the participants' attitudes and feelings as they relate to your purpose.
- ✔ Summarize your desired outcome and begin according to the agenda.

Preparing for a Session with Someone from Another Culture

In addition to all the standard preparations that precede any negotiation, you must make some special considerations when you are negotiating with someone from another culture. Follow the tips in this section, but don't shortchange any of the other steps of preparation just because you are in an international situation. In fact, a good rule for international settings is: *When in doubt, be polite and considerate according to your own culture.*

Whom do you invite?

Knowing whom to invite can be a very delicate matter — get the help of an expert. Most big-city governments and every state have protocol officers that can give you some tips. We also recommend that you read culture-specific books, because practices vary all over the world. In different countries, the role of women ranges from purely secretarial to fully participating members. In some Asian countries, women participate fully during the business portion of the meeting, and then the men go out by themselves. If you aren't sure, you can defer to the lead negotiator from that culture. In fact, deferring to the lead negotiator in such matters can help you build rapport.

Hiring an interpreter

If you think that you and the other party may need an interpreter to communicate with each other, say so before you start the negotiation. Hiring an interpreter midstream could appear as a disparaging commentary on the other party's ability to be clear, or speak ill of your ability to understand what the other party is saying. If you have any doubt about understanding the other party (and if you can afford it, and if the size of the deal merits the expense), hire an interpreter early. After all, the other party won't be insulted if you later decide that you don't need the interpreter.

Interpreters work in one of two ways: *Simultaneously* and *consecutively.*

- ✔ **Simultaneous translation:** Working with simultaneous translators is expensive, but it's a heady experience. You feel as though you are at the United Nations. It's a little like being inside a badly dubbed movie. You have to watch the speaker for the body language and the facial expressions. For the words — usually delivered in a sort of monotone — you listen to the translator who is about two beats behind the speaker. As expensive and impractical as simultaneous translation is, the measure does lend importance to the negotiation.

- ✔ **Consecutive translation:** Much more common is the consecutive translator (also called a *delayed* or *sequential* translator). This type of translator listens to a response and then summarizes it for you in your language. Never hire such a person unless you carefully check references, preferably with people you know well. You need loyalty, confidentiality, strong technical skills, and a detachment from what is going on.

You may opt for the extra expense of a simultaneous translator if you need a translator. Having a simultaneous translator impresses the heck out of the opposing party. One way to hire simultaneous translators is to contact the local courthouse where such translators are common. You must work around the courts' schedules.

If you follow these simple guidelines, your first time out with a translator should be a positive experience:

- ✔ Never share a translator with the other side.
- ✔ Leave plenty of time to brief the translator before the negotiation begins. Treat the translator like a professional.
- ✔ Be alert to the translator's need for more breaks than you need.
- ✔ Never crack jokes for the interpreter to translate.
- ✔ Don't use slang expressions.
- ✔ Speak in short sentences using simple word choices.
- ✔ Never raise your voice.

Be alert to the possibility that the translator may be taking too big a role in the meeting, sometimes rising to the position of some sort of broker or agent. The biggest indicator that this may be happening is that the translator and the other subject will be talking back and forth without including you.

A funny example is the small film *Bottle Rocket*. The translator is brokering a conversation between an American surfer-type and his new, Spanish-speaking girlfriend — to humorous results. If you plan to use a translator in your negotiations, we recommend you rent this video. You'll laugh as you learn.

Usually, the situation can be immediately corrected by just telling the interpreter "not to get out in front" or "not to get ahead of you." You hired this person. A gentle reminder should do the trick.

How quick to the kill?

Be very sensitive about how quickly you turn the meeting from the informal to the business at hand. Every culture has its subculture, and even within that, individuals vary. Take the lead from the opposing party. Don't launch right into business unless you know that is what is desired. When in doubt, go slow.

In the United States, people tend to be eager to get down to business and seem to be in a constant search for the *bottom line*. In Japan, on the other hand, this kind of single-minded haste is considered disrespectful. For example, jamming someone else's business card into your pocket without looking at it may be common in the United States, but is highly offensive in Japan. If someone from Japan hands you a business card, look at it, read it, take it in, and then put it respectfully into a safe place such as a wallet or pocket that doesn't have a lot of other things in it. Never write on a business card given to you by someone from Japan.

Think of the films you watched in biology class about the mating ritual of certain animals: the gentle but definite dancing, singing, and investigating. When all the preliminary ceremony is done, the final moments can be quite brief. This is the picture we keep in mind during negotiations across any cultural barrier. When it is safe to talk about the deal, go right ahead. But don't rush the mating process; this ritual serves the valuable function of building comfort and trust.

If a meal is involved

We don't doubt that you, gentle reader, always remember your manners when you go out for a meal. But if the meal is with a foreign guest, you may have to *learn* new manners. This is especially true if the meal is on foreign turf.

In what country do you eat with your hands, but licking your fingers is rude? Where do you eat with your right hand, but never eat with your left hand? Where do you insult the cook if you do not slurp your soup? Where should you leave a morsel of rice on your plate to show that you don't want more food? Where do you pass the fork back and forth between your hands depending on whether you are cutting or moving food to your mouth? Ethiopia, Saudi Arabia, Japan, China, and the United States are the correct answers.

The point is that every country has its idiosyncrasies when it comes to eating. Even different households begin a meal differently, from a prayer to a toast to everybody diving in! It never hurts, in such circumstances, to wait a beat while the host leads the way. Follow the lead of the well-bred native.

Michael Says • Michael Says • Michael Says • Michael Says • Michael Says • Michael Says • Michael Says • Michael Says • Michael Says

Passage to India

I once negotiated with a producer from India in my office. My client was out of patience with this producer and, in anger, had said that this would be the last offer. He told me not to waste any more time. I shared his frustration. When I reluctantly put in the call to set the meeting, I had to listen to the producer complain about how curt my client had been to him. Then he complained about the last offer. I cut to the chase and set the meeting. In closing, he complained about how I had never accepted his invitation to have tea.

As I returned the phone to its cradle, I understood what he was saying for the first time. Unfortunately, that is often when inspiration dawns. In this case, however, it was not too late to fix a terrible mistake. The producer lived just outside of Pittsburgh, but he had immigrated to the United States from India as a young man. He brought much of his culture with him. Fortunately, I had traveled in India, including his hometown.

When Amin arrived at my office, we sat on the sofas in the corner. My assistant brought hot tea — steeped, not from a bag. We talked of many things, but not one word about his film. I must confess to getting a little antsy when we hit the half-hour mark. Our time together was almost up. We had verbally visited India, but we had not advanced my client's position — or so I thought. As if to stir me from my fretful reverie, Amin said, "You know, Michael, I could accept the entire deal if it were for one year and not five."

I was stunned. I took a deep breath, thanked him, and explained why my client needed five years. We went back and forth and back and forth. Finally, I came up with a contract term based on gross revenues, and everyone was satisfied.

Michael Says • Michael Says • Michael Says • Michael Says • Michael Says • Michael Says • Michael Says • Michael Says • Michael Says

Part II
Drawing Lines and Making Goals

By Rich Tennant

"Your time is almost up. If you don't agree to our terms,
I'm gonna head back to the corral."

In this part . . .

Before you start the negotiation, you have some soul searching to do. Setting limits is a life skill that comes into play at this time and puts you in charge of the negotiation. After you set your limits, you are ready to determine your goals and make your opening offer. How to make all these critical decisions is the topic of this part.

Chapter 4
Setting Limits . . . and Sticking to Them

. . . .

. . . .

*I*n negotiating, as in life, setting limits and then sticking to them is one of the most important and most difficult lessons you can learn. This chapter tells you how to set limits and then use those limits to take charge of every negotiation in your personal and professional life.

If you're like most people on this planet, at one time or another, you stayed in a relationship too long because you never set your limits. You agreed to do something you didn't want to do because you were unable to stick to your limits. Or you ticked somebody off because they failed to make their limits clear.

Set your limits before you enter a negotiation. Setting limits early saves an enormous amount of time during the actual course of the negotiation because you already know your options. And knowing your options makes you more decisive during the discussions. Rapid decision making depends more on having your limits well in mind at the start of a negotiation than it does on intellect.

After you set limits, establishing your negotiating goals (discussed in the next chapter) is much easier. Limits and goals are equally important. When you carefully and realistically predetermine your limits, they serve as rudders, guiding the negotiations through rough waters. Dirty tricks being thrown at you? Full steam ahead! Unfair tactics? Full steam ahead — as long as you set your limits and know your goals.

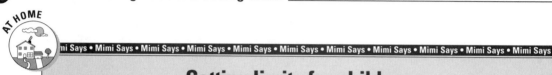

Setting limits for children

It comes naturally to set the same limits for your own children that your parents set for you — those are the limits you've known all your life. For example, curfew was always a rigid limit for me as a child, so giving my stepchildren a curfew came automatically.

It was a school night, the week of final exams — a crucial week in my stepdaughter Wendy's junior year. The results of these exams would impact Wendy's grades, and she needed high grades for her college applications to balance out some low grades from her freshman year. Wendy had studied and was ready for her French final the next day.

She burst into our bedroom at 11 p.m. asking, "Dad, can I borrow your car to go pick up Kathy? She and her mom were arguing, and she left the house."

I instinctively started shaking my head no. My limits were crystal clear. "It's after 11:00 — no car," Michael said. "It's finals week, and you have a test tomorrow," I said. Her eyes filled with

tears, and I heard her mutter something about "heartless" as she flounced out of the room.

I followed her, explaining that her limits and our limits had to be respected. Her priority was to be alert tomorrow. She said that was "selfish," and Kathy couldn't help it if her mother picked a fight with her. I knew they fought often — verbal fights; Kathy was not in danger. I said to Wendy, "What a selfish thing for her mother to do. I would never fight with you late at night during finals week. I want you fresh and unstressed the next morning. You want that, too. Kathy and her mom had control over that. They don't have the same limits we do." And she let me kiss her goodnight. I don't remember being kissed back.

When I was raised by my academically oriented family, limits were clear. Curfews were based on priorities. Friends were not first priority; school was. My responses to Wendy were automatic, firm, and clean. I often think of that time. I use that memory to inspire me to be as clear about other limits as I was about that one.

What It Means to Set Limits

Your limits define what you are willing to give up in order to get what you want. Setting limits means establishing the point at which you are willing to walk away from the negotiation and pursue some alternative course.

Your limit may be the highest price you'll pay for a car, the lowest salary you'll accept from a prospective employer, the farthest you're willing to drive before it's your spouse's turn to take over, or the latest curfew you'll allow for your teenager. If your limits are crossed: no car, no job, no trip, no date — no dice.

In business negotiations, setting limits may not seem necessary because the marketplace can define the boundaries of the discussion. People generally have an idea about the value of goods or services; they know what others are paying for comparable homes, cars, or cleaning services. They assume the discussion will not go beyond an acceptable range — what they consider to be a fair and reasonable value for the product or service under negotiation.

Not true. Even business negotiations can go off track. Especially in times of economic downturn, you find limits being tested.

Think about the last three times you became upset about something in your personal life. It's almost a certainty that at least one of those situations was caused by the fact that your limits were crossed. You probably didn't articulate those limits in advance. For example, your neighbor arrives for a chat. You have only a few minutes to spare, but you fail to tell your visitor. Your blood pressure rises while the neighbor talks for an hour.

Unfortunately, setting limits is a very difficult task for most people. It takes practice. Start small: Set a limit of 60 seconds the next time someone calls to chat when you don't have time. That should be enough time to take care of the pleasantries necessary to maintain the relationship and still get you off the phone.

Setting limits is worth the effort. People who consistently make bad deals usually do not set limits before the negotiation starts. They don't know when to walk away. You must know your limits and know how to enforce them. Knowing that you're prepared to walk away gives you the strength and confidence to be firm, even if the other party isn't aware of your limits or your ability to enforce them.

The Consequences of Not Setting Limits

Whether you have consciously set your limits or not, in every negotiation, you have a point beyond which you won't go. There's also a point beyond which your opponent won't go. If you don't set your limits ahead of time, you discover them as your patience becomes strained. Often, people explode or feel stepped on when this line is crossed. Much of setting limits is really figuring out what your limits are — before they come up and hit you in the face because someone crossed them.

In your personal life, you usually discover your limits when anger or hurt feelings signal that your boundaries have been crossed. If you identify these limits ahead of time, you can avoid the anger or hurt by stating your limits and enforcing them.

In most negotiations, limits are never tested. But your limits and the other party's limits loom over every negotiation like peregrine falcons circling high above, ready to swoop down for the kill. You are much better off coming to terms with this reality before a negotiation ever starts.

If a negotiation terminates because demands crossed the limits of one party or the other, the end happens as swiftly, silently, and unexpectedly as a pigeon hit from behind by a diving predator. The surprise factor is stunning. Usually, one or both parties feel betrayed or angry or both. In truth, setting your limits in advance can completely avoid the problem. Each party is aware of the limits that form the negotiating boundaries.

INSIDE SCOOP

ael Says • Michael Says • Michael Says • Michael Says • Michael Says • Michael Says • Michael Says • Michael Says • Michael Says

Of Landon, limits, and landlords

Michael Landon was excellent at setting limits in business. One of Michael's limits was that he would not continue to negotiate with someone who was acting out of pure greed or avarice. Requests substantially outside the normal range were suspect, and phrases like "Oh, you can afford it" were death knells to a deal.

I was proud to represent Michael on all his productions for the last decade of his productive life—including his final movie for television, *Where Pigeons Go to Die*.

The location manager found a great farmhouse to use for the shoot and made a standard agreement with the owner. For a fixed fee, Landon Productions would have the full use of the main house for a week before the shoot to add a loft to the house, *age* the house (paint the indications of time and weather), and make other minor changes. They would not disturb the tenant, who rented a small building on the property, and they would assure normal access in and out of the rental unit. They would return the property to its original state except the loft, which the owner wanted to keep. Overall, the agreement was a standard deal for when a film crew is staying at one location for an extended period.

After a few days of watching large amounts of money being spent, the tenant decided that he wanted some money himself. Because filming always involves an element of inconvenience, Michael authorized a modest payment. When the location manager passed the offer along to the tenant, he failed to explain why the offer was more than fair or how good Michael was about setting limits. Nor did he explain the probable consequences of turning down Michael's offer.

The tenant was unsatisfied with the amount offered and sought out a local lawyer to obtain "his money." I gave the local lawyer a healthy education about Michael's way of doing business. Michael always gave a warning before ending negotiations so that the other person could change position, but my personal opinion was that we had already offered the tenant too much money to settle the case. The tenant's lawyer pressed on, speaking of the great inconvenience to his client and stating that he had visited the set and "saw all the money being spent." I gave him a friendly warning about the adverse consequences of taking such an approach, but the lawyer persisted.

Michael instructed me to repeat the offer one more time, explain our position again, and then steadily reduce the offer if they did not accept it. We increased security on the set and followed up with Michael's approach.

The matter settled quickly, but Michael would have been totally comfortable paying the tenant nothing and accepting whatever wrath that response would evoke. He had his limits, and he knew how to enforce them.

Michael was one of the most generous men I ever met, but he did not like being exploited. He knew how to set limits.

Setting limits is the cornerstone of good parent-child relationships. It should be no surprise, then, that Michael, who was my very best client when it came to setting limits, was also the one with the most children.

Setting Limits in Four Easy Steps

When you know how to set limits and have confidence in that ability, the entire negotiating process changes. You can hang tough or walk away from a negotiation when necessary.

Kenny Rogers may have said it best (sung it best?) in his hit song *The Gambler*, which was about the high-stakes negotiation that takes place around a poker table. Rogers croons this important truth:

> *You gotta know when to hold 'em,*
> *know when to fold 'em,*
> *know when to walk away, and*
> *know when to run.*

Notice that the word "know" appears in each line of the chorus. Being able to set limits is directly tied to knowledge, and knowledge is the result of preparation. (Chapter 2 explains the extremely important skill of preparation.)

This section contains four steps that master negotiators around the world use to set limits. Like the Kenny Rogers song, each of these steps includes the word "know."

Know that you have other choices

Texas billionaire Nelson Bunker Hunt is often quoted as saying, "There is always another deal around the corner."

One reason Bunker made so many good deals during his life is that he was always willing to walk away from a deal if it was not right. He was good at setting his limits and then sticking to them. Bunker's slogan must be part of your core beliefs. Keep repeating his quote until it becomes a part of your belief system:

"There is always another deal around the corner."

Poor negotiators tend to attach themselves to the notion that they must close every negotiation with a purchase or sale. Good negotiators, on the other hand, often walk away. Walking away from a bad deal is just as important — maybe more important — than closing a good deal.

Whether the object of your affection is a stock, a piece of real estate, or a potential lover, you must have in your heart and in your mind that you are not stuck. The biggest prison is the one you build around your mind if you limit your choices.

"There is always another deal around the corner." This phrase must be your mantra. Repeat it until it becomes part of your core belief system. Own it. This truth can influence your entire life and bring positive results to all your future negotiations.

Start making this your mantra today. Don't wait until you are in the middle of an emotional situation to convince yourself that you have other choices. That strategy is not going to work easily. The truth of this mantra can only be grasped in the crisp light of a clear and uncluttered day — not in the depths of a specific problem.

Know what the other choices are

A few years ago, The Harvard Negotiating Institute came up with something they call BATNA — the Best Alternative to a Negotiated Agreement. BATNA is a core element in their negotiating course. This program defines what alternatives you have if you can't close a deal. (Flip to Chapter 24 to find out how to reach the Harvard Negotiating Institute Web page.)

I urge you not only to develop your best alternative, but the second best and the third best. List all the alternatives available to you should the negotiation fail to close on the terms you want. Don't edit your list. Make it as long as possible. Life is always about exercising options. What are your options if you walk away from this deal? You have nothing to lose and everything to gain by listing your choices. Don't inhibit yourself. Instead, list all your options, even if you don't think they are very valuable or practical. You have plenty of time to edit them down later.

Before you enter the negotiation, you should also try constructing a similar list for the other party. The more you know about the choices available to the other side, the more strength you have in the negotiation. Consider these exercises as a part of your preparation for the negotiation (discussed in Part I of this book).

If you are buying a new car, your alternatives may include going to another lot, choosing another model, choosing another make, or delaying the purchase. If you are interviewing for a job, your alternatives may involve accepting a lower wage, accepting another job, continuing your search, going to another city, changing professions, or going into business for yourself.

Whatever the alternatives are in your situation, list them clearly and completely. If you find that you can't list any alternatives, you need to do more preparing. One result of being well prepared is the ability to create this list of alternatives before a negotiation begins.

Know your "or else"

Once you have created the list of alternatives, decide which alternative is most acceptable to you. Pick your personal *"or else."* Decide what it is you want to do if the negotiation doesn't close. Think about that course of action. Play the scenario out in your mind.

Knowing what your "or else" is — that is, knowing what your favorite option is, if the deal does not close — defines your limits for each negotiation. Suppose that you are willing to pay $300,000 for a house before you set your "or else." Then remind yourself that you have choices and list all the choices that you have. After you write down your list, you may decide that you can accept another house that is cheaper. This way, you can be firm or even lower the $300,000 price you were willing to offer. On the other hand, if you decide that no other house would be right for you, the price could go up rather than down.

Know how to enforce your limits

Limits are not much help if you cave in every time you set them. In fact, caving in too often can gravely affect a relationship. Parents who constantly lay down the law only to pick it up a few minutes later usually end up raising brats — confused, unhappy brats at that. Now you have one more reason to practice enforcing your limits!

Check out the sidebar called "The Haggler" for a fun way to get the practice you need at setting and enforcing limits in a negotiation.

Establishing Your Resistance Point

One reason you must be very certain to set limits is that the limits that you set automatically define your *resistance point.* Your resistance point is close to your limit but leaves enough room to close the deal without crossing your limit. At the resistance point, you let the other party know that they are getting close to your limit — that you will soon be walking away.

Don't remain silent until the other party crosses the limit and knocks the negotiation out of the sky. You need to begin your complaints before that critical moment. Resist any proposal that too closely approaches the limits you set.

How far out in front of the limit you set your resistance point is a matter of your own personality and comfort zone. However, if you have not set limits, you cannot know when to start putting up a strong resistance. You can bet that the other party will be hurt and angry when you walk out if they haven't had a clear warning from you in advance. Your counterpart needs to hear that the negotiation is approaching a resistance point before the discussion concludes.

ACTIVITY

The Haggler

The four steps to setting limits are simple, but they do take time and practice to master. In the beginning, practice the steps in situations outside of your business or personal relationships. It is particularly fun and somewhat easier, psychologically, to walk away from a deal when you're on vacation. You are browsing at your leisure, and you see something you want to buy. Be sure that you are willing to buy the item, because you may just close the deal. Be equally sure that you are willing to leave the shop without the item, because that is the point of this game.

Note the price. Determine what you are willing to pay for it, which must be much less than the indicated price. Don't just grab a number because you want to play a game with the shopkeeper. Give serious thought to the true value of the item. If the item is already a bargain, maybe this is not the right shop for this exercise. When you have set a price, engage the shopkeeper in a dialogue — not a summer clerk who can't bargain with you. Don't say what your bottom-line price is. Instead, offer less than you are willing to pay but above what you think the shopkeeper paid.

If the shopkeeper tells you that bargaining is against store policy, explain that you would really like the item, but you feel it is overpriced. State that you are from out of town and can wait until you get back home, but you would like to make the purchase here, if you can agree on terms. Generally, the owner makes a concession. If not, ask whether anybody is available with whom you can discuss the matter further — you may not have engaged the decision maker. (If you're new at this approach, you may be more comfortable making your first effort in a shop where bargaining seems okay, such as an antique shop.)

If no further negotiation takes place, say thanks and politely walk out. Closing even this non-negotiation in a formal way is important. Don't just slink away like a beaten hound. You offered the shopkeeper an opportunity to move some merchandise. Make sure that the shopkeeper knows the opportunity is passing. Don't apologize for not overpaying for the item.

The shopkeeper may well respond with a lower offer. Don't automatically accept. Remember that, although you are willing to purchase the item, you are seeking the experience of hanging tough, even walking away from a deal. You may increase your offer slightly but don't move too fast toward the end point. After all, you want to practice!

If the shopkeeper quickly meets your unstated limit, keep the negotiation going. Adjust your price downwards, toward your last stated position. When a buyer with cash meets a willing seller, what follows may surprise you even in shops where you think bargaining is strictly forbidden.

As the back and forth haggling goes on, you may be surprised at how hard it is to kill a deal if you are genuinely ready to walk away. Frequently, your hand on the doorknob brings out the lowest possible sale price. Outside this exercise, when and whether to cave in is purely your own decision. For this exercise, do not pay one penny over the price you first set. Remember that you are trying to determine limits and enforce them.

Never Paint Yourself into a Corner

If you state your limits immediately when negotiations commence, you violate a fundamental tenet of sound negotiations. You probably already learned this rule while fixing up your first apartment: Never, ever paint yourself into a corner. In negotiations, you paint yourself into a corner by taking a strong stand and not leaving yourself an alternative, or an *out*.

In other words, don't start a negotiation by telling someone that you will not pay one dime more than fifty bucks (or whatever) unless you know that other stores offer the same product within your price range. Such an announcement paints you into a corner when no alternative exists.

This chapter should help you set limits, not shout limits. In fact, the final instruction a judge reads to the jury before sending them to deliberate a case is not to announce their position too quickly. In California, those final words are

> "The attitude and conduct of jurors at the beginning of their
> deliberations are very important. It is rarely helpful for a juror,
> on entering the jury room, to express an emphatic opinion on
> the case or to announce a determination to stand for a certain
> verdict. When one does that at the outset, a sense of pride
> may be aroused, and one may hesitate to change a position
> even if shown that it is wrong. . . ."

Too bad no one reads these words to us as we commence each day.

Re-examining Your Limits

Set your *bottom line* (that is, the point beyond which you will not go) before you ever start negotiating. In fact, set a bottom line as soon as you have the data to do so. But don't be afraid to take a second look at the limits you set.

When you have set your limits, write them down. Writing them down doesn't mean that they won't change, but having a written record does mean that you can't fudge later and pretend that you aren't adjusting limits.

Slowly changing limits during a negotiation without mindful consideration is a very common mistake. If you are conscious of what you are doing and keenly aware of the reasons, changing limits can be a positive and appropriate course of action. However, if you don't write down your limits — your "or else" — you risk adjusting them by inches when a foot is needed. Slipping and sliding creates confusion in your mind and in the minds of those with whom you are negotiating.

Sometimes, the Best Deal in Town Is No Deal at All

Setting limits is tough. Walking away is even tougher. You may actually be afraid that something bad is going to happen if you walk away from a negotiation. Walking away often feels like failure. Don't worry — nothing terrible will occur if you walk away.

You can find out much about negotiation by walking away from a deal or two just for the practice. Life does go on. Try it. It's okay, and it can be fun.

 Knowing how to walk away is critically important in your personal negotiations. How many people do you know who are miserable because they don't have the strength or the experience to set limits with children, spouses, or parents? People stay in bad relationships longer than is healthy because of their inability to set limits and stick to them.

Michael Says • Michael Says • Michael Says • Michael Says • Michael Says • Michael Says • Michael Says • Michael Says • Michael Says

A sailing lesson becomes a negotiating lesson

During my Basic Training at the United States Marine Corps Officers' Candidate School in Quantico, Virginia, I joined the Marine Corps Sailing Team, an unofficial group who sailed a small Marine Corps-owned sailboat in weekend regattas up and down the eastern seaboard. I had been sailing for years, and joining this group seemed like a cheap and effective way to meet interesting people and have immediate status at events where I would not otherwise be admitted. Sailing would also provide great weekend relief from Officer Candidate School.

At my first opportunity, I went down to the docks to sign up. The skipper was all Marine — he wouldn't consider anyone who hadn't taken his course. Lesson one: Get into the boat with an instructor, sail toward the horizon, and turn the boat over as fast as you can.

You learn a great deal about a sailboat by trying to turn it over. The task is not as easy as you may think. In fact, the assignment can be difficult without a good strong wind. Righting a small capsized boat, on the other hand, is not very difficult, if you've had practice.

Now I am not advocating brinkmanship in negotiating or sailing. I have never intentionally (and rarely unintentionally) capsized a boat since that afternoon in Quantico. But that experience taught me an important lesson that applies to negotiating: Capsizing a boat (or killing a deal) isn't so easy, and righting a boat afterward (or finding another deal) isn't so hard.

This exercise also caused me to lose any fear I had of capsizing a boat. Don't be afraid to tip the boat over. And don't be afraid to walk away from a bad deal.

Michael Says • Michael Says • Michael Says • Michael Says • Michael Says • Michael Says • Michael Says • Michael Says • Michael Says

Chapter 5

Making Goals — Reach for the Stars

. . . .

In This Chapter

▶ Setting good goals

▶ Evaluating the goals you set

▶ Making an opening offer

▶ Adjusting your goals during a negotiation

. . . .

You've got to have a dream.
If you don't have a dream,
how you gonna have a dream come true?

These words are from the song "Happy Talk," in the Rodgers and Hammerstein musical, *South Pacific.* Bloody Mary sings them to Liat and the Lieutenant just after they tell her that they have fallen in love.

Rodgers and Hammerstein taught us a thing or two about goal setting. The entire show is about chasing after your dreams and all the wonderful things that happen when you do. The essence of this great musical is that if you don't work toward your dreams, you regret it for the rest of your life. Sometimes, your dreams — or, in negotiation terms, your *goals* — dawn on you intuitively. Other times, you discover them through more dry, rational processes.

Do you feel fulfilled? Are you achieving what you want in life? If not, the problem may be that you are not setting goals. Or perhaps your goals are too general. Setting goals — in your life and in your next negotiation — requires spending some time. Goal setting is a natural extension of proper preparation (see Part I). Goals are the flip side of limits, discussed in the previous chapter.

You may be scared to set goals (and even more fearful of writing those goals down) because you are afraid of failing. But any athlete can tell you that failure is part of winning. In baseball, if you can make it to first base in just four out of ten times at the plate, you are considered a really good hitter.

You don't have to achieve every goal you set. But if you want to grow consistently, you do have to set goals for yourself and for your next negotiation. Setting tangible goals is important if you are to be successful. In specific negotiations, the process is essential.

Setting a Good Goal

Setting goals for yourself, for others, or for your organization is a practical activity that demands preparation and disciplined focus. Setting goals is not wishful thinking. It is not fantasizing. It is not daydreaming. A *goal* is any object or end that you strive to obtain. For example, becoming rich and famous may be the result of achieving certain goals, but fame and fortune are not the goals themselves. Deciding to write a bestseller is not setting a goal; it is daydreaming. Deciding to write a great book, on the other hand, is a goal (an ambitious one, but a goal nonetheless). Research shows that individuals who set challenging, specific goals do better than those who do not.

Distinguish between a goal and a purpose. If your purpose in life is to become an Olympic champion, set all your goals with that ultimate purpose in mind. There are many steps along the way to becoming a champion of any kind. Think about your purpose in life; your negotiating goals should contribute to that purpose deal by deal.

Don't confuse goal setting with the process of deciding what to put forward as an opening offer. (We discuss opening offers at the end of this chapter.) You must set your personal goals yourself, before a negotiation begins. Get all the information you can, but set your own goals. Keep a practiced eye on your goals during the course of the negotiation. Be ready to modify, adjust, and change as you uncover new data during the discussions.

Decide whether a goal is a *good* goal when you set it, not after the fact. Sometimes, people say, "Shucks, we didn't set our goal high enough." If you have ever said that, one or more of the qualities described in the following sections was absent from the goal-setting process. Each of these qualities is important. You don't have to wait until after the negotiation to find out whether your goals are well set. You can judge your goals at the moment you make them by determining whether they contain the following qualities.

Active participation by every team member

If you are representing someone else or you are part of your company's negotiating team, goal setting is a shared activity. Your first negotiation is with the other team members to be sure that the goals are realistic and understood by everybody on the team.

Odds are that you have someone on your team that you would prefer to leave out of a planning session. Perhaps this person's pace is slower than yours, and you're afraid the team's work will slow down. Or the person may be cantankerous and hardly ever agree with the group. Don't succumb to the temptation to exclude that individual. This person can end up being a stumbling block later when you are close to a decision deadline. Be sure that everyone who is a member of the negotiating team participates to the extent possible in setting the goals. Some people may not be verbal, but make sure that they are on board, even in a passive way. You need everyone to agree on the goals. Then they are more likely to *own* the goals — and the results.

Even with a personal goal that seems to be your decision alone, you can benefit from consulting with your family or friends. These are the people who are affected by the decision. If your friends and family are made a part of the goal-setting process, they can be invaluable in helping you reach your objective. For example, if you want to write a book, your loved one can join right in, if not with content, with helpful encouragement so you don't let less important things get in the way. Telling another human being makes your goal real.

Michael Says • Michael Says • Michael Says • Michael Says • Michael Says • Michael Says • Michael Says • Michael Says • Michael Says

Talking about goals

Even when setting a personal goal that you think is your decision alone, you can benefit from consulting with those whom that decision impacts. When I came home from speaking in Toronto with my first two . . .*For Dummies* books under my arm, I shoved them into Mimi's hands and exclaimed, "I want these people to publish my book!"

After Mimi looked over the books, she agreed that my easy-to-follow, six-step approach to negotiating lent itself to the . . .*For Dummies* format. In fact, Mimi prodded me to make the initial call sooner rather than later. She continued to prod and support so that I wouldn't let other priorities get in the way while negotiating for the opportunity to write this book. The fact that another person bought into my goal early on helped make it achievable. Sharing progress with a supportive partner fired my own enthusiasm for the project.

I soon realized that many of my stories contained the phrase "my wife, Mimi." In the middle of the process, the . . .*For Dummies* people floated the idea of a credit for Mimi on the cover.

As we worked together on the redraft of the materials I had written, a full-blown co-authorship began to grow. We had been teaching negotiating classes together. It was a natural progression to the fully co-authored book you are reading.

Mimi's unwavering support of my negotiation philosophy helped get this book published. Long before I signed any publishing agreement, Mimi introduced me as the author of a "soon-to-be-published book on negotiating." She absolutely believed in this goal, and soon I started believing in it, too. Setting your goals is step one. Sharing your goals can help make them a reality.

Michael Says • Michael Says • Michael Says • Michael Says • Michael Says • Michael Says • Michael Says • Michael Says • Michael Says

Related to this specific negotiation

Many people out there are frustrated at not being heard. If you ask them to participate in goal setting, they may go hog wild. Before long, the list of goals contains demands that are outside the particular negotiation in which you are involved. This result is especially true in workplace negotiations because, when asked to contribute, frustrated employees may feel that this is finally their chance to relieve their frustration. Allowing people with specific agendas to take your goal off course can keep you from getting what you want.

This caveat does not contradict the good advice in one of my favorite mantras: "There is no harm in asking." If your goals relate to the specific negotiation, you can choose to add an unrelated matter to the discussion. You can raise an unrelated issue appropriately but be prepared to abandon it quickly if the reaction is too adverse. Although asking for a few extras probably won't hurt, you should be conscious that you are doing so so you don't sabotage the primary goals you are trying to achieve in the negotiation.

Few rather than many

The negotiation itself dictates the number of specific goals you should set. It's amazing how many goals some people can squeeze into even a simple negotiation. Recognize that you cannot get everything done in one negotiation. For example, if your priority is to get a raise, don't demand flextime and an assistant as well. By putting too much on the table at one time, you just confuse people. Your boss's eyes will glaze over, and you may not get anything at all.

Specific rather than general

Your goals should not be so abstract that no one — including you — can tell whether you achieved them. To avoid any ambiguity, quantify your goals as much as possible.

If you're selling your home, for example, saying, "I want as much as I can get" is not a good goal. This is probably a true statement, but it doesn't help you achieve anything. A well-stated goal for the price portion of the negotiation must include an exact amount, like $125,000. If you can't be that specific, you'd better do some more preparation. Go to Chapter 2 and read a bit about preparing for a negotiation.

Challenging yet attainable

It is absolutely certain that you never achieve more than your goals. Experiments testing this thesis have shown it to be true. Surprise! At the same time, you must ground your goals in the real world. Otherwise, you're just daydreaming.

If you're asking $125,000 for your house, and no house in your neighborhood has ever sold for that amount, you'd better have some good reasons for setting your goal that high. Maybe you're in a rising real estate market. Maybe your house is larger or noticeably nicer than any other house in the neighborhood. Maybe a large office complex is under construction nearby, making your location more desirable than ever before. Any of these factors make a record-breaking price for your home attainable. Without special factors like these, you're wasting your time by starting with such high goals.

Likewise, you want to be sure that the $125,000 is challenging. If every house on the block sells for $125,000, that price isn't much of a goal — unless your house is noticeably more run-down than the others (in which case, you may want to consider some landscaping or painting first). You may have to do some research to find ways to justify asking a higher price than the others in the neighborhood. If you find out that major construction is planned for the near future, for example, you can make that part of your sales pitch.

Too many of us suffer from setting our goals too low. Shoot high or not at all — you can be sure that the other side will never ask you to raise your goals. But remember that you don't have to become rich and famous before breakfast. Goals that are *too* high for the deal lead to frustration and failed negotiations. For the specific negotiation at hand, consider the marketplace, current values, and your available options.

You can quickly see that setting a challenging yet attainable goal requires that you have a good deal of information — information you always need before you start negotiating. Setting your goals is one way you know whether you are prepared for your next negotiation.

Think of that big thermometer that the United Way puts up before every fundraising drive. The number at the top of the thermometer represents a figure generally a little higher than the previous year, but not too much higher. A better economy, more members participating in the fundraising drive, or a special event (such as building a new pool) justifies an increased amount. As members of the group raise money, they fill the outline of the thermometer with red paint to show exactly what has been contributed. Whether the organization reaches its goal or not, the thermometer looks very red at the end of the campaign, and those who contributed feel good.

Mimi Says • Mimi Says • Mimi Says • Mimi Says • Mimi Says • Mimi Says • Mimi Says • Mimi Says • Mimi Says • Mimi Says • Mimi Says

Setting goals till death do you part

Michael and I met and married only a few years ago. It was a first marriage for me, and I was in my early 40s; Michael was in his early 50s. We discussed our long-range and short-range goals early and carefully. The first night we met he shared the fact that he had teenage daughters. I told him I didn't want children of my own. So we made sure, before even starting a relationship, that our short-range goals didn't involve having and raising small children — rather, raising his adolescents to be happy, productive adults.

I am amazed at the number of couples who expect that the decision on whether to have children will resolve itself. People often assume that their partner will come around to their way of thinking.

My sister knew better. She and her husband really did negotiate for ten years before they married. The negotiation centered on whether they would have children and what religion the kids would be, because it was an interfaith marriage. They clarified their goals, and their kids are happy and unconfused. My sister and brother-in-law have led groups of interfaith couples who need to negotiate agreed-upon goals.

Our long-term goals for retirement were important, too, at this stage of Michael's and my life together. We agreed on the big picture: traveling for a year and then settling outside the United States near water and mountains in a less-developed country with a tropical climate. We had to negotiate the details: what we would do in this ideal setting. Michael wanted to own and run a bed-and-breakfast. After years of training managers, I knew that I didn't want to manage people during my retirement! My idea was to lie on a beach, meditate, and write more books. Over the past few years, we have reached a compromise. We will own our own house first and expand to one guest house, to see how that goes. We can both live with that goal. So far, so good.

Mimi Says • Mimi Says • Mimi Says • Mimi Says • Mimi Says • Mimi Says • Mimi Says • Mimi Says • Mimi Says • Mimi Says • Mimi Says

Weighted in terms of importance

Be sure to rank your goals in terms of importance. Ideally, you want to achieve 100-percent consensus about the official ranking of your goals. However, different individuals may hold onto their personal agendas. In those cases, let the majority prevail and note explicitly the view of the minority. By making special note of the minority view at the beginning, you record it for the duration. Later, you can allow the repeat discussion but remind the advocates of the minority view that they were outvoted.

It is a rare negotiation in which you achieve all of your goals. You must know which are the most important. This decision can become contentious. Teams often abandon the critical step of prioritizing in the name of keeping the peace. Unfortunately, such teams are only deferring the argument to a later point in time — and probably a worse time, such as when the team needs to hang together, when not enough time exists to deal with a side issue, when the stakes in the outcome seem higher because they are more immediate, and when a distraction from negotiating is the most damaging. What a disaster! Bite the bullet and get the team together on this important issue when you settle upon the list of goals.

Long-Range versus Short-Range Goals

Set your goals for any particular negotiation with an eye on your long-range life goals, but keep your feet planted firmly on the ground. You want to accomplish the immediate objective of the current negotiation; you also want each negotiation to advance you toward achieving your ultimate life goals. Your goals in any negotiation should help you march along the life path you have set for yourself.

For instance, we had a long-range goal of publishing a comprehensive book on negotiating. When we opened discussions with the . . . *For Dummies* people, other proposals were on the desk. This became a very specific negotiation with a very specific short-range goal: choose us! They did. Our long-range goal was still out there. The successful resolution of the short-term negotiation put us one step closer.

Once that negotiation was resolved, another specific negotiation involved the publishing contract. For that we hired an experienced New York lawyer who did his magic quickly and effectively. Basically, the contract was accepted as offered with some clarifications, but very little substantive changes. As we send off the final manuscript, we face a whole new round of very specific negotiations with various bookstores, magazines, and talk shows to help us promote and sell the book.

The Opening Offer

The *opening offer* is nothing more and nothing less than the first specific statement of what you are looking for in a negotiation. After you have set your goals for the negotiation, you can consider the opening offer. Don't look for any hard-and-fast rules or magic formulas. To determine your opening offer, you should draw heavily on the goals and limits you set and the information you have gathered while preparing for the negotiation. Obviously, your opening offer should be higher than the goals you have set for yourself. But it should not be so outrageously high as to be off-putting to the other side or make you look foolish or inexperienced. Figure 5-1 depicts this relationship graphically.

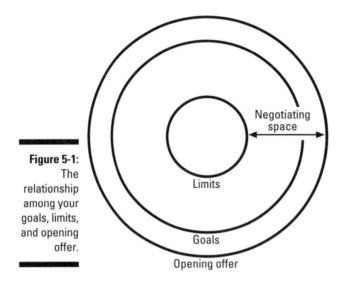

Figure 5-1:
The
relationship
among your
goals, limits,
and opening
offer.

Whether the amount you state in your opening offer is higher or lower than the amount of your goal depends on whether you're the buyer or the seller (you determine how much higher or lower through good preparation):

- ✔ If you're the seller, your opening offer should never be lower than the goal you set.

- ✔ If you're the buyer, the opening offer should never be higher than the goal you set.

We have found over the years that many people are quite anxious about the opening offer. They are fearful that they will mess up the entire negotiation by blurting out a demand that is too modest or too ambitious. Use your anxiety level as a measure of how well prepared you are. Part of being well prepared is knowing relative values. If you know the value of what you are offering, the opening offer is easy to deduce. You just decide how much negotiating room you want to leave yourself.

Have your opening offer in mind even if you don't plan to state it openly. This approach speeds your reaction time to whatever offer the other side makes.

Opening offers and the style with which they are given vary around the world. Two widely disparate examples are Japan and almost anywhere in the Middle East. As with everything else in this book, read and then behave in a way that is most comfortable for you and fits with your own personality.

Opening on a high or a low

One agent in town always negotiates from numbers much higher than where he plans ultimately to end up. I always accommodate him by asking for outrageously low numbers, knowing this is a process he likes to experience.

On the other hand, I successfully and quickly sold my house in Beverly Hills during the recent lousy real estate market by pricing it a mere $5,000 over the price I thought would be the ultimate sale price. I based the amount on the sale price of a nearby home just two months before. That house was almost the exact same size as my house, but without a pool. So I added a small amount for the pool and planted little blooming flowers all along the walkway. The feeding frenzy that resulted caused the house to go out at exactly the asking price! I made this deal during an unprecedented downturn in the Southern California real estate market.

Japan

No one sits down and goes right to the bottom line in a negotiation in Japan. Rather, an extended discussion ensues. Often the negotiation involves one or more meals. Entering too quickly into the details of a negotiation is not wise. The Japanese know that things change; no one can foretell the future with accuracy. They allow for change in their written contracts. They don't try to address every possible legal contingency when preparing a contract. They keep the risks associated with this legal flexibility minimal by refusing to do business with anybody they don't trust.

To negotiate with someone from Japan, you need to establish trust. This bond takes time — time at dinner, time over drinks. This is not wasted time, although by American standards it may feel that way. It is building time — building trust.

Middle East

Middle Easterners often make a fast and (what seems to Americans, at least) an outlandishly high offer. This approach is the hallmark of negotiating in the Middle East. The tradition is to throw out numbers that are wildly beyond the point at which a person plans to end up. You are expected to react with great animation, but no anger and no personal attacks — such displays would end the discussion immediately.

What follows is a ceremonial back and forth with numbers that tend to be pretty far apart. Both parties move around the targeted price with posturing and prancing. It is almost as if they are testing the waters to see whether making a deal with you is safe. If you pass this test, the Middle Easterner reveals the true price. If you do not pass this test, the true price is never revealed — you either pay the exorbitant price or move on.

Unfortunately, many Americans don't understand the difference between the initial ritual and the actual offer and acceptance that comes much later. If you find yourself in the Middle East, take part in the ceremony with enthusiasm. This participation is essential for a workable relationship. Every country has its own nuances, but the overriding aspect of negotiating in every Middle Eastern country is the large spread between the asking price and the actual price at the beginning of the negotiation.

Breaking the Stone Tablet

Write down your goals but do not chisel them in stone. Goals can change throughout the course of a negotiation and throughout the course of your life.

During a negotiation, you should state your goals as just that. If you state your goal as a take-it-or-leave-it demand, you are creating a terrible dynamic. Goals are goals. We discuss *limits* in Chapter 4. We discuss *opening offers* in the preceding section. If you keep these three different concepts separate in your mind, your negotiations begin — and end — on a much happier note.

Even if you never change your goals, you should review them just before you close the deal. Then look at your goals again after closing the deal. If they were too high, or maybe not high enough, consider what information you didn't have before you set your goals that caused you to miss the mark. Don't kick yourself if you decide that your goals should have been higher. Remember why you made the deal you made and learn from the experience.

Part III
Maintaining
Emotional Distance

The 5th Wave   By Rich Tennant

"Well that's just great! We're this close to landing 'Godzilla –
The Mini-Series,' and you lose your emotional distance over
syndication rights!"

In this part . . .

You're all fired up to negotiate . . . so why are we telling you to cool down? The fact is, putting some emotional distance between yourself and the negotiation actually gives you the upper hand. Look in this part to find out how emotions can work for and against you in a negotiation, and how to find your personal pause button to put those emotions on hold.

Chapter 6
Pushing the Magic Pause Button

. . . .

. . . .

*A*ll master negotiators possess a certain skill that intimidates, inspires awe, or just plain leaves others in the dust. This essential negotiating skill is hard to discern as you sit with a master negotiator, but over the years, we have discovered that the ability to maintain emotional distance from whatever is being discussed is what differentiates the master negotiator from the very good or merely lucky negotiator.

The best way we know to maintain this emotional distance in a negotiation is through a technique we call *pushing the pause button.* Knowing when and how to push the pause button not only endows you with an aura of composure and confidence, but also gives you control over all the critical points of the negotiation.

The Pause Button Defined

Pushing your pause button is just a method of keeping some emotional distance during high stress situations — at home, at work, anywhere you need a little space. We teach this method in our negotiation courses to explain the concept that waiting is good — that doing nothing is sometimes the right action. We tell our students, "If you're getting stressed out, don't just do something . . . sit there."

Pushing the pause button just means putting the negotiations on hold for a moment or an hour or an evening while you sort things out. Everyone owns a pause button, so to speak, and everyone pushes it in a different way.

When you push the pause button, you freeze-frame the negotiation — much as you freeze-frame the video on television screen with your remote control. You step away, physically or psychologically, to review the work you have done up to that point and check over your plan for the rest of the negotiation. You take a break. It may be purely mental; it may be imperceptible to the other side, but you give yourself whatever time it takes to review matters before you continue.

This focused review is a separate activity from the other basic elements of negotiation. It gives you an opportunity to regroup, catch your breath, and be sure that you aren't missing anything. The pause button gives you that little bit of emotional distance that allows you to make the decisions you want to make in your business and your life.

Pushing the pause button gives you the opportunity to review the entire process of negotiating and to make sure that you aren't overlooking anything. It allows you to avoid getting boxed into a corner. By pushing the pause button, you keep your emotions from ruling (and ruining) the negotiation.

Knowing how to use your pause button is so important that we include a pause button on the Cheat Sheet at the beginning of this book. Tear out this pause button and carry it with you until you develop one of your own. Whenever negotiations get heated, having this card with you should serve as a reminder to press your internal pause button. (The back of this card lists the six basic skills of negotiation. After you press pause is a good time to review these skills as they relate to the negotiation at hand.)

Telling the Other Person That You Need a Pause

Everyone has a different way of pushing the pause button. Sometimes, how you push pause depends on the situation:

- Ask for a night to think the negotiation over. Most people will respect your request to "sleep on it."

- Excuse yourself to the rest room. Who's going to refuse *that* request?

- For a short break, just lean back in your chair and say, "Wait a minute, I have to take that in." For a dramatic touch, try closing your eyes or rubbing your chin.

- In a business situation, having someone with whom you have to consult before giving a final answer is a convenient excuse for pressing pause. Simply say, "I'll have to run this by my partner (or family or consultants or whatever) and get back to you at 9:00 tomorrow morning."

Michael Says • Michael Says • Michael Says • Michael Says • Michael Says • Michael Says • Michael Says • Michael Says • Michael Says

A nine-year-old experiences the pause button

My mother sent me to spend one summer with my uncle, who lived in Georgia. Quickly, I noticed how cautious he was to answer questions to which my mom would give a quick yes. Very often, when I made a request, he would ask a few questions. (I now recognize that he was merely preparing himself because I was a new commodity for him.) If he still was not ready to answer, he would light his pipe!

He would ceremoniously tamp the tobacco in the pipe, ritualistically light it with a long wooden match, and then draw deeply, holding his breath for what seemed like an eternity, before slowly exhaling the thin blue smoke into the silent, anticipatory space. Occasionally, he would go through all the motions again, though I was sure the pipe was lit.

Whatever followed seemed like wisdom redefined. How clever! The wisdom was not so much in the decision that he announced but in my uncle's comfortable and not-so-obvious pushing of the pause button.

Buying even a little time to review and distance oneself from the negotiation is the critical difference between the master negotiator and the merely good negotiator.

Michael Says • Michael Says • Michael Says • Michael Says • Michael Says • Michael Says • Michael Says • Michael Says • Michael Says

Admitting early in the negotiation that you don't have final authority is often beneficial. Make it clear that someone above you must approve the decision. That way, the other party won't get angry with you. Working this information into the beginning of your negotiating institutionalizes the pause button and sets the tone for a thoughtful, considered negotiation.

Taking notes is helpful at many points in a negotiation. One of the best times to pull out your pen is when you need to pause. Writing down statements that are confusing or upsetting is an excellent way to push the pause button. Rather than blurting out an inappropriate or angry response, tell the speaker to hold on while you write down the statement. Asking the other party to check what you've written to be sure that you got it right can be enormously effective if the words upset you because they indicate a bias against you or your company. The process of putting those words to paper almost always causes the other party to backtrack, amend, or, better yet, erase the words altogether. You'll find that most people don't want their biases on paper for all the world to see.

Knowing When to Pause

Your first practical opportunity to use the pause button arrives before you participate in the first session of a negotiation. Ask yourself whether you are as prepared as you need to be. Then, when the first sentence is uttered, you're ready to listen because you have pushed that pause button. When you speak your first words, you are more clear for having taken that break.

Use the pause button at each critical moment to review the negotiation or to decide when to close a deal. Definitely use the pause button whenever you are feeling pressured or under stress.

Of course, the pause you take is only as valuable as what you do during it. Ask yourself specific questions during these brief respites. Circumstances differ for every negotiation. Usually, you need to ponder a specific point. You may want to use the time to check over the other five essential skills in a negotiation:

- ✔ **Prepare:** Do you need any additional pieces of information?

- ✔ **Set limits:** Are the limits you previously set still viable considering the additional information you have acquired during the negotiation?

- ✔ **Listen:** Did you hear everything the other person said? Did it match up with the body language and everything else that occurred during the negotiation?

- ✔ **Be clear:** Is there anything that you wish you had expressed more clearly or directly?

- ✔ **Know when to close:** Have you had plenty of time to live with the final proposal before accepting it?

When you become conscious of pushing the pause button and what to do during the pause, such a quick review as the preceding one is almost automatic. Sometimes, you are just giving your mind a break. Sometimes, you are pushing the pause button for everybody involved in the negotiation, especially if things have gotten a little heated.

Parties can get caught up in the emotions of a negotiation. They're afraid to lose face. They become angry or distrustful of the other party. They fall in love with the deal and ignore facts that are important to decision making — especially if the decision ought to be to walk away. They let their own moods, or the moods of the other party, rule the negotiating sessions, causing the negotiations to wander off course. These problems disappear when you use a pause button.

If you want to watch a negotiator with his hand firmly on the pause button, rent the HBO movie *Barbarians at the Gate*. This film stars James Garner as the president of Nabisco and depicts his efforts to buy the company. Unfortunately for him, another buyer — played by Jonathan Pryce — is better prepared and carries a pause button with him everywhere. Watch him make millions of dollars by delaying a deal one hour. This is not a family film. The swearing and gratuitous sexual references earned this film an R rating. This movie is a fast-paced, exciting lesson in high-stakes negotiating. The main things that separate the winner and the loser are preparation and the effective use of the pause button.

Don't be an animal — remember your pause button

The pause button is one thing that separates us from the animals. My cat Linguini didn't have a pause button. Whenever he heard the sound of the electric can opener, he went nuts: meowing, jumping, clawing my legs. He was unable to push the pause button and think, "Before I expend all this energy, is that my tuna fish or yours?" (He didn't know the difference, but I did — about a buck thirty-three!)

Of course, sometimes even we humans forget that we have pause buttons — especially when someone else is pushing *our* buttons. For example, you ask a coworker to do something, and she responds, "That's not my job." Feeling your blood pressure rise, you may be tempted to blurt out, "Well, it's not mine either, blockhead!"

This response may come to your mind, but it needn't come out of your mouth. You have a pause button. When you push it, your realize that, if you utter your first response, you won't get the job done and you may alienate the coworker. (Remember, friends come and go; enemies accumulate.) So instead you say, "I understand."

And you do: The person feels overworked and underpaid — don't we all? Then you may say, "I know that you're swamped, but this thing has to get done to meet the deadline. Can you give it any time at all?" And the negotiation begins. Now you have a chance of getting what you want. I'd like to see a cat manage that!

The moral of this story: Every cat ought to have a paws button.

Pausing before a concession

Every request for a concession calls for pushing the pause button. Your moment of reflection gives the concession some significance. You must treat the concession as significant, or you aren't perceived as having made a concession — the other party doesn't realize they have gained anything. No concession is unimportant. By emphasizing each concession in your own mind, you have not given ground for naught.

This is not just an act. A pause, no matter how slight, before making a concession gives the concession some importance. Of course, you want to be sure that you always have something to give up in order to hold onto what is important to you.

The obvious and easiest example is conceding a price too quickly. Too often, a quick concession robs the other party of the good feelings that they rightfully deserve after making a good bargain. It leaves the other party feeling that they priced the article too low and that they could have gotten more if they'd been smarter. Although that may be true, what advantage is it to you that they feel that way? None. Worse, now they're out to prevent that mistake from occurring the next time you negotiate, or they compensate by taking a hard line on another aspect of the deal.

Pausing under pressure

Some negotiators use pressure to get what they want from you. Don't give in to these pressures. Tell whoever is bullying you into reaching a decision that, if you're not allowed to use your pause button, then you're not going to negotiate with them at all. Sometimes, the pause button is your only defense against being pressured into making a decision based on someone else's deadline.

Decisions made under artificial pressures — especially time pressures imposed by the other side in a negotiation — are often flawed, simply because the decision maker does not have sufficient time to consult that most personal of counselors, the inner voice. (Chapter 10 can get you in touch with your own inner voice.)

Unfortunately, many women still allow themselves to be pressured into making a decision before they are ready to do so. Too many women have been socialized to answer every question at the moment it's asked. A woman may forget that she has the right to take the time she needs. Anyone trying to keep her from using the pause button is, in effect, trying to interfere with her decision making. If you find yourself in such a situation, give yourself permission to pause. Don't say, "I can't decide." Say, "I am going to think over everything you've said and get back to you tomorrow."

If you're feeling pressure to reach a decision immediately, you can even push the pause button to assess whether or not you need to push the pause button. Take a few moments to consider whether the pressure for a speedy response is reasonable. Certain external circumstances do require immediate decisions. They are few and far between.

If You're Not the Only One to Pause

Your awareness of the pause button sets you apart from other negotiators. But don't worry if the other side is also aware of this technique. Don't think of the pause button as a top-secret weapon because, when your negotiating counterparts have their own pause buttons, the negotiations proceed even more smoothly and come to a more satisfactory resolution.

Sometimes, you have the strong sense that the other person needs to push the pause button. Never say so in so many words. Instead, be very explicit about your need to take a break. Mince no words. "I need a break." or "You know, things are getting a little heated in here. Can I take five?" or "Let's call it quits for a while. Can we get together tomorrow morning to pick this back up?"

When someone else asks for a break, be very cautious before you resist it. If a person needs thinking time or needs a moment to regroup, allow it. In fact, take a break yourself. But be alert. If you conclude, after one or two breaks, that the other party is unfocused or is not paying attention, you may decide to try to extend a session. You have to distinguish between the other party using a pause button and the other party just being restless or tired.

Allowing the other party to push the pause button, or pushing your own pause button, makes the negotiating process more focused, effective, and pleasant for everyone involved.

Pushing the Pause Button to Save Lives

The most dramatic example of good use of the pause button is during a hostage situation. A hostage situation usually arises because something went wrong in a robbery. With today's swift communications techniques, officers often arrive on the scene of a crime as the perpetrator is coming out the front door, which sends the criminal running back into the building. When that happens, the scared criminal is trapped and has a brand new problem on his hands: the unplanned holding of whoever is inside the bank or store.

Law enforcement officials now have to negotiate for the release of hostages. The police have a simple mission: Do nothing to endanger the hostages or to prevent getting them out safely.

The television cameras generally focus on some cool cop trained for the task of lead negotiator. This person was trained at the two-week FBI school in Quantico, Virginia, or at any one of a number of state institutes. Where does all that cool come from? Truth is that no one can be counted on for constant cool.

That's why a member of the supporting team is in charge of the pause button. This member's main task is to continually monitor the entire situation to be sure that all the officers involved keep their cool — no grandstanding, no heroes, just a lot of hard work. This officer insists on taking enough time to get the captor's demands in detail. Without such a pause, a captor rarely thinks through and states demands so specifically. If the demands are laid out clearly and unemotionally, the negotiation closes successfully more often than not. The captor usually walks out with his hands over his head.

Next time you see such a situation on television, try to find the person standing calmly near the lead negotiator. That person is probably the keeper of the pause button. Wouldn't it be great to have one person in your life in charge of keeping the cool? But you're on your own; you have to pack your own pause button. Don't leave home without it.

Heavy Subjects

When negotiating about something to which you have an emotional attachment, you must be sure that you have the pause button well in hand. Use it every step of the way so that your emotional side doesn't trigger a decision before its time. Be sure to check the limits you set before sitting down at the negotiating table so that you don't make a bad deal because of emotional stress.

No single skill can be as helpful to you as the pause button in any situation laden with heavy emotional overtones. Almost by definition, you cannot fully prepare ahead of time for these situations. Your judicious use of the pause button can compensate. Pushing the pause button produces better results . . . or at least results that you feel better about.

Divorce

Because the pause button is so important when negotiating anything with heavy emotional overtones, a professional third party is usually called in during a divorce — a lawyer, for example, or a family counselor. The couple assigns one person to monitor the situation, to check and recheck, to be sure that emotions are not getting in the way of effective decision making, and to push the pause button when necessary.

A man who screams "Oh, all right, let her have it all!" at his divorce lawyer is almost certain to rue the day that he ever said the words. A woman who sighs, "Oh, all right — for the children's sake," will surely grow to resent the decision . . . and sometimes the kids who prompted it.

The sharp divorce lawyer simply does not close the deal until the fresh light of morning shines on the decision. If you are ever in this situation, remember the pause button. Be sure that your lawyer has one firmly in hand, also. This is no time for misguided show-offs.

Sickness

When a parent is fatally ill, the children usually disagree on the meaning of phrases such as heroic methods. Each child has a different idea of what Mama wanted (depending largely on what the child wants). Time seems so precious. The decisions seem overwhelming.

Prayer or meditation can be a great pause button, even for the devoutly nonreligious among us. Answers emerge from quiet time and not from the pressured consultation with medical professionals, although that is an important part of preparing to make such decisions.

Taking a pause to assess the damage

Even with a total wipe-out of an item that you know the price of, you should push the pause button. When my computer was stolen from my office, I immediately submitted the price of the equipment. The adjuster offered the purchase price with a very small reduction. He even added a little bit for software. I said, "Fine, send over the papers." When I walked out of my office, my secretary exploded. "Are they going to send someone over to reenter all the data?" We had some backup data, but not everything.

I went back into my office, called the adjuster, and said it would be a day or two before I would have a final number. He objected. "I thought we just settled this." I replied that I didn't know the extent of the loss and told him that I'd call him in a few days. When it comes to the pause button, better late than never.

Fire, earthquakes, and other disasters

Insurance claims — whether due to fire, accident, earthquake, or illness — are inherently stressful situations. The adjuster who shows up immediately after a tragedy is not only practicing good customer service, he is also taking advantage of a window of opportunity to settle your claim under the most favorable negotiating circumstances for the insurance company. Right after a tragic disaster is when you are the most likely to have misplaced your pause button. Chances are highest to get a yes to a settlement figure that doesn't include many things you would remember if you had more time. Time is your friend. Use it.

If you find yourself in one of these unhappy circumstances, listen to whomever the insurance company sends out. Try to get the insurance company to make a partial payment without your releasing all your rights. You may continue to find new elements of damage and loss for months to come.

Selling something you love

Even selling can require a degree of emotional distance. If you decide to sell something to which you have a special attachment, push the pause button. Be very clear with yourself as to why you are selling this item.

Sometimes, it seems easier to avoid thinking about the sale at all. Your first reaction when someone tells you to think carefully about why you are selling something you love may be, "Oh, I don't want to think about it." But that is exactly why you *have to* think about it. With time and consideration, you may be able to come up with a special arrangement. For example, you may find a friendly patron who will act as a pawnbroker, purchasing your boat, horse, or *objets d'art* at wholesale and giving you the right to buy it back when you're on your feet again. Or a family member may be happy to purchase the item from you; at least then you can visit it occasionally.

When you must part with treasured personal items, you may never completely resolve the feeling of loss. But when you take time to consider why and to whom you are going to sell something, you can often soften the blow for yourself.

INSIDE SCOOP

hael Says • Michael Says • Michael Says • Michael Says • Michael Says • Michael Says • Michael Says • Michael Says • Michael Says

Sometimes, it's just TV

Fortunately, my work-a-day world does not involve life and death situations. When I worked with Michael Landon, he loved to goad me every time I got too intense about an issue.

"It's only television," he would say, with a twinkle in his eye. It was his way of telling me to push the pause button, get some emotional distance, and not take the matter too seriously.

When I once countered to Michael that, to me, negotiating his deals was like brain surgery, Michael said, "No, to you it's billable hours . . . to me, it's just television."

Michael Says • Michael Says • Michael Says • Michael Says • Michael Says • Michael Says • Michael Says • Michael Says • Michael Says

Chapter 7

Handling Hot Button Issues

*E*verybody experiences emotions and responses. Just because you are involved in a negotiation doesn't mean that you'll remain cool, calm, and collected throughout. In fact, the more important the negotiation is to you on a personal level, the more likely it is to stir up your emotional responses.

The ability to respond emotionally is a part of every healthy human being. When you feel emotions welling up inside you, having control means that you choose to use these emotions to your advantage, rather than allowing them to send you to the locker room in defeat or cause you to blow up. This chapter discusses the emotions that commonly arise in any negotiation — at home or at work — and suggests ways to handle them in yourself and others.

Dealing with Your Hot Buttons

To negotiate masterfully, you must stay in control of your emotions. This means having the confidence to take control in the first place and the skill to channel your emotions effectively as the negotiation progresses. You can usually do this — with one exception — when people or situations push your hot buttons. *Hot buttons* are stimuli that trigger a response of resistance and cause you to be tempted to go out of control.

Negotiators (and, in fact, humans in general) deal with many different emotions all the time. In this chapter, we discuss the most common hot buttons that come up during (and often get in the way of) negotiating.

Pushing the pause button on anger

Negotiations naturally involve a risk of being upset. When people don't get what they want, one natural response is to get angry. Everyone knows what it feels like: the pressure literally builds inside the body. You feel like exploding — and sometimes you do. However, you have the ability to express anger calmly, but firmly. Anger is often useful in helping determine your limits. (Truth be told, you usually get angry because you allowed someone to cross your limits.)

When you are genuinely angry at something that happened in a negotiation, letting the other side know is usually best. This advice doesn't mean that you go ballistic. If you don't consciously and calmly express your anger, it will slip out anyway, in a more destructive way. Here is what you do: Use "I" statements. For example, say, "I feel really angry because . . ." Avoid "you" statements such as, "You are wrong because. . . ." They invariably escalate the emotional charge in the situation.

INSIDE SCOOP

Michael Says • Michael Says • Michael Says • Michael Says • Michael Says • Michael Says • Michael Says • Michael Says • Michael Says

Using anger to reset limits

Not too long ago, I was negotiating the details of a major stage presentation scheduled to appear at one of the leading theaters in Los Angeles, whom I represent. The producer and I had a two-page agreement covering all the big stuff — dates, ticket prices, and such. But we were having a devil of a time with the details.

My client was talking directly with the producer over some technical points. Tempers flared. With a rising voice and a "we'll teach you a lesson" tone, the other party told my client that the production would just bypass Los Angeles altogether. Such a rescheduling would actually have been more convenient for the other side than sticking to their promise to come to Los Angeles on the agreed dates.

After a couple of weeks, things had settled down. My client didn't want to "make a stink about it." I convinced him that constructive comment was useful. The next time I talked to the lawyer for the other side, I told her how wrong I thought her client's approach was. I calmly said that threats to break our written agreement really made me angry, that my client was angry as well, and threats had no place in our relationship.

Her initial reaction was the same as my client's: "Oh, that has all blown over. We didn't really mean it." I reiterated my position clearly and firmly. When she tried to minimize it, I told her I wasn't looking for an apology, but I felt I had to stick with the point until I was sure that she understood. By minimizing the situation, she made me think she didn't understand that all of our discussions had to take place on the premise that each side would live up to its commitments in the written (and signed) short-form agreement. She paused, and then said, "I understand."

We never heard such a threat again. We have negotiated more shows with the same company and expect to continue to work with them for years to come.

Note that the first outburst (in which the other party threatened to bypass Los Angeles) nearly blew the entire negotiation and damaged the relationship. My statement (noting that my client and I were both angry about the way we'd been treated) went a long way to clear the air. Although no one apologized, we reached an understanding and — to date, at least — no more threats were made.

Michael Says • Michael Says • Michael Says • Michael Says • Michael Says • Michael Says • Michael Says • Michael Says • Michael Says

Remember, a prime factor in effective negotiation is the honest communication between the parties. If you are truly angry about something that has happened, you need to tell the other side. People are not mind readers. They don't know when they have stepped over the line unless you tell them. Let some time go by, but don't let the point go, especially if your relationship with the other party is one that matters to you.

Expressing enthusiasm

We don't believe in secrets or trickery in negotiations. One of the themes of this book is that your counterpart should be as well prepared as you are — it's more fun that way. Here are two guidelines about expressing enthusiasm during a negotiation.

- ✔ Don't be afraid to show that you really want something . . . that you like it . . . that you think it is terrific . . . that you would do anything to own it, and so on.

- ✔ Always resist the temptation to gloat or make an outburst when you think that you have won a point. Gloating is expressing excessive satisfaction and tends to tell your counterpart that you defeated him or her. Gloating suggests to the other side that he or she should not have made the deal. It is better to stay humble (not arrogant) even when you won every point. You don't want your counterparts to feel exploited. Just tell them how much you enjoyed working with them.

Passion pays off

Expressing enthusiasm is important when a distributor is interested in an independent film. Harvey Weinstein, who heads Miramax Films along with his brother Bob, is a master at this technique. The first thing he does when he sees a film he wants to distribute is convince the filmmaker that he really, really loves the film, that he understands the concept, that he knows how to distribute the film, *and* that he would never dream of changing one frame of it.

This approach works.

Harvey's ability to obtain the rights to distribute the best films in the independent film world is unmatched. The pictures he has distributed — *The Crying Game; The Postman; The Piano; Sex, Lies and Videotape,* and many, many more — are classics of independent filmmaking. Nobody, but nobody, is better at convincing filmmakers that they should entrust their babies (oops, films) to his tender, loving hands. He pursues, cajoles, and persuades with passion and purpose. He is tireless.

Almost every real estate agent we have ever worked with has said, "Don't let the sellers know that you really want the house." Nonetheless, we have never bought or sold a house from or to someone without expressing how terrific the house is. (Look at the "Knowing the seller pays off" sidebar in Chapter 2 to understand the value of an unabashed disclosure of how much you want what the other person is selling.)

Many people are afraid that if they reveal how much they want a negotiation to end in their favor, they will be taken advantage of. But as long as you properly prepare (Chapter 2) and set your limits (Chapter 4), you cannot be exploited. In fact, letting others know how much you want what they are selling can give you a great advantage. You can even get the seller to become sympathetic to your position once you reveal how much you want the item in question.

Showing how much you want something is particularly important with something like a house. Most home sellers have grown attached to the home they're selling. They are feeling a sense of remorse at having to sell the home. People don't just sell their homes because the ashtrays are dirty. Often, people are forced to sell their homes because of some traumatic event, such as a divorce, a job change, a death, the kids' departure, and so on. In these cases, you are much better off if the seller knows that you really, really want the house, that you love it, and that you will not change an inch of it. Even when the reason for the move to another home is positive, the seller is not going to be happy with derogatory remarks about the old homestead.

Now we're not saying that you should fake a gush of adoration when none exists, or be anything but honest in an expression of your feelings. We simply want to wipe away any fear you may have about expressing your eagerness in a negotiation. If you have otherwise prepared and set limits, virtually no risk is involved in honestly appreciating the object of the negotiation. You are able to walk away if the terms of the sale are not right.

Acting assertively

Do you find it difficult to express what you want and need to your boss? Are you unable to respond at times when you think you should? Are you frustrated by a feeling of powerlessness in some day-to-day negotiations? You do not need to change your basic communication style to make your needs known. You can be direct softly and appropriately.

The art of being *assertive* is a crucial skill, involving the ability to confidently and comfortably express your wants and needs without hurting or being hurt. Many people didn't learn the art of being assertive as children. In fact, many people had their assertiveness deprogrammed. As a result, they are ill-prepared to meet the challenges of the workplace, where people need to get results through other people. Priorities compete for attention, and the squeaky wheel often gets the grease, especially in ego-driven environments.

Life's all about confronting challenges, standing your ground, and, most of all, having the courage to state clearly what you need and want.

In your life, you face the same choices over and over again — you must choose between telling the truth to someone who needs to hear it or keeping the truth tucked away unsaid. You must choose between being comfortable and safe, or risking discomfort and even the loss of some of your perceived popularity in order to set your limits and get what you want. The payoff for taking the risk is better relationships built on trust and honesty.

Dealing with discouragement

Many professional negotiators work in the sales field. Selling, even when it's done well, involves a great deal of rejection and failure, which can lead to feelings of frustration and discouragement.

Our son-in-law is starting a career in selling. We are thankful that his company is preparing him for those moments when he feels that no one will ever buy from him again, that he will not be able to provide for his family, that he is a failure. Selling is a tough occupation.

Tom Hopkins is a master trainer of salespeople. In his book *Selling For Dummies,* he spends a great deal of time discussing these emotions. His advice for when discouragement creeps into your negotiating environment is the best in the field. The part of the book entitled "You Won't Always Win" deals with what to do with such feelings and, to some extent, how to avoid them. Nobody at IDG Books asked us to plug this book. The truth is, this was the first book we read in the . . .*For Dummies* series. We were impressed with the quality of the information, and that's what drew us to IDG Books Worldwide as a publisher for our material.

The gist of Tom's advice is to consider failure to be a learning experience; that is, failure is really feedback that enables you to change direction. As we like to say, "Every 'no' puts you one step closer to 'yes'. Gathering in the 'no's gets you to the ultimate 'yes'."

In a protracted negotiation, you must be prepared to face frustration again and again. Anything worth doing has the potential for triggering a great deal of frustration. Nothing of value is handed to you on a silver platter. Seeking a challenge is part of the human condition.

Not failures — steps before success

My grandfather was a friend of Thomas Edison. He wrote Edison's biography in 1929 after writing two books about the history of electricity and its spread throughout the country. He tells the story of Edison's invention of the light bulb. Before he finally succeeded, Edison tried 2,386 different times to sustain light using electricity. "Wasn't that discouraging?" he was often asked. "No," was his constant response. "Each time something did not work, I knew I was one step closer to success."

No one could use this new invention until Edison invented a distribution system, meters to measure the use of electricity, and devices to be sure that customers got the same strength of electricity no matter how far they were from the source. Edison experienced failure far more often than success — unless you consider each so-called failure to be a step toward the successful end.

Edison was able to do this because he kept the ultimate goal in mind. With the light bulb, his purpose was to find that elusive combination of filament and containers that would sustain light. He didn't care what the specific combination turned out to be, so he kept going when any particular combination failed to work. He knew that he would eventually find the answer. You can handle your own small setbacks when you stay focused on the larger objectives.

Dealing with Difficult People in the Workplace

Often, what causes you to become frustrated or angry in a negotiation is not a specific event, but a certain kind of individual. You know the types — people who have the potential to get your dander up and throw a meeting off course. Here are some guidelines for handling such people.

Handling the office jerk

Some people don't seem to care if they hurt someone else or tell a joke at someone else's expense. When you are the target of such behavior, remembering that the perpetrator is almost always acting out of insecurity is difficult. You wish you could ignore the situation, and sometimes you can. But more often you need this person's help or input in some part of your job. Your reactions are typically anger and resentment.

Sometimes you think of the perfect response after an attack, when it's too late. Here are some tips to keep in mind so that you can respond appropriately on the spot to deflect that person and stay in control.

- ✔ **Don't resist the person's remarks.** Instead, validate them. For example, if someone says "You keep forgetting that price over and over again. Have you lost your mind?" You say, "It must seem like that to you, doesn't it?" Refusing to strike back eventually bores your attacker. When there is no fuel for the fire, there *is* no fire.

- ✔ **Acknowledge the truth.** The comments that hurt most are those that have an element of truth in them. For example, if you know you're not the most prompt person in returning phone calls, you will be especially sensitive when someone accuses you of that neglect. The more you know yourself and your flaws, the better prepared you are when someone points them out to you. You can then make it easier to acknowledge the kernel of truth without agreeing with the way it was said. You can say, "Yes, sometimes I don't return calls as fast as I would like to." You must then determine which attacks deserve an apology or explanation from you and which don't.

- ✔ **Show the person off.** If someone makes a disparaging remark to you in front of a group of people, call attention to that person. That is, with an expansive gesture towards the jerk, address the group. Say something like "Well, that didn't sound very nice to everybody, did it?" or "Gee, these people aren't going to get a good impression of you." Then pause and let peer pressure take over. Someone in the group is sure to say, "Hey, yeah Joe, cut it out."

If you use these techniques to show you're not a victim, the jerk at work usually decides to pick on someone else.

Confronting the passive-aggressive coworker

Meet the passive-aggressive personality: *passive* because these people don't speak out directly or act openly, but *aggressive* because they are focused on getting what they want, even if it is at the expense of others. They can be hostile, and the anger eventually surfaces in other ways. Passive-aggressive people get even in ways that are so indirect that it is difficult to pin these people down. For example, they may leave work half-finished, do it late, or do it inaccurately. Some common excuses are "I forgot," "I didn't know it was due *then,* " "I didn't know it included *all* of this."

The passive-aggressive person seems to be cooperative, is often calm and willing to help, and may never complain. But somehow the work you counted on or the task they promised to do doesn't get done. Aggressive behavior can surface in many other ways with these people. Talking behind your back and leaving angry notes or messages are two other ways their resistance is expressed.

How can you handle these people? Follow these two general rules when dealing with passive-aggressive people:

✔ Don't rely on such a person to do anything critical. This is not an individual you should, for example, hire to work for you, marry, or allow to handle your insurance. The reason is that you never know how this person will take out his or her emotions on you, and you frequently don't even know what those emotions are. These people aren't straight with you. And they can end up making you as angry as they are.

✔ Take your personal feelings out of the equation. Don't overreact to this person's tactics — accept that this is how passive-aggressive people treat everyone.

We don't recommend that you get involved with a passive-aggressive person if you can help it. However, if you must work with a passive-aggressive individual, follow these guidelines for remaining cool and objective:

1. **Put it in black and white.**

   Have the person write down all your expectations — or, better yet, write them down yourself and keep a copy. Be very specific in your notes. Then, the person can't say, "I didn't know."

2. **Clearly state the consequences if certain actions aren't performed — and have the individual write these consequences down.**

   Even if you are not this person's boss, you can still point out consequences — such as what your attitude will be if the person doesn't meet expectations. For example, you may say, "If you don't deliver the figures by this deadline, I won't be inclined to rush my schedule to help you out in the future."

3. **Follow up.**

   Don't let a long time go by before checking up on this person. Keep documenting all conversations by writing down what you said and the response.

4. **Give the person the benefit of the doubt.**

   Be positive. Watch out for any temptation to get nasty. Keep your cool.

What if you are a passive-aggressive individual at times? How do you know if you are? Answer these questions with a yes or no:

✔ Do you utter "tsk" and sigh loudly so that someone else can hear?

✔ Do you mutter under your breath just loudly enough, so someone will ask "What did you say?" and then you reply, "Nothing"?

✔ Do you find you forget to do things you really don't *want* to do?

✔ Can you think of at least three things you recently did above and beyond the call of duty for which you *should* have but didn't receive notice or thanks?

✔ Do you judge people as thick if they can't read your mind?

If you answered yes to at least three out of five of these questions, you exhibit passive-aggressive tendencies. Cut it out! Start using direct "I" statements, such as "I want . . ." and "I need. . . ." Why? People most often ignore nonassertive signals — they tend to respond to direct communication. The more your signals are ignored, the more frustrated and unhappy you become.

Staying in control during a meeting

Intense meetings can get pretty emotional for everyone. However, if you don't keep your own and everyone else's emotions in check by curbing inflammatory behavior, you won't get anything accomplished. The following are four types of people that can throw your meeting off course unless you stay in control.

Dealing with dominators

Dominators are people who disrupt your negotiation because they need to dominate the conversation. You need to be strong and firm in dealing with these people. Here are some suggestions:

✔ Credit the speaker's knowledge of the subject and constructive contributions.

✔ State the need for opinions from other participants.

✔ Ask the group or another individual for views or reactions.

✔ Intervene in personal attacks by partially paraphrasing objective information.

✔ Find a natural break or pause and intervene.

Restraining the ramblers

Ramblers are people who go off on tangents and bore the other participants. Usually, these folks just need attention. You need to take control and not sacrifice the attention of many to accommodate the needs of one person.

✔ Confirm your understanding of the point of the story.

✔ Restate the urgency of the objectives and the time constraints.

✔ Direct a question to another participant or to the entire group and refocus on the objectives.

Curtailing the competing conversers

Sometimes people have side conversations while you are trying to make progress on the meeting agenda. That creates several problems. You lose the attention of the people in the competing conversation. You lose control of the meeting. The side conversations tend to multiply. You need to nip that distraction in the bud and take control.

- ✔ Pause and look directly at the conversers.

- ✔ Ask the conversers to share their ideas with the group.

- ✔ Restate the importance of the objectives and state that the group will accomplish more if one person speaks at a time.

Addressing the arguers

Some people feel a need to argue with whatever is being presented. It doesn't matter what subject is being discussed, up goes their hand and out comes a slightly contrary view of the matter. Be aware of those people and use the following guidelines:

- ✔ Address the person who is presenting the argument. Use *paraphrasing* (restating in your own words) to express your understanding of the remarks he or she has made. If more than one person is involved, do this for each person.

- ✔ Restate the agreed upon agenda in order to move the discussion back towards your desired outcome. Summarize points of agreement to re-establish a positive tone.

Tips for Handling Stressful Situations

There you are — in the same negotiation . . . again. A few people are stubbornly saying the same things they said last week, and you can't see any progress. "I hate being here," you begin to think. You start to worry about being late to your next appointment. Your face feels hot, and your temple starts to throb. Just then, someone says something about the computers being down (again) and that's why the new figures aren't ready yet. On top of it all, the room is terribly warm and, remember, you're never supposed to let them see you sweat. "These people don't know how to control the temperature," you think, glaring at strangers across the table. You feel your neck and shoulders tighten, and the throb in your right temple intensifies and spreads across your forehead. "My day is ruined," your internal voice declares. And it may be.

Stress is an internal response to an external event. All the people and situations in a negotiation make up the *external* event, and all your mental and physical reactions (including stress) are *internal* responses. Because the external events seldom are under our complete control, how can you change your internal response? Pretend to be happy when you're miserable or to like the people you can't stand? Not likely.

At WAR with yourself

Stress is caused by resisting what's going on around you. When you resist a stalled negotiation, a rude person, or an uncomfortable situation, you respond with three emotions: worry, anger, and resentment.

Notice that the first letters of these three words describe the stress response perfectly: WAR; that is, the war within you. If you look at a stressful event, you find that the worry, anger, and resentment are not a part of the event itself; the event is merely the trigger that sets off these three emotions *inside* you. Reread the example at the beginning of this section about meeting stress and try to distinguish the emotions from the events:

- ✔ **Worry:** You worry about being late. Are you going to a beloved, joy-filled place or to a place you'd rather not go, where you feel anxiety and pressure to perform? What's the worry really about — fear of reprisal or punishment? Is it perceived lack of choice on your part?

- ✔ **Anger:** You feel anger at people who you suspect aren't hearing you. Is the suspicion familiar? Do you often mistrust people — and yourself? Or is your anger related to the notion that you do more than most people and aren't properly recognized for your effort? Do you feel the duties you have in life are fairly distributed, or do you feel you do more than your share? Many external events can bring this anger to the surface.

- ✔ **Resentment:** You feel resentment at these people who don't know how to control the temperature in their own office! Are you often impatient with people who don't do things exactly as you do?

These emotions are human and normal. You gain control when you are aware of your emotions. When you ignore the WAR, the stress and tension builds up inside of you. Awareness puts you in charge of your reactions.

Stop, look, and listen . . . before you have a cow

Are you someone who always seems to be stressed out? For example, do you resent strangers in the supermarket who always seem to be standing in a faster-moving line? How can you stop fuming and seething in the supermarket line and become the person pleasantly chatting with the customer ahead of you?

Take a look at your first reaction: resistance. Consider the opposite of this reaction — acceptance. Learn to accept. We don't mean for you to think, "Oh goody, a stalled negotiation!" We're talking about a recognition, such as, "Ah — a stalled negotiation. That's one of the things that drives me crazy, and now I must deal with it." Use humor to accept your circumstances. Only when you accept a situation can you effectively act upon it. If you're busy resisting it, you're paralyzed.

Acceptance involves three steps: stop, look, and listen.

✔ **Stop:** Push the pause button. (See Chapter 6 for more about the pause button. You can use it to gain control over an automatic emotional response.)

✔ **Look:** Recognize that you are now experiencing one of your stress triggers. Then recognize that you have a choice about whether or not to get upset. *Look* also means to look at what you really want and ask, "Is being emotional going to help me get it?" Usually, the answer is no.

✔ **Listen:** Pay attention to what your inner self is telling you to do. (In Chapter 10, we tell you how to get in touch with this inner voice.) Generally, if you don't like the deal you're being handed in a negotiation, you have three alternatives: adapt, alter, or avoid.

- *Adapt* means adapting yourself to the situation. Listen to what the person is saying. You may have unrealistic expectations about the time it takes some people to reach a resolution, and you may have to adapt to a delay.

- *Alter* means changing the situation. Find alternative routes to your goal; prepare better before the negotiation starts.

- *Avoid* can usually be eliminated right away. Unless you avoid negotiations altogether, you can't avoid people and situations that may cause you to be overly emotional.

Your inner voice will tell you whether to adapt, alter, or avoid. Follow its advice and you will no longer feel stress.

The best tool to handle emotional people is the empathetic statement. A sincerely empathetic statement shows that you are listening. Listening by making an empathetic statement defuses emotional people because often such people are being emotional to make their points heard. The empathetic statement is calming, comforting, positive, and specific. A good one takes only six seconds. "I understand how frustrating it is not to get the information when you want it." Six seconds. "I understand how easy it is to get impatient with that machine." Six seconds. "It sounds like you're very upset. It looks like you need our full cooperation." Six seconds. Not only do you defuse the other person, you now have time to think of a response to achieve your goal while staying within your limits.

The Challenge of Negotiating in Long-Term Relationships

Negotiating within the context of a valued on-going relationship is different in three significant ways from a one-time agreement:

- ✔ **You know this person.** You know this person's hot buttons, so you know how to punch below the belt.

- ✔ **You can't walk away.** This isn't like buying a used car. If you don't get what you want, you can't just walk down the street and find someone else.

- ✔ **You have baggage — life baggage.** If your spouse, long-time coworker, or boss turns a phrase that reminds you of one of your parents, all of a sudden you two can end up in a shouting match over a bit of nonsense. You're no longer reacting to the other person; you're reacting to some memory from your childhood that was triggered by some word, posture, or tone.

Given these special circumstances, how do you keep your cool in a heated negotiation with a loved one? You have to start with an agreement that every-thing is negotiable, and that you *will* work things out. Start by developing some rules for fair fighting. We prefer to call it *negotiating,* but when things get over 50 decibels, we admit that it's fighting. We laugh at the fact that, although we teach people how to avoid overreacting, we charge into the fray right along with the best of them. How does that happen? You teach what you most need to learn.

Tips on quarreling

We hate the word *quarreling,* but we use it in deference to those who think that *fighting* is too strong and *negotiating* is too impersonal. Here are our tips for taking the sting out of quarreling.

Develop your own set of rules for how to process your differences. On the job, this may be difficult, but within the family these rules are essential. Here are some of ours:

- ✔ The After 10:00 Rule: Don't bring up any super-sensitive subjects after 10 p.m.

- ✔ Temporarily walk away: Take an announced *time out* when things get sticky. (See the No Answer game in Chapter 9.)

- ✔ Resist the urge to make the other person wrong by quoting outside experts.

✔ Don't be afraid to visit a counselor. This tip is very California, we know. We live in a community with a higher density of psychologists, psychiatrists, family counselors, therapy groups, seminars, and support groups than anywhere in the country. "Sharing" has become a cottage industry in Los Angeles. Still, a professional person can help guide a couple into calm seas and give you the tools you need. A good counselor can help you build your own style for resolving conflict.

✔ Find something to laugh about afterwards. This activity is tough if it doesn't come naturally, but the results are worth the effort. If you can't see how ridiculous most of your arguments are, you are destined to continue having them forever.

✔ Speak up about the things that bother you before they build up to the point at which you are a walking volcano. With loved ones, people tend to wimp out of asking for what they want because they are afraid of an emotional confrontation — usually an *imagined* emotional confrontation. However, by keeping these issues bottled up inside, you're just prolonging (and intensifying) the inevitable.

Special preparations

One reason emotions can rise so quickly in some long-term relationships is that people fail to properly prepare. Emotions are less likely to flare if both partners prepare. Solid preparation makes the whole process more logical. Preparation enables you to devise alternative solutions. We spend extra time on this aspect because many people don't even think about preparing for intensely personal negotiations.

As important as preparation is to negotiations in general, preparation is *especially* important in any negotiation that takes place within the context of a long-term relationship. Because you live with or work closely with a person, you may assume you know the person. But this familiarity shouldn't stop you from asking questions about that person's wants and needs. Remember that people change. Curiosity is respectful; making assumptions is not.

At a minimum, ask questions in order to decide whether this is a good time to negotiate with your loved one. Chances are the person is not going anywhere, so relax. Find out how prepared your loved one is. Then, when the time is right, negotiate.

Don't give up — negotiate!

This principle was brought home to me on a business trip in an airport food court. I chose the Chinese food stall and got an order of *lo mein* (Chinese soft noodles). I was enjoying my dinner and reading a novel when I felt someone standing next to me. I looked up to see a young woman staring longingly at my *lo mein*.

She said "That looks good."

"It is," I replied.

She said, "I'm having pizza."

I said, "I don't like pizza."

She said, "Neither do I." Then she looked over her shoulder toward the pizza stall, and I followed her gaze. Her husband and her two young, fidgeting sons stood in line.

I wanted to shake this woman right there in the airport food court and scream, "You don't have to have pizza — you can have *lo mein!*" At the same time, I wanted to hug her and say, "They can have pizza; you can have *lo mein*. You can all have what you want, and you'll *all* be happy." I stifled the impulse. She was resigned to settling for things she didn't want.

If this young woman had been in my class instead of in an airport, I'd have explained to her how she could use all six basic skills of negotiating in less than two minutes to make a deal with her husband. This is what I would say to her:

✔ **Prepare:** Look around the food court quickly and decide you want Chinese food. Then prepare for any possible conflicts with or objections from your husband. You have an advantage — you know this person very well. What is important to him? Would being without the kids in line be valuable to him? Is getting food quickly a high priority?

✔ **Set limits:** You don't like pizza. Your limit may be that you will not eat what you don't like. If your spouse won't respect your limits, perhaps you should reevaluate the relationship.

✔ **Push the pause button:** Give yourself time to plan your strategy and what you will say. Be respectful of his processing, even if he takes longer to mull over your proposal than you would. Know you have permission to meet your own needs. Reject the notion that you can't do anything that has the potential to upset someone.

✔ **Listen:** Hear what he says when you first tell him you want Chinese food, even though he and the boys are going to have pizza. Then, listen again when you offer to take the kids or provide some other motivation for him.

✔ **Be clear:** You love him; tell him that. Tell him that the relationship will be *better* when you both get what you want. Assure him that getting your needs met in this situation won't take more time *or* cost more money.

✔ **Close the deal:** This is a cinch if you've done the other steps. Kiss him. Acknowledge him. Thank him. Make the deal worth it for him. Everyone wants to be appreciated.

Part IV
Do You Hear What I Hear?

The 5th Wave — By Rich Tennant

"Just because your office is bigger than mine is hardly a reason to use such big words."

In this part . . .

Listening is one of the most underrated skills in negotiating. Most people believe that they get what they want through talking, not listening. But the truth is, successful negotiators spend more time listening than they do speaking. This section gives you pointers on how to listen more effectively, and how to use what you hear. Find out how to listen to your own inner voice as well as to what others are saying. Discover how people say volumes without ever opening their mouths. Even if you consider yourself to be a good listener, this section can help you sharpen your skills and open the door to a new dimension in negotiating.

Chapter 8

Listening Your Way to the Top

L isten with your ears, your eyes, and every pore in between. Absolutely fundamental to all interpersonal activities, listening is an essential negotiation skill that gives you a leg up in all kinds of situations.

Good listening skills can change your business life and your personal life. How many women have left their husbands with the basic complaint: "He never listened to me?" In your personal life, failing to listen leads your partner to feel unimportant, ignored, and unloved. In your business life, not listening leads to failed deals, bad deals, and no deals.

Listening is fundamental to every negotiation. Often, it is the first skill invoked in a negotiation. When someone approaches you personally or professionally and starts a negotiation, this person is seeking your acquiescence, approval, or action. You may not have anticipated a negotiation, but now you have no choice. All you can do is listen.

Active Listening

Listening is more difficult than most people realize. Listening appears to be passive, but it is actually an *active* sport. You must be alert to listen. Listening is something you *do* — not something that gets done to you. Some people treat listening like a full-body massage. They relax into it, let the words wash over them, and, at the end, they wake up to say how much they have enjoyed it. Enjoyed? Yes. Listened effectively? Probably not. Listening takes work and energy. It can be exhausting — especially with certain people. (Please, no names!)

At its simplest, *listening* is accurately taking in all that the other party is communicating. *Active listening* involves all the senses and many screening devices. At its most sophisticated, it is getting the other party to open up, to communicate more information, and to express ideas more clearly than is the norm for that person. You may find that the other person opens up merely because they realize that someone is truly listening.

Often, people who describe their marital breakup as something they "did not expect," "did not know was coming," or "did not have any clue about," were simply not listening actively. If you've had this experience in a relationship, you should know that active listening is something you can learn. Start practicing right away.

In your very next conversation, use two active listening tools: restatement and paraphrasing. Both of these tools involve checking in with the person who is talking to find out whether you are hearing what he or she is saying.

- ✔ **Restating:** Repeat, word-for-word, a short statement that the other person has just made to you.
- ✔ **Paraphrasing:** Recount, in your own words, the longer statements that the other person has said to you.

In either case, introduce your efforts with respect and good humor. Try starting with the phrase, "Let me see if I got that right. . . . "

Are You a Good Listener?

The reason most people don't listen more effectively is that they don't *want* to listen. They just want to talk. You must decide that listening is worth doing; then you must do it.

Most people consider themselves to be good listeners. Anything less than being a good listener is considered a personality flaw. The fact that our culture universally values good listening and considers it a positive quality in a person makes it all the stranger that people don't work harder at being good listeners. No one ever says, "I hate the way that person always listens to what I have to say!"

As a general rule, you should listen more than 50 percent of the time. If you are speaking 50 percent of the time or more, you are speaking too much and not listening enough. If both people have this as a general rule, what a sweet situation it would be: Both parties trying to listen to the other more than they speak, each being willing to let the other talk. Such a negotiation may take a bit longer, but what a wonderful (and more effective) process it would be — sounds like Nirvana.

Various indicators in your personal life tell you just how good your listening skills are. The following sections can help you take a listening inventory. No matter how you rate yourself now, your listening skills can improve. But they won't improve overnight, no matter how motivated you are. Listening is a skill characterized by slow growth.

The interruption index

Our experience is that people who interrupt a great deal are generally not very good listeners. When we talk of interruption here, we're not referring to the loving completion of sentences by people in relationships — emphasize the word *loving* to understand the difference.

To find out whether you're an interrupter, simply ask yourself how often others say to you, "Please don't interrupt," or words to that effect.

Conversely, being interrupted tends to bother good listeners more than it bothers people who are not good listeners. Does it bother you if someone interrupts a joke you are telling or a point you are making? If the answer is no, there's a pretty good chance that you need to work on listening skills.

 Research shows that men interrupt women far more often than women interrupt men. Some of this discrepancy springs from a perceived power differential. Interruptions represent power. Someone who interrupts you is taking away your power to speak. Obviously, this kind of behavior cancels out any possibility of listening.

Ask a friend

Ask a loved one or a subordinate whether you are a good listener. You should ask this in absolute seriousness. Find a quiet time when you are not likely to be interrupted. This is not an inquiry you can make on-the-fly and expect to receive a thoughtful response.

Be a good listener during this conversation. Don't take the first flip answer that you receive. Ask for examples of when you listened at your best and when you listened at your worst. Make notes. Be thoughtful. Don't defend yourself. This conversation is not about right and wrong. You are not there to convince anyone that you are a good listener. You are there to learn how you can be a better listener, no matter how well you listen right now. You are there to listen.

Play repeater

Set an egg timer at the dinner table. When it rings, each person has to repeat the last sentence uttered before the timer rang by the person sitting to their left. Take turns going all around the table. The more people at the table, the better. Often, real confusion sets in as to what was said.

You can tighten up the house rules as everyone improves their listening skills. For example, repeat the last two sentences, and then three, and so forth. Alternatively, designate one person to read a poem or story out loud. That person stops reading without warning and selects someone at random to repeat the last phrase read by that person. It isn't long before this game is worthy of real prizes. The results can control who has to clear the table and who does not.

If you are successful in drawing the other person out, you may hear some pretty horrendous versions of your listening skills. You may be surprised, but don't be insulted. None of us listens as well as we think we do.

Thank the person as soon as you have had enough. Say that you want to talk again about your communication skills and actually follow up when you are ready. Never challenge the impressions or information the other person has given you, no matter how off-base you think the assessment is. This defense mechanism only stunts your growth.

Six Barriers to Being a Good Listener

Most people try to be good listeners, and most people consider themselves successful. Yet accusations such as "You are not listening to me!" abound. Unfortunately, a number of barriers to listening apply to a greater or lesser extent to everybody at some time or another.

Naturally, *you* are one of the lucky few who has overcome these barriers. But if you want to find out what keeps some of your friends from listening more effectively, you may want to read the following sections.

The defense mechanism

One reason people don't listen carefully during a negotiation is purely psychological. Generally speaking, people don't want to get bad news. Some people state this derisively, as in, "Oh, he just hears what he wants to hear." Shibboleths like that almost always have more than a kernel of truth in them. In fact, everyone filters out bad news to one extent or another.

Every animal has stunning built-in survival mechanisms. One of the most important survival mechanisms is to hear danger coming. A predator, a fire, even a storm all have advance warning signals that those wishing to avoid danger must hear and assess.

Although humans have retained many useful self-defense mechanisms, such as blinking, ducking, and flinching in the face of danger, we seem to have lost a very important one — the ability to hear danger coming. Perhaps we've decided that simply not hearing the danger is a better approach than hearing and, subsequently, having to deal with it. Not so. This is one case where the other animals are more advanced than humans are. Only when you hear and can accurately assess the danger you face, are you in a position to avoid or defuse it. In fact, you should force yourself to probe even deeper if you suspect that bad news is lurking.

Mimi Says • Mimi Says • Mimi Says • Mimi Says • Mimi Says • Mimi Says • Mimi Says • Mimi Says • Mimi Says • Mimi Says • Mimi Says

A case of the "yeah, buts"

One of the most self-destructive ways to listen in business and personal situations is listening with what I call the "yeah, buts." This condition occurs when you are defensive about what the speaker is saying, and the first response out of your mouth is "yeah, but." Whether you are listening to a customer, boss, or spouse, you've got to put the automatic "yeah, but" response on hold. Watch out for responses like these:

"Yeah, I know, but you're not our only customer."

"Yeah, but honey, you're always on my case about that."

"Yeah, but *you* always use that tone of voice with me."

These responses cause defensiveness in your listener. You want to say "I hear you," or "I understand" first. Then pause. Then say, "Here's the situation," and explain. You will get more positive results this way.

Mimi Says • Mimi Says • Mimi Says • Mimi Says • Mimi Says • Mimi Says • Mimi Says • Mimi Says • Mimi Says • Mimi Says • Mimi Says

Weak self-confidence (the butterflies)

Many people who talk too much when they should be listening do so out of nervousness. Talking a great deal is often a mask for, or a result of, old-fashioned butterflies.

Butterflies are lethal to good listening — they cause a person's mind to race around searching for an answer, observation, or anecdote while the other person is speaking. A mind in motion blocks listening as effectively as a mouth in motion.

By and large, the same people who talk too much usually don't even listen to themselves. Interrupt them and ask them to repeat something they just said, and they can't do it. They talk, but they don't listen — not even to themselves!

An unfortunate side effect often occurs when your mind is racing during communication. The person speaking takes your silence for listening, not preoccupation. Then, when you give an inappropriate answer or, worse, a loud "Huh?," that person makes an immediate and inaccurate assessment of your IQ.

Understand that butterflies are not free. They are expensive. If your butterflies cause you to lose control of your mouth when you need to be listening, they can cost you a job, a sale, a contract, or a date.

Entire courses on how to handle the butterflies are available. Several techniques are useful to drain off the energy. Our personal favorite is a few quick push-ups before taking the podium. (Imagine our surprise when Jack Palance did just that as he was taking the podium at the top of the Oscar telecast in 1992.) More universally useful exercises are a few deep breaths, or stretching the body, arms, or hands. Anything you do to release the energy helps. Remember, butterflies are just nervous energy not channeled in positive ways.

Rechanneling anxieties into positive energy makes you look confident and in control in listening situations as well as when you speak. Energy can voluntarily escape your body through five channels:

- ✔ Eyes
- ✔ Hands
- ✔ Feet
- ✔ Body
- ✔ Voice

Releasing your energy through eye contact is better than talking too much. Leaning forward and listening harder is better than talking too much. The key is to recognize that these feelings of anxiety are actually energy that your body is generating to help move you through a dangerous situation. If it sounds somewhat primordial, it is. The better your skills, the less threatened you feel and the less nervous energy your body must manage.

The energy drag

Sometimes, people are just too tired or too lazy to listen. Listening takes energy. Listening can be thought provoking. Thinking, too, takes energy. Consider how you listen to your children or spouse in the morning, and how you listen after a long day at the office. Whatever your style, those two times of the day are going to produce different results.

If your energy is flagging, you have a hard time listening. Be aware of that fact. You probably have said or heard, "Slow down, I've had a heck of a day." That is the sound of a good negotiator, someone who knows that you can't always listen at top speed. If the speaker needs to slow down in order for you to fully participate and pay attention, just say so.

Habit

Maybe you have, over time, developed the habit of talking or thinking ahead when you should be listening. If this is the case, you can treat this habit like smoking; you can quit.

Changing this behavior pattern is difficult because you have to do it on your own. No nicotine patch is available for effective listening. The more status and power you have, the less likely people are to tell you that they think you're not listening. They notice. They react. They just don't tell you. It's like bad breath; many notice, and few comment.

One interim step you can take in the process of becoming a better listener is to stop talking out loud and start talking inside of your head. This technique is not as good as listening earnestly, but you are at least talking less. Eventually, you can segue into true listening.

Thinking without speaking is not easy for many people. You can think much faster than anyone can talk. Speech rate is about 100-150 words per minute. You can listen at over 500 words per minute. It's only natural that your mind may race ahead of the words you hear and even take in other conversations. You have to be very careful that, when this happens, you refocus on the speaker.

The preconception

Beware of the preconception. A *preconception* is an expectation that prevents your mind from staying open and receptive. Like its relative, the assumption, the preconception is an enemy to listening. Both problems seem to prey on people in long-term relationships.

A preconception is a notion that just because a person has behaved one way before, he or she will act that way again. If a person blusters once, for example, you may well jump to the conclusion that the individual will display the same behavior during the next negotiation. "Oh, he's just that way" may be an accurate statement of fact. But if that conclusion is used as an explanation for every outburst, it may well mask the reality that the blustering party is quite angry at some aspect of your behavior. The blusterer may be genuinely frustrated this time at not being able to reach a deal or may be reacting to pressures from places not related to the negotiation.

Not expecting value in others

Many people don't listen simply because they are not expecting others to say anything of value. Every human being has something to contribute. Sometimes you must do some digging, but everyone has some special knowledge. In a negotiation, the other party has a great deal of beneficial information. But if your normal mind-set is that the people you talk to have very little to contribute, turning that around and listening effectively may be difficult.

Listening can be like sifting through sand on the beach. This is truer at a cocktail party than at a scheduled negotiating session. To be the best possible listener at the negotiating session, you can practice at cocktail parties. The next time you have to go to a party, keep repeating, "Buried within this chatter is something of value." If you want to find it, you can.

When some people speak, what they have to say and how they go about saying it is, to put it bluntly, boring. Spending the energy to listen to such people may not seem worth the effort. But even these people often have valuable information and insight. Your job is to draw such speakers out. Question them until you hit some nugget of interesting information.

In fact, good listeners tend to attract much more interesting company than others. It's also true that, by listening carefully to the company you keep, you learn much more about the subjects that makes them interesting.

Listening Your Way up the Corporate Ladder

In negotiation, silence is golden — in fact, it is money in the bank.

Remember, you can't listen and talk at the same time (not to yourself or to anyone else). Many a negotiation has been blown — and many a sale lost — because someone kept talking long after discussion was necessary or desirable. Conversely, many an opportunity to gain valuable information has been lost because the listening activity stops too soon.

One of the best ways to control a meeting is to listen and insist that others listen. If a big talker is monopolizing the negotiation, that person probably doesn't even recognize that others want to contribute to the discussion. Stifle your instinct to grab the floor yourself. Instead, point out someone else who looks as though he or she is trying to talk. "Jane, you look like you had a comment on that." Jane appreciates it, others appreciate it, and you suddenly control the meeting. Sometimes, others can make your point for you. If you find that you still have something to add, the group will probably let you do so. You are now a hero, even to members of the other negotiating team. When you do say something, everyone listens out of appreciation — if not admiration.

Various studies have shown that successful people listen better than their counterparts — especially on their way up. Ironically, great success sometimes causes a person to be a less sensitive listener, usually to that person's detriment. The most visible example is the President of the United States, who must listen well during the rise to political power. However, a sitting President can easily become cut off from the very people who helped in the ascent. The isolated President is a common feature of the American political landscape.

To become successful in the business world and stay successful, you must be a good listener. Here are some examples of the importance of listening effectively while you're on the clock:

- ✔ Many managers face setbacks in their careers when they prejudge an employee before they hear all sides of the story. If you want to gain respect as a manager, gather all the data from all the parties before you take any action.

- ✔ New employees need to listen first when they enter a meeting or a department. Get the lay of the land. Resist that first verbal contribution, which will be everyone's first impression of you, until you know that the contribution is a good one.

- ✔ Salespeople lose sales when they talk more than they listen. The successful ones use empathetic statements to show they understand what the customer is saying and how they are feeling.

Listening around the World

Communication patterns differ around the world. In some cultures, listening is more important than in others. The *way* people listen even varies from one country to the next. The first rule of international negotiation is to keep in step with the customs wherever you happen to be.

As soon as you have mastered all the generalities about the country or culture in which you are about to negotiate, remember the second rule of international negotiating: *It ain't necessarily so.* Generalizations are just that; not everyone conforms. You are negotiating with an individual, not a nation. The person with whom you are negotiating may have played football at Duke University after going to high school elsewhere in the United States. Don't forget to find out about the *individual* as well as the nationality.

Listening in Bali

Nowhere in the world do people listen the way they do in Bali. The practice can be unsettling to visitors to the rural areas of Bali. The natives there stand quietly and fix the focal point of their gaze at a point just behind your eyes. You feel as though they are looking into your soul. They don't exert any pressure upon you to hurry up and finish what you are saying. When you do finish, there is a slight pause before the other person starts to speak, lest you have an afterthought.

We spent a week in a guest house in a village that is not even on the map. The nearest phone was in the next village. Of all the beautiful sights and sounds and smells that flooded over us that week, nothing impressed us more than the way the natives of Bali drink in a person's words.

Listening in America

Americans are decidedly on the other end of the listening spectrum from the Balinese. Evelyn Waugh, the great English satirist, once noted, "Americans do not so much listen as they stand around and wait for their turn to talk."

Waugh's observation is accurate, but it's interesting also in that much of America's style is inherited from the British empire. All indications are that the Brits are not such great listeners either; they are just more polite about it.

Listening in Japan

In Japan, listening is more than ceremonial. Particularly at the early stages of a negotiation, a great deal of listening takes place. Many writers comment on the amount of time the Japanese want to spend getting to know you before they do business with you. That's true. They want to listen to what you have to say — about yourself, about other deals you have made, about the people you admire and why, and the people you do not admire and why not. The listening goes on so long that it is ultimately a subject of note to every commentator who does business in Japan.

If you are negotiating in Japan, you must listen particularly keenly for a no. The Japanese rarely phrase rejection as bluntly and quickly as do Americans. A more likely response is something like, "that is difficult." To an American accustomed to doing business in America, that phrase means that the door is wide open. Yankees can do anything with a "that is difficult." In Japan, the same phrase means that the door is probably bolted shut.

Chapter 9

Hearing Aids for Everybody

S ometimes, you may just want to say, "All right, already! I'm tired of people telling me that I'm a bad listener. I try, but I keep getting involved in miscommunications. Just tell me what I'm doing wrong."

This chapter tells you how to listen effectively. Forget the theory. Forget the models. Follow the simple suggestions in this chapter to become a better listener — immediately.

Tips for Becoming a Good Listener

The following are four things you can do right now to improve your listening skills. These techniques are easy to use and bring immediate results.

Clear away the clutter

To be a good listener, you have to clear out the clutter. This is not just a question of good manners, it is an absolute necessity if you want to focus on the person speaking to you. Noise clutter, desk clutter, and even mind clutter all interfere with good listening.

Think about the worst listener you've encountered in your life. If you have a teenager, you probably don't have to look far. Consider the all-too-typical teen's room: Stereo blaring, *Beverly Hills 90210* on the television set, things strewn everywhere. No wonder your teenager can't hear you. Your words may temporarily penetrate the chaos, but the full content of your message doesn't get through.

Why not learn from your teenager's mistakes?

✔ When you talk to someone, don't just mute the television set, turn it off.

✔ If you have something else on your mind, write it down before you enter a conversation. With a note as a reminder, you won't worry about forgetting to address the issue — and your mind is free to concentrate on the rest of the conversation.

✔ Clear your desk — or whatever is between you and the speaker — so that you can focus on what the speaker is saying.

✔ Don't accept phone calls while you are talking with someone else. Interrupting a conversation to take a call makes the person in the room with you feel unimportant — and makes what you have to say seem unimportant.

When a coworker comes to your office, don't feel that you need to engage in a discussion right away. If knowing that you need to finish a task may distract you from listening effectively, you may be better off delaying the conversation. If the project you're engaged in will only take a moment to complete, try saying, "Just a minute, let me finish this so that I can give you my full attention." If it's going to take a while, ask to schedule a meeting for later that day. Your coworkers would rather wait until you can listen than have you tending to other business while they're trying to talk to you.

The same rule holds true for phone conversations. Never try to negotiate on the telephone while you're reading a note from your secretary, catching up on filing, or playing a computer game. Trying to do two tasks at once simply doesn't work. True, your ears can be engaged in listening while your eyes are occupied with something else. However, your brain cannot simultaneously process the conflicting information from your eyes and from your ears. Both messages lose out.

To be a better listener, clear the clutter away — from your ears, your desk, and your mind. Nothing gets in the way like stuff. Get rid of it.

Count to three

Here's an extraordinarily simple device to help you listen more effectively. Just count to three before you speak. This slight delay enables you to absorb and understand the last statement before you respond.

As you practice this skill over time, actually counting may not be necessary, but the pause always pays off. You absorb the message, and you give the other party one last chance to modify the statement or question. Even if your response is simply that you must consult with your client, spouse, or boss, pausing for three beats helps you better comprehend and remember what the other person said.

Wake yourself up

If you are truly interested in what the other party is saying, look the part. If you feel yourself getting drowsy, don't give in. Sit up straighter. Stand up. Get the blood flowing in whatever way works for you. Don't think that you can effectively hide flagging interest without changing your physical position.

In your very next conversation, just for the fun of it, assume the most attentive position you can. Observe how this change in behavior improves your listening skills. Follow these steps for enhancing your next conversation:

- ✔ Uncross your arms and legs.
- ✔ Sit straight in the chair.
- ✔ Face the speaker full on.
- ✔ Lean forward.
- ✔ Make as much eye contact as you can.

Michael Says • Michael Says • Michael Says • Michael Says • Michael Says • Michael Says • Michael Says • Michael Says • Michael Says

Using the edge of your seat

Mimi and I both love movies and theater and attend many shows in Los Angeles. But even during this activity that I so enjoy, my attention sometimes begins to drift. If I feel myself losing interest in a performance, I physically lean forward in my seat. Sometimes, I actually slide forward a bit.

When I sit on the edge of my seat, my interest seems to renew itself — a strange reversal of the normal cause-and-effect relationship. By *looking* bright-eyed and bushy-tailed, I actually *become* more alert. My friends confirm that they have experienced the same outcome. Try this technique the next time nature seems to be overpowering your ability to stay focused.

Michael Says • Michael Says • Michael Says • Michael Says • Michael Says • Michael Says • Michael Says • Michael Says • Michael Says

Write it down

Taking notes is a great listening aid. Regardless of whether you ever refer to your notes again, the mere act of writing down the salient points boosts the entire listening process. Writing information down engages other parts of your brain, as well as your eyes and fingers, in the listening process. Fully absorbing an entire conversation merely by listening is almost impossible.

Making notes is important throughout every step of the negotiating process. Immediately after a negotiating session, review your notes to be sure that you wrote down everything you may want to recall, and that you can read everything you wrote down. Remember from your student days how confusing old notes can be: strange abbreviations, unintelligible squiggles, large coffee stains.

When you are comfortable with your notes, consider providing a status report to the other side. A confirming memo is an excellent way to assure that you listened well. Writing down what you think you heard and verifying the material with the other side is a positive experience for both parties.

However, if your counterpart believes that you recorded the conversation incorrectly, he or she may get angry and repudiate your version. You still win in such a case. Your memo serves an excellent purpose if the response reveals that you and your counterpart have conflicting views of the proceedings. Immediately thank the other party. Point out that you wrote the memo to be sure that you listened well and interpreted the discussion accurately.

You may not have listened carefully, but it's just as likely that the other party is correcting a sloppy communication to you. People often change or refine their position once they see it in black and white. Let that modification happen gracefully. When the other party provides a new version of the negotiation, simply change your notes. Don't argue about the past conversation. Fighting over who said what never furthers the negotiations; identifying the opposing party's position does. Remember: You write it out to get it right.

In family meetings, recording negotiations and agreements is often just as important as it is in business meetings. Make a habit of writing down house rules of conduct for young children, chores for older children, and even agreements between spouses or loved ones. That way, everyone is clear on the expectations. Your life is easier and behavior is more consistent.

Conversing between the Sexes

We always take a break in our negotiating seminars to present some material on the different ways in which men and women communicate. Obviously, there are lots of exceptions to any broad generalization. We do not theorize about whether these differences are the result of culture, environment, social pressures, or the power structure. We leave that for the academicians. We just relay the information about the state of things as they exist today and what you as an individual can do to get more of what you want in life — including better communications with those you love and labor with.

Tips for women

Here are three tips for women when listening to men:

- ✔ **Don't talk when he's talking.** Many women think that because they are marrying their best friends, they can talk to their husbands the same way that they talk with their best women friends. As their husbands talk to them, they interject comments. Usually, the husband abruptly stops talking. The women, confused by this response, ask what's the matter, and the husbands accuse them of interrupting. (Can you tell that we know about this phenomenon first hand?)

  The women don't think that they're interrupting, they think they're *adding*. For women to add to each other's sentences is acceptable. However, most men need a space in which to enter a conversation, and they want to keep their space until they are finished talking.

  Listen silently instead of vocalizing little affirmations such as "uh-huh," "oh, yes," and "wow, yeah." Women use these phrases to encourage the speaker to keep talking. A woman speaker interprets these comments the way they are intended. A male speaker may view them as an interruption.

  Another problem is that sometimes, when you verbalize such affirmations, a man thinks that you are agreeing with the content of what he is saying, rather than letting him know you understand what he means.

- ✔ **Believe what he is saying.** If we had a dollar for every time a woman told us, "He said this, but here's what *I* think he meant," we'd be rich. Many women believe men speak on many levels, and they try to find hidden meanings. In our experience, men usually say what they mean and mean what they say, and they expect women to do the same. They don't spend two minutes of their time calling another guy to say, "Here's what she said at breakfast this morning — what do you think she meant?"

- ✔ **Be patient.** A man's pace may be different from yours. He may talk more slowly or pause more often than you do. Let his thoughts flow. Don't speak during his pauses.

Tips for men

Here are three tips for men when listening to women:

- ✔ **Listen to her all the way through.** Sometimes, women talk in order to process information or to figure out what they want to do, instead of thinking in silence and then stating a conclusion. If you sense that this is happening, just let her thoughts progress. Don't rush her — prompting her interrupts her thought process and causes her to feel slighted.

- ✔ **Give her your full attention.** Don't just mute the TV; turn it off. Don't just look up from the sports page; put the newspaper down. Turn to her. Look her in the eye. This response shows you care about what she is saying.

- ✔ **Be patient.** Her pace may be different from yours. She may want to cover more subjects in the same conversation than you do. Remember that men and women communicate differently. Make an effort to accommodate those differences.

MEN & WOMEN

Mimi Says • Mimi Says • Mimi Says • Mimi Says • Mimi Says • Mimi Says • Mimi Says • Mimi Says • Mimi Says • Mimi Says • Mimi Says

The times are a changin'

I lecture all over the country on the differences between male and female communication. When I started on the lecture circuit 15 years ago, someone in the audience always objected to the assertion that these differences exist. They only wanted to hear about the fact that women have not had equal power in the workplace.

As an ardent feminist, I've worked to change the imbalance of power between the sexes. But today, most people recognize that differences between men and women exist, and they want to know what to do with that information.

Bookstores are packed with books on the subject.

As you read about the differences in how men and women listen, don't forget that we live in a time and place that spawns a lot of examination of these differences. *All* men and *all* women are not conditioned to speak and listen the same way. Managers and employees, husbands and wives, and friends are all trying to bridge the gaps that do exist. It is important to assess each *individual's* level of comfort as you follow the tips in this section.

Mimi Says • Mimi Says • Mimi Says • Mimi Says • Mimi Says • Mimi Says • Mimi Says • Mimi Says • Mimi Says • Mimi Says • Mimi Says

Tickle It Out

Effective listening requires probing. No one says everything you want to hear in the exact order, depth, and detail that you prefer. You have to ask. No phrase describes the job of questioning better than *tickle it out.* Questions are a way of coaxing out information that you want or need.

In a trial, the question-and-answer format rules the proceedings. Attorneys and the judge can talk to each other in declarative sentences, but all the testimony is presented in the somewhat artificial format of question-and-answer. In court, as in a negotiation, the purpose of every question should be to obtain specific information. If the question isn't answered directly, it needs to be asked in another way. The rules in the courtroom are pretty specific; as a matter of etiquette, you should apply the same rules in a business meeting. For example, courtesy prohibits you from barraging the other side with rapid-fire questions; court rules prevent the same thing.

Developing the ability to ask good questions is a life-long effort. If you have the opportunity to observe a trial, notice that the primary difference between the experienced attorney and the less experienced attorney is the ability of the former to ask the right question at the right time. Almost without fail, the key question is not a bombastic, confrontational inquiry, but a simple, easy-to-understand question designed to extract specific information.

An excellent example of tickling it out occurred in the O. J. Simpson murder trial during the questioning of police officer Mark Fuhrman. Lengthy, soft-spoken questions led up to the simple query, "In the last ten years, have you used the 'n' word?" "No," the officer replied. "Are you sure?" the attorney asked. "Yes, sir," Mark Fuhrman responded. There were no fireworks, no victory dances at that point, but the quiet exchange permanently altered the trial. Eventually, the truth about Fuhrman's behavior smashed against that statement so explosively that every other piece of evidence was damaged. Fuhrman and all his coworkers were hurt by those brief words so gently tickled during questioning.

About the only place you can regularly see trained people posing careful questions is on the cable channel, Court TV. Tune in. Obviously, various attorneys have different skill levels. Some are better than others. Watch and listen as they ask their questions. Watching these men and women in action sensitizes you to the good and bad aspects of questioning.

Battling the jargon

Don't be shy or embarrassed about asking someone to clarify a statement. Many people use jargon or shorthand when they talk, so you can't always be sure of what they mean. For example, when we met with the head of marketing for the . . .*For Dummies* trade series, she started talking about the AMC. We teased her about the jargon which, to us, meant *American Multi Cinema,* a large chain of motion picture theaters. She quickly identified AMC as the *advanced marketing chapter,* which is sent to various buyers months before the entire book is ready for print. This situation was easy to handle because Stacy, the Brand Manager, was happy to clarify. We just needed to ask.

A slightly more difficult situation arises when you are both in the same industry, and the other person assumes that you know the meaning of words that he or she is using. You may feel embarrassed to ask for the meaning under that circumstance, because you think that you *should* know. There are a few good ways to handle this situation. Our favorite response is this statement, "Just to be sure that we are using our shorthand in the same way, tell me exactly how you define XYZ." When the other person gives you his or her definition, use it. Here are three useful responses when the other party defines a term for you:

- ✔ That's great! We use that phrase the same way.
- ✔ Glad I asked; we use that phrase a little differently, but we can go with your definition.
- ✔ Thanks, I just learned something new.

If you really think the other person is miles off the target and some real damage may be done if you use the word their way instead of your way, say: "We should define that term in the written agreement so others won't get confused. You and I know what we are talking about, but we want to be sure that everyone else does, too." Don't get into a battle over definitions.

There's a third situation in which you may run into jargon. Some people use jargon to impress others with their knowledge, power, or position. We have noticed these types among the ranks of doctors, lawyers, and accountants. As often as not, they use this device on their own clients. Use the preceding techniques to get clear on the conversation, but if the problem is chronic, look for another professional to serve your needs.

Clarifying relativity

Just as important as asking others to explain specific pieces of jargon is requiring that they define *relative* words. Relative words are nonspecific descriptive words that only have meaning in relation to something else.

Here are some examples of relative words that can create a great deal of confusion:

- ✔ Cheap
- ✔ High quality
- ✔ Large
- ✔ Many
- ✔ Soon
- ✔ Substantial

Don't be shy about asking for clarification when someone lays one of these words on you. If the person insists on using generalities, as some people do, press for a range. If you still don't get a specific answer, supply two or three ranges and force the person to choose one. For example, you can say "Do you mean more like ten, or maybe about hundred, or would it be closer to a thousand?"

How big's your pocket?

I wish I could say that I always eliminated the confusions that occur when vague terms are used. The truth is that people don't always have time to do so. Sometimes, you just want to get out of a conversational situation, and the last thing you want to do is prolong things by making absolutely sure that you have all the details correct. Other times, being specific just doesn't seem that important.

I recently had a meeting with a wealthy investor. When we were through discussing the subject of our meeting, he mentioned that he had given "pocket money" to one of my clients. I took that, quite literally, as a small amount of reimbursement for nonspecific expenses. I thought, "Oh, that's nice" and said as much. In the South, we call that kind of money "walking around money."

Later, I learned that he had written a check for $100,000 and was annoyed and frustrated with my client at the way the money was being spent. He was also unhappy with me for not rectifying the situation after he had informed me about it. Needless to say, I was shocked to learn all of this from a trusted friend that the investor and I had in common. Fortunately, we were able to remedy the problem right away.

If his comment had been the subject of the meeting, I would have sought clarification at the moment. As it was, I didn't give the comment much thought, and his annoyance continued to simmer until I heard the complaint clearly two weeks later and was able to fix it. This story is a happy one because I learned the details fairly quickly. The situation could have smoldered and seriously damaged my client's and (unfairly) my own relationship with that investor. And why? Lack of clarity. When my client explained carefully and completely how the money was being spent, the investor was not only satisfied, he advanced more money. Some of the best time you can spend in almost any situation is that extra moment it takes to make sure that everyone is communicating clearly.

Asking Questions: A Real Power Tool

When you listen attentively, you make an incredible discovery. Sometimes, the person is not delivering the information you need. The chief tool of the good listener is a good question. Questions are marvelous tools for stimulating, drawing out, and guiding communication.

Asking a good question is a learned skill requiring years of training. The foundation of good question-asking is knowing what information you want to obtain. Here are eight handy guidelines for asking better questions — questions that are likely to get to the meat of things:

- **Plan your questions in advance.** Prepare what you're going to ask about but don't memorize the exact wording, or you'll sound artificial. A script is too restrictive to flow naturally into the conversation. However, it pays to outline your purpose and a sequence of related questions. If you plan ahead, you can follow the speaker's train of thought and harvest much more information. Pretty soon, the speaker is comfortably divulging information. The question-and-answer format acts as an aid rather than a block to good communication.

- **Ask with a purpose.** Every question you ask should have one of two basic purposes: to get facts or to get opinions (see Table 9-1 for examples of each). Know which is your goal and go for it, but don't confuse the two concepts.

- **Tailor your question to your listener.** Relate questions to the listener's frame of reference and background. If the listener is a farmer, use farming examples. If the listener is your teenager, make references to school life, dating, or other areas that will hit home. And be sure to use words and phrases the listener understands. Don't try to dazzle your five-year-old with your vast vocabulary or slip computer jargon in on your technologically handicapped, unenlightened boss.

- **Follow general questions with more specific ones.** These specific inquiries, called *follow-up questions,* generally get you past the fluff and into more of the meat-and-potato information. This progression is also the way that most people think, so you are leading them down a natural path.

- **Keep questions short and clear — cover only one subject.** Again, this tip helps you shape your questioning technique to the way the mind really works. People have to process your question. This is no time to show off. Ask simple questions. Questions are just a way to lead people into telling you what you want to know. If you really want to know two different things, ask two different questions. You are the one who wants the information; you are the one who should do the work. Crafting short questions takes more energy but the effort is worth it. Pretty soon, the other party is talking to you about the subject, and you can drop the questioning all together.

✔ **Make transitions between their answers and your questions.** Listen to the answer to your first question. Use something in the answer to frame your next question. Even if this takes you off the path for a while, it leads to rich rewards because of the comfort level it provides to the person you are questioning. This approach also sounds more conversational and therefore less threatening. This is one reason we urge you to plan your questions not to memorize them.

✔ **Don't interrupt; let the other person answer the question!**

Table 9-1	The Two Goals of Asking Questions
To Get Facts	*To Get Opinions*
"When did you begin work on the plan?"	"How good is this plan?"
"How many employees are available?"	"Will the schedule work?"
"What are the dimensions of the house?"	"What do you think of the design?"
"Which car reached the intersection first?"	"Who caused the accident?"

A sharp negotiator may try to use a series of questions to compel you to toward a specific conclusion. Each question is designed to elicit a positive response — a "yes." This sequence of questions leads to a final query posed in the same manner. When you respond in the affirmative to this final question, the negotiation is complete — and you have agreed to your counterpart's terms. Chapter 17 shows how questions can be used to close a deal.

Some people use questions to intimidate or beat up on others. Someone may ask you, "Why in the world would you want to wear a hat like that?" You may be tempted to take off the hat and use it to pummel that person. The best answer, in such cases, is no answer. Let a few beats go by and then go on without answering or acknowledging the question. Some conduct is unworthy of any of your time or energy. Don't try to educate such a person on the niceties of living in a civilized society. It won't work. Keep your eye on your own goal and ignore the diversion.

Avoid leading questions

To get the most telling answers and objective information, don't ask leading questions. *Leading questions* contain the germ of the answer you seek. Here is a typical example of a leading question:

TOP (The Other Person): "I have only used that golf club a couple of times."

You: "How did you like the feel of the great weight and balance on that club?"

Because your question contains a glowing editorial of the golf club, the other person will have a difficult time saying anything negative about it, even if that's what he or she feels. A nonleading question, such as "How do you like it?" is neutral and more likely to elicit the truth.

Here are some more examples of leading questions:

- ✔ "Don't you think that such-and-such is true?"
- ✔ "Isn't the usual price XYZ?"
- ✔ "Everyone agrees that this widget is best, don't you?"

If phrased in a nonleading way, these questions are more likely to extract accurate information or honest opinions. Here are the same three questions reworded:

- ✔ "What do you think about such-and-such?"
- ✔ "What is the usual price of XYZ?"
- ✔ "Which widget do you think is best?"

Leading questions don't help you improve your listening skills or get the highest quality information. As a sales tool, however, you may *want* to lead the person to purchase an item on terms favorable to you. When you are closing a deal, the leading question may help lead the other person right to a close. In this section, we are looking at questions you ask to find out what the other party is thinking, *not* to affirm your own views or serve your own financial interests.

In court, leading questions are not allowed. Witnesses are forced by the laws of evidence to give their own views, not to mimic what the lawyer wants. That is because in court — as in this section — the focus is to find out what factual information the witness has to offer.

Don't assume anything

We all know that the word "assume" makes an "ass" out of "u" and "me." When people make flagrant and obvious assumptions, they tend to make a joke about it. What most people don't realize is how many times each day they make routine assumptions about the intention of the other speaker, without double-checking with that person.

Good listening requires that you don't assume anything about the intention of the speaker. This rule is especially true in conversations with family, friends, and work associates. You learn how they use words and often know their verbal shorthand. This familiarity can lead you to presume that you understand a friend's, family member's, or coworker's point — without carefully considering what this person is actually saying to you. Be wary of jumping to conclusions about the speaker's intent, especially with the important inner circle of people closest to you.

Lawyers say, "Don't assume facts not in evidence." This legal principle covers a group of questions that are not allowed in a court of law. The most famous example of this type of question is

"When did you stop beating your wife?"

This question is actually a trap because the wording implies that you beat your wife in the past. This famous example demonstrates why such questions impede good communication. The question immediately puts someone on the defensive, and responding accurately is impossible if the underlying assumption is false. If the speaker's purpose is to draw out the truth, these three questions are more objective:

- ✔ "Did you ever beat your wife?"
- ✔ (If yes) "Have you stopped beating your wife?"
- ✔ (If yes) "When did you stop beating your wife?"

In business, leading questions are often viewed as improper. At a minimum, they are challenging. This is often hostile. Here is an example:

"Why does your company insist on overcharging on this item?"

Now break down this question so that it doesn't assume any facts not in evidence. Again, to get at the information objectively requires three questions: It also eliminates the hostility.

- ✔ "What does your company charge for this item?"
- ✔ "What do other companies charge for this item?"
- ✔ "Why do you think this discrepancy in pricing exists?"

Note that, in this example, you and the other person may have different pricing information. Breaking the question down into three parts offers an opportunity to clear up this difference without getting into an argument.

At home, leading questions often get viewed as accusations. Because of the emotional ties, such questions can be even more off-putting than they are at work. They can launch an argument pretty quickly. Consider this leading question that often pops up on the home front:

"Why won't you ever talk about it?"

This particular example shows how such question seems to assume an unwillingness to communicate. Try breaking this question down so that it contains no assumptions. Guess what — it takes three questions again. As you read these questions, play them out in your mind trying to picture the reaction of someone you are close with.

- ✔ "If you're not willing to talk about it now, would you be willing to talk about it under different circumstances?"
- ✔ "What are those circumstances?"
- ✔ "How can I help create those circumstances?"

Ask open-ended questions

Unlike simple yes-or-no questions, *open-ended questions* enable the respondent to talk — and enable you to get much more information. In Chapter 15, we discuss using yes-or-no questions to help close a deal. Yes-or-no questions limit choices and force a decision. On the other hand, when you want to find out a person's opinion or gather some facts during the course of a negotiation, the more you get the other person to talk, the more information you learn.

Here is a simple closed question requiring a yes-or-no answer:

"Do you like this car?"

An open-ended question, on the other hand, encourages the person to start talking:

"What do you like best about this car?"

Try some classic open-ended questions when you need to get information. These questions invite the other party to open up and tell all:

"What happened next?"

"So how did that make you feel?"

"Tell me about that."

Notice in the last example that you can ask a question in the declarative format (as a request rather than as a traditional question). That technique can be very useful if you are dealing with a reluctant participant. People who won't answer questions will sometimes respond to a direct order.

Ask again

When a speaker fails to answer your question, you have two choices, depending on the situation.

- ✔ Stop everything until you get your answer or a clear acknowledgment that your question will not be answered. Silence can be golden at these opportunities. Most of us are uncomfortable with silence. An individual may feel compelled to answer a difficult question if you remain silent after posing the question. "The next one who speaks loses."

- ✔ Bide your time and ask the question later. If the question was worth asking in the first place, it's worth asking again.

Which of these two techniques you use depends on the situation. If the situation is fast paced and the information you requested is fundamental to decision making, use the first technique. You can choose the second technique (to bide your time) whenever you know that you will have another opportunity to get the information, and you don't need the information right away. Biding your time is always easier and less confrontational, but if you really need a piece of data, don't be afraid to say, "Wait, I need to know. . . . "

A good way to handle someone who doesn't answer your question is to make a little joke out of the situation with a statement such as, "You're leaving me in the dust," or "I need to catch up." No matter how serious the subject matter of the negotiation, a little humor never hurts, especially if you don't spare yourself as a subject of that humor.

If the person makes a little joke back to avoid the question, you may have to shift back to a serious mode. Persevere until you either get an answer to your question or you realize that you must go elsewhere. If the other party is not going to answer your question, make a note of that fact so that you won't forget to use other resources to get the answer you need.

Don't waste your asks

If you're lucky, the opposing side will answer most of your questions before you ask them. That's why you shouldn't spew out your questions like a Gatling gun. Have patience. Only ask essential questions. If you don't care about the answer one way or the other, don't ask. You are granted only so many *asks* in the world. Don't use them indiscriminately.

Every child learns the futility of repeating the question, "Are we there yet?" At a negotiating table, you may never "get there" if you have overstepped the asking line. The consequences: The listener becomes oversensitive to your probing which often translates to defensiveness and resistance to answering your queries. When someone becomes defensive in one area, they will be defensive in other areas and, therefore, unreceptive to your general position. That's a high price to pay for asking too many questions.

Not asking too many questions is particularly important when you are negotiating across cultures. The other person knows as well as you do that your different backgrounds can cause problems. Asking excessive questions puts the other person on the defensive. You artificially heighten concerns about communication, clarity, and camaraderie. A question puts the person on the spot. If someone doesn't understand your question, that person has to reveal this confusion and may feel stupid. The corollary is that the occasional well-framed question helps you gauge how well you are being understood.

To become a really good questioner, take some time after a negotiating session to think about the questions you asked. Identify the extraneous questions. Remember that every question should serve a purpose. You are not looking for damage that was done in that particular negotiation, you are evaluating the quality of the questions.

Accept No Substitutes

You are listening. You are asking all the right questions at the right time. You are patient. So why aren't you getting the information you need? One of the following possibilities may exist:

- The person simply doesn't want to answer your questions. Maybe company policy prevents disclosure of the information. Maybe the person feels uncomfortable discussing a particular subject matter.

- The person is not good at answering questions. The avoidance is not deliberate or devious. Because of bad habits, sloppiness, or laziness, the person neglects to respond to your inquiry.

- The person is a pathological liar.

In each of these cases, the result is the same. You are not getting a valuable piece of information. The question is "What are you going to do about it?"

- In the first case, make a note and find out the information elsewhere.

- In the second case, use the same techniques as you would for a deliberate dodge. See the next section.

- In the third case, run. Never negotiate with a liar — you can't win.

The next three sections discuss ploys people use to avoid providing accurate answers. When you are alert to these substitutes for honest information, you can demand the real McCoy.

Persistence pays

I once had a negotiation drag on for months because the other party didn't want to give me a specific piece of salary information — even though the initial response was a promise to provide the figure the same day! I represented someone whom a studio was hiring to fill a newly created position, so no salary history was available. I didn't want to negotiate from my client's previous salary because my client had been working outside the studio system for an organization that paid low wages. So I asked the simple question: How much do you pay the person she will be reporting to and how much do you pay the two men who are already in the positions on the same level of the organization chart, even though the duties are different?"

The more time passed, the more I realized the importance of the information I was seeking. I finally called people all around town and came up with the critical information, but I didn't inform my counterparts. Finally, I gave the price I would settle for, but only after I knew this figure was at the very top of their range. We closed shortly thereafter.

The desire of the studio not to disclose what they thought was confidential information caused them to pay more than they had planned. For two years, that desire also kept them from admitting what a good deal my client had gotten. But, of course, I already knew that anyway.

If you can't get information the easy way — through the direct question — do your own research. Research until you get the information you need. Never let yourself be trapped in Dodge City.

Don't tolerate the dodge

Politicians, as a group, seem specially trained to provide anything but an answer when asked a question. For example, if you ask about the state of public education, your representative may launch into a dissertation about family values. Don't accept the dodge when you ask a question. Recognize this tactic for what it is and repeat the question, this time insisting on a real answer or an exact time when you can expect an answer.

When people say that they have to look into something and get back to you, about the only thing you can do (without making a rather obvious and frontal assault on their honesty) is wait. However, you *can* nail them down to a specific date and time. If the question is important enough for the other side to delay (or not answer at all), the issue is important enough for you to press forward. Asking, "When can I expect an answer from you?" is a direct way of obtaining that information. Be sure to make a note of the reply.

Don't accept an assertion for the answer

A person who doesn't want to answer your question may try instead to emphatically state something close to what you are looking for. This technique is common when you are asking for a commitment that the other party doesn't want to make.

The confirmed bachelor, upon being asked for an emotional commitment, may give a little speech about how important monogamy is to him and how having a family is a primary life goal for him. These are reassuring words, but not a commitment. Be sure you get the response you seek — not platitudes in the general subject area.

Sometimes, an assertion about the past is substituted for an answer about the future. For example, you ask whether a company plans to spend $50,000 on advertising in the next year. You receive an emphatic statement that the company has spent $50,000 each year for the past four years, that sales are rising, and that any company would be a fool to cut back now. Don't settle for such assertions — push for an answer. Say something like "Does that mean that your company has made a final commitment to spend $50,000 for advertising this year?"

Because assertions are sometimes delivered with a great deal of energy or passion, you may feel awkward insisting on the answer to your question. Not persisting with the inquiry can be fatal to your interests.

Don't allow too many pronouns

Beware the deadly pronoun: he, she, they, especially the infamous *they*. Pronouns can send you into a quagmire of misunderstanding. Every single day, it seems, we have to say to someone, "Too many pronouns." During a negotiation, force your counterpart to use specific nouns and proper names. This preventive measure avoids a great deal of miscommunication.

With pronouns, you must guess which "they" the speaker is talking about. Don't guess. Just throw up your hands and say, with humor, "Too many pronouns." We have never met anyone who begrudged our taking the time to clarify this issue. More often than not, the request is greeted with a chuckle. The potential for confusion is obvious, and everyone appreciates the effort to maintain clarity.

INSIDE SCOOP

No answers, no insurance

At a negotiating seminar we conducted in Palm Springs, an insurance saleswoman passionately related a very common occurrence. She was trying to land a big employee insurance contract with a large corporation. She figured out how she could supply the exact same insurance coverage for substantially less money than the company had been paying.

She asked the buyer point blank, "Can I get this account if I can save you substantial money?"

He looked her right in the eye and said the company would absolutely like to save money on insurance. She pressed on. "The contract will go to the low bid." She was surprised because she knew the company was paying way too much to a broker who had been servicing the account for years. So she repeated the question. "Absolutely" was the assuring answer. "We will buy our next policy based on price alone."

She worked very hard and presented a plan to save the company $25,000. The buyer took her hard work to his long-time friend, the company's current insurance salesperson. When he met the price, he got the contract.

The buyer's assertion was accurate. He never said he wouldn't give his good friend the opportunity to match the bid. The hardworking saleswoman was angry, hurt, and frustrated.

She asked the right question initially, but she accepted a bald assertion in place of the answer she needed. She needed to take time to ask the key question: "If I can show you how to save your company $25,000, will you buy your next policy from me?" To be even more certain, she could have said, "I don't want my quote taken to Joe Blow so that he can match it. Anybody can cut their prices one time to beat me. I will deliver low premiums year after year." She should have gotten an answer to that question before showing exactly how she could save the company all that money.

If she had taken that extra time, she could have saved a great deal more time in the long run — or at least made the choice to take such a risk. As it is, she is feeling cheated out of a commission.

Look for Evidence of Listening

As you listen to the other party in a negotiation, be alert to the occasional indicators that the other person is not really listening to you. If the other person says something like "uh-huh" or "that's interesting," find out immediately whether this response is an expression of genuine interest, a way of postponing discussion, or — equally fatal to communication — a signal that he or she is fighting the dreaded doze monster. Those little demons that tug at the eyelids in the middle of the afternoon cause odd, nonspecific utterances to fall from the lips.

If you suspect the latter, ask a probing question or two to ferret out the truth. Asking, "'Uh-huh' yes you agree, or just 'Uh-huh' you heard me?" is a good way to flush out the noncommittal uh-huh.

When someone says "That's interesting," find out exactly what makes it interesting. Don't be afraid to keep things lively. This approach is much better than having the conversation die right there at the negotiating table.

If you decide that, indeed, your conversational partner is simply not listening, take a break. Often, a quick stretch or, in a more serious case of the afternoon slumps, a walk around the block helps revive everybody. If a distraction is causing the lagging interest in what you are saying, deal with it. Discuss the preoccupying problem or have the distracted party make that critical call.

Let the Silence Begin

Most everyone knows *how* to listen; most people just aren't willing to listen enough of the time. They aren't clear on *when* to listen.

Stories about salespeople talking too much are legion. A good salesperson must be able to sense the time to stop talking and wait for a response. There is an old saying, "The person who talks next loses." That axiom is used in many training courses. Failing to listen to the customer is probably the chief reason sales are lost. The seller keeps talking until the buyer is turned off or at least has gained control of the impulse to buy.

If you want others to listen to what you have to say, you must listen to what they have to say — this is one of life's simplest equations.

No Answer

You know that it's time to play No Answer when you hear voices rise and doors slam. Playing No Answer is particularly effective in your personal life when you and your significant other are not listening to each other; the subject matter is so highly charged that neither side lets the other finish a statement. We began using this technique early in our marriage.

When the dust settles after an argument, suggest that your partner take five or ten minutes to say everything they need to say about the dispute in question. You listen without any comments whatsoever and, in this case, without taking notes. Try to really listen, instead of preparing your rebuttal. Listen mainly for the message under the words.

You must then wait one to three hours. During the elapsed time, go about your normal business without mentioning anything about the dispute. Then, you can take your turn to voice your concerns without interruption from the listener. The cycle can be repeated as often as necessary. Usually the process exhausts itself rapidly because now two adults are listening rather than two children fighting. This technique actually works.

Chapter 10

Your Inner Voice Is Your Best Friend

● ●

In This Chapter

▶ Discovering your inner voice

▶ Using your inner voice

▶ Listening to warning messages

● ●

And this above all, to thine own self be true
And it must follow as night the day,
You cannot be false to any man.

–William Shakespeare

Your *inner voice* is your intuitive self talking to you. Call it a hunch, intuition, or a sixth sense, too many people ignore this inner voice. When you seek your inner truth, you are more likely to be honest and ethical in your dealings with others. We think that's what old Shakespeare was trying to say.

Your inner voice tells you when a deal is sour. Your inner voice tells you to go forward with an agreement, although the money may not be right. *Listen to that voice.* Go to a quiet place and get in touch with what is really going on inside. Talk it out with a trusted adviser if you like, but nothing and no one can give a message as powerfully accurate as your own inner voice can.

One reason that women frequently make such good negotiators is that they tend to have better intuitive skills than men. Some men belittle *women's intuition* as less useful than a quantifiable response to the objective data being presented. However, studies show that successful people, be they men or women, rely heavily on intuition. Learn to trust and value what your inner voice says; don't dismiss it because of self-doubt or the skepticism of others.

Finding Your Inner Voice

Everyone's mind works on two levels: the conscious and the subconscious. Your inner voice is your subconscious. For those interested in the scientific explanation for the inner voice, this section explains the biology of it all. Please, no dissecting.

The conscious and subconscious mind

The mind constantly processes millions of pieces of data quickly and efficiently. The brain feeds the results into a storage device unmatched by any filing system in the world. The *conscious* mind uses this data for speech, recognition, and every other human activity. The actual processing of the information, however, is completely outside our conscious experience. We are unaware of the process because it is *subconscious*.

This subconscious realm is the source of your dreams. The meaning of dreams is not always obvious, especially to the layperson. Psychiatrists are so interested in dreams because dreams are like windows to the subconscious mind.

When you go to sleep, your conscious mind quiets down. Messages, in the form of dreams, barrage you from your subconscious mind, not because your subconscious mind becomes more active, but because your conscious mind becomes less active.

The phenomenon is much like viewing the stars in the heavens. People say, "The sky is full of stars tonight." In fact, the number of stars in the sky hasn't changed. You just can't see them when the glare of the sun obscures them, the night's cloud cover conceals them, or the city lights dim them. Remove the obstructions and millions of stars are visible to the naked eye. We recently visited Death Valley, where you can walk by the light of the stars even if the moon is not visible. It is amazing. We could see the stars because nothing blocked our view.

When you fall asleep, your conscious mind also takes a rest. The noisy thought processes of your conscious mind no longer block out the activity of your subconscious mind. Your dreams are a product of this activity. Sometimes, your demons come tripping out. The welcome and unwelcome activity of your conscious mind plays out much more vividly at night than during the day.

The brain scans millions of pieces of data at lightning speed (and maybe even faster). The result is fed to the speech and reasoning centers of the conscious mind. Only then are we aware of the process and only then can the results be put to use.

Running toward your inner voice

I remember the first time I heard my inner voice. This voice sounded different from the chatter of my inner critic judging what people looked like, what they were wearing, and how their voices sounded. It was 1982, around mile eight of a ten-mile run in my training regime for my first marathon race. It was the longest run I had attempted to date, and I could hear my thoughts slowing down. I thought of a knotty problem with a friend and an impending discussion to negotiate our conflicting views of a vacation we were scheduled to take. I heard my inner voice slowly talking to my friend with understanding and a patient tone. Suddenly, I knew I was listening to the perfect words I would need to say to resolve our conflict, and I realized the situation could be settled.

Some people say it was the extra adrenaline pumping through me, giving me an endorphin high. But now I hear my inner voice when I'm sitting still. At first, I thought I needed a beautiful place — like the beach or mountains. And I thought I had to be alone. But as time went on, I found I could hear my inner voice anywhere (even walking up and down the supermarket aisles). I can summon it by asking myself a question, internally, and then just listening to the answer. Sometimes, my inner voice wakes me up in the early morning hours. I reach for the pad near my bedside and write what it says without editing. Then I go back to sleep. When I awake and read my notes, I can hear my inner voice again and my notes make sense.

For example, a greeting may be issued: "Hi, Judy. How are the kids?" By the time a message of greeting arrives at the speech center, a great deal of processing — evaluating, accepting, and rejecting — has occurred without interference from the conscious mind. In fact your speech center may be otherwise engaged even as the recognition process is occurring. Your brain gives you a final answer instead of a piece of the puzzle. Your processing centers have done all the work — without words, without anxious thought. The process is almost instantaneous and highly accurate because no data is overlooked.

This speedy, subconscious processing of massive amounts of data is what really goes on when we resonate with a hunch or an intuitive feeling about something. Many people develop this aspect of their brains, either by accident or by design, to a very high degree. However, everyone's brain functions in this way.

If you did not have a subconscious that could send such messages, you could not function in the world. You would have to be institutionalized. If you can read this book, you can read your subconscious. Unfortunately, no one teaches you how to read those messages in school. Readin', writin', and resonatin' is not currently the accepted grade school curriculum. Although this discussion of the phenomenon is hardly complete, you may feel more trusting next time your subconscious provides an answer to a complicated problem.

The architecture of the brain

Sometimes, a picture is worth a thousand words. We scribble felt-tip cartoons to highlight points in our negotiating seminars. Figure 10-1 is a nice, professional drawing to show where all those inner thoughts come from.

Look first at the brain stem right at the base of the skull. Scientists sometimes call this the *reptilian brain,* because all vertebrates from reptiles to mammals have one. This part of the brain oversees reproduction, self-preservation, and the vital functions of the body.

The *limbic system* seems to be the source of motivation as well as vivid emotions such as fear and aggression. From an evolutionary point of view, the limbic system and the brain stem are the oldest parts of the brain. Together, these two areas of the brain generate subconscious thought.

Overlying all of this is the *cerebral cortex* (as in, "Herbert is too cerebral," meaning he's too logical or too brainy). The *cerebral cortex,* sometimes called "the gray matter," is the part of the brain that is logical, alert, and in contact with your daily surroundings. The cerebral cortex is your conscious mind. It tries to find a cause for every effect and an effect for every cause. To a certain degree, the cerebral cortex can modify the instinctive reactions of your subconscious mind.

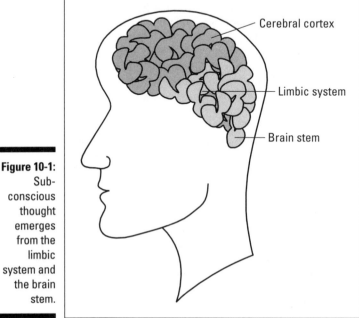

Figure 10-1:
Sub-
conscious
thought
emerges
from the
limbic
system and
the brain
stem.

So now you have it. Your very own picture of a human brain. Proof, right here in black and white, that the subconscious mind does exist. You are not crazy when you come up with a solution to a problem and you cannot explain logically each step in the process, but you know you are right. Your subconscious mind gave you the answer.

How You Can Use Your Inner Voice

The inner voice is most adept at sending messages of warning. This feature remains in all of us from primitive days when our survival depended on keen senses. The messages to run, duck, hide, be quiet, or stay still had to be honored if cavepeople wanted to stay alive. The warning cry is the one emitted most strongly by the inner voice. What a great tool! It can guide you away from dangerous decisions you may make in your life.

Remember that the inner voice is easily masked. If it were not, you would go crazy from all the voices in your head. Consequently, you can talk, read, process data, and perform myriad tasks while your subconscious mind is busily doing its thing. Therefore, if you want to get in touch with your inner voice, you must quiet your conscious mind. For some people, this would involve a mind-relaxing activity such as running, walking, or fishing. Other people must sit quietly for a few minutes. Do whatever works for you in order to let those inner messages surface.

If this is a new idea to you, you may have to practice. You have to be extra alert until you get used to accepting the complete messages that come from the subconscious without explanation. As you do, the messages come to you more often and more clearly. Don't be discouraged as you attempt this process and remember that listening to your inner voice is a personal process. Your subconscious is your own storehouse of information, unlike anybody else's. It is where your entire life is captured. You can enjoy great success if you can use that information by following your inner voice.

The disadvantage of articulating answers and decisions brought to you by your subconscious is that you are unable to discuss the process that occurred or describe the logic that was used. You were not conscious of the process while it was occurring. You cannot explain the entire process to someone in the same way you can explain a conscious, logical path from problem to solution. The logic occurs too quickly and uses too many bits of data to explain rationally.

How many people in your life can question you about how you arrive at your decisions? The longer the list, the less comfortable you are with decisions that you cannot rationally explain. Very successful people have fewer people to answer to, which is one reason they can get away with intuitive problem solving. When the boss says, "I smell a rat!" nobody asks for a detailed analysis. Subordinates accept the intuitive process. "Put it in a memo" is simply not an appropriate response to the boss's hunch . . . intuitive process . . . inner voice.

Hearing Two Voices

Be assured that you do not have two different inner voices inside you. You only have one of these phenomenal subconscious centers. When people talk about *conflicting voices* within themselves, they are frequently experiencing their conscious mind testing the solution provided by the subconscious mind. Almost without exception, the solution provided by the subconscious part of the mind survives this testing, but the solution provided by the conscious part of the mind is easier to rationalize and explain. The conscious thought process is reducible to words.

The other phenomenon that may give you the idea that you have two inner voices is your memory of voices from your childhood, mostly from your mother or father. Your inner voice tells you to go forth. A parental voice, indelibly etched in your memory, says, "Don't do that. That is dangerous. You will fail." As adults, we need to recognize the play of memory messages. Look skyward and say, "It's okay. I can do it. And if I fail, that's okay, too. I need to try — for me."

If the owner of that parental voice is still alive, look skyward anyway. Don't act out this conversation with a real person. The last thing you need is a protracted discussion with a dubious critic at just the time you need to gird up your loins and sally forth on a new adventure.

Inner critics aren't all bad. Having an inner critic is good when you need that kind of feedback. Decide between your inner voice and your inner critic and do what is right for you.

Paying Heed to Special Messages

The inner voice works best as a warning system. Sometimes those warnings come through loud and clear. When that happens, heed them. Messages that are both loud and clear are special indeed. These messages are rarely wrong.

Shady characters

Although hardly anyone states it so bluntly, one thing you want to know about the other party in a negotiation is whether or not you can trust the information that person gives you. What is this person's reputation for honesty and accuracy? If you are trying to negotiate efficiently, you must find out the general trustworthiness of the assertions from the other side.

MEN & WOMEN

Sometimes you feel like a nut . . . sometimes you don't

We women often have trouble distinguishing our inner voice from our inner critic. Frequently, a woman's inner critic doesn't give her permission to follow her instincts if they run counter to a man's. Some women have been socialized to be cautious of acting differently from the way a man expects them to — especially in dating situations. As a result, women often chicken out of potentially successful negotiations with men.

A woman once told me a story that illustrates this point nicely. Her boyfriend came over to watch a movie and brought a big bag of peanut M&Ms "to share." The woman had told him previously that she was allergic to nuts, but she chose not to remind him. Instead, she just carefully ate off the chocolate and spit out the peanuts!

Quite a romantic evening, huh? The story may sound funny, but I find it sad. Wanting to please a man you care about isn't sad, but not wanting to demonstrate separateness is. This woman imagined that expressing her individuality would threaten her boyfriend (note that she seemed to have no trouble telling her preferences to another woman). In fact, most men aren't bothered by such expressions, but rather appreciate your ability to express your preferences.

Imagining that *any* expression of your own needs will create a problem is sad. Research indicates that men want to be appreciated. So why do we women back out of telling them what we want? Why do we give in before even trying to negotiate? We say, "Do what you want; it's okay." The implied message is "What I want isn't important."

Gloria Steinem points out that we are empathy sick — we have walked in someone else's shoes so much that we've forgotten how to fill our own. You need to do unto yourself as you would do for others. Start listening to your inner voice to find out what it is that you want — not what you think others expect.

Sometimes, you hear that someone is not dishonest, just ignorant, inefficient, or inexperienced. These qualities may sound better than dishonesty, but they have the same consequence to you. As a negotiator, you cannot afford to blindly accept anything that such a person says to you.

A different but highly related issue is whether you can trust the client represented by the person with whom you are negotiating. Even if you trust the negotiator, you may feel that you need to be extra careful in dealing with the party on the other side of the negotiating table.

The best advice we can offer is not to do business with a person you don't trust. No lawyer in the world can protect you from someone determined to do you in, cheat you, or steal from you. No cop or security system in the world can protect your house from a sufficiently determined thief. President Kennedy once prophetically observed, "There is no secret service agent who can guarantee a president's life, if someone is willing to give their own life in exchange."

Sometimes, you are forced to do business with someone you don't trust. In such a case, be sure to focus on the parts of the contract that will protect you if something goes wrong. Decide where a lawsuit would be filed and in which courts. Your lawyer can be a big help here. Make provisions for when and how you can check the books for accuracy. In such a case, you must prepare a much more detailed contract than you normally would.

Having clauses that protect you is always important in case you come to honest differences that you did not anticipate. Such clauses are the special province of an experienced attorney. For example, if someone is to pay you money under a contract, you want a fast and certain way to collect in case of default. The negotiator who does not consider this aspect of the deal is not doing a good job. Negotiating for big payments is futile if the payments are, as a practical matter, uncollectible. You may want to insist that all funds under negotiation be held in a special account until the contract is finalized.

If you want to include clauses to protect yourself but can't get the other party to agree, you must decide whether you want to do business with this person. Listen carefully to why the other party is not willing to provide certain mechanisms that put your mind at ease about payment. If that person insists on maintaining an unfair out, think twice before entering into the agreement. Be clear in expressing the importance of these provisions and why you must have them.

If everything else seems good about a deal, walking away based on these points can be difficult. The other side knows that and will often turn the issue into a *trust test:* "If you trust me, you'll make this deal with me." Look such a person right in the eye and say, "I trust you well enough to enter this deal. But I don't know what good or bad fortune is going to visit you over the next year while I am needing steady payments. You may quit the company (or sell your business). You may get killed. I just don't know what the future holds."

Questionable deals

If your inner voice tells you that you don't want to make a deal, stop the negotiation. Relax. Examine that message. Either your subconscious will send you a more detailed message, or your conscious mind will work it out logically.

Ask yourself why you have reservations. What is the reason you don't want to buy this boat? Is it that you'll never use it? Or that you may move soon? Or perhaps because it's not as big as your neighbor's boat? Sometimes, you can resolve these reservations; other times, you can't. Don't go forward with a deal if your inner voice tells you not to.

Pre-buyer's remorse

If you experience buyer's remorse before you even buy, stop everything.

Heed any strong messages that a given course of action is wise or unwise. Mold your conduct to that message. You don't have to stand up in the middle of a meeting and announce to the assembly that your inner voice is telling you that the discussions are over. In fact, you may decide to keep the source of your decision to yourself. You should heed the message and begin to concentrate on closing the discussion. Wrap up the deal. Use the message without necessarily announcing it to the room.

Try to develop your ability to listen to your inner voice. It is the most important voice you can possibly hear. No one knows you better than you do. People who learn to hear their inner voice — unfiltered by reason or rationale — are always happier with their decisions (and thus less likely to experience buyer's remorse) than those who are not able to do so.

Chapter 11

Listening to Body Language

. . . .

In This Chapter

▶ Deciphering the body language of others

▶ Using your own body language effectively

▶ Putting your knowledge to work in a negotiation

▶ Recognizing resistance, boredom, and nervousness

▶ Exhibiting openness, interest, and confidence

. . . .

*W*ithout ever being conscious that you are reading body language, you can recognize such emotions as fear, sadness, happiness, love, and hatred in another human being's unspoken communication. Words aren't necessary to express these feelings.

Honing your ability to use and understand body language is one of the most enjoyable ways to improve negotiating skills. Look for the activity icons sprinkled throughout this chapter. Even if you are already doing some of these activities instinctively, begin practicing them consciously. Doing these activities can help you become fluent in body language in the same way you learn any other language — through practice.

Everybody's Bilingual

In addition to the words you speak, you also use another, silent language — body language. *Body language* refers to all the ways people communicate *without* speaking or writing. We are born with an ability to communicate nonverbally. In fact, we spend the first few months of our lives communicating without words.

People can send and receive body language from four different parts of the body. In order of expressiveness and reliability, these are:

- Facial expressions and eyes
- Arms and hands
- Legs and feet
- Torso positions and posture

Human beings receive most nonverbal cues from the face. Because people primarily look at each other's faces during communication, humans have evolved to understand facial cues the best. Professional card players rely so heavily on controlling their facial expressions that the term *poker face* is used to describe the ability to hide feelings behind a mask of nonexpression. Interestingly, photographic studies show that even the most practiced card sharks cannot prevent the pupils of their eyes from expanding when they open a really good hand. The general rule for arms, hands, legs, and feet is that closed positions (crossed arms and legs) signal resistance and open positions signal receptivity.

The torso position can be the hardest to read because posture and seating position are often a matter of individual habit. Moreover, people don't always have the opportunity to observe each other's full torso during a meeting. Nevertheless, the torso can be a valuable source of meaning to the experienced observer.

Many expressions of the human body are the same throughout the world. Facial expressions are especially similar. Smiles are an international greeting. Laughing is an international expression of happiness. A person in deep thought anywhere in the world looks like Rodin's famous sculpture *The Thinker*. Crying and anguish are universally understood and look the same on anyone's face regardless of race, sex, or national origin. These forms of body language seem to be a *natural* part of the human condition. Other gestures are *learned;* that is, some gestures are culturally and socially determined. Here are some examples:

- In some societies in India, people shake their heads up and down to mean "no" and from side to side to mean "yes." In the Western world, the opposite is true.

- In Japan, people point to themselves by pressing their index fingers against their noses. Americans convey the same meaning by pointing to their hearts using a finger, thumb, or hand.

- The only men in the world who prop a foot up on their opposite knee are from America. Non-Americans who see this position for the first time are taken aback. They are accustomed to men crossing their legs by putting one knee over the other.

Some elements of body language are even admissible as evidence in the courts of most states, under certain circumstances. For example, flight can be considered evidence of guilt. If the courts are paying attention to these acts, you can't afford to do less.

Here's an activity for the next time you're at an airport or bus terminal. Watch callers talk on the telephone. See if you can guess who is on the other end of the line, just by observing the callers' body language. Notice the positions of their bodies. If a person is cradling the phone affectionately, with head cocked and body hunched to make the conversation as private as possible, a romantic interest is probably on the other end. If the person is shifting from foot to foot and looking around, a spouse or significant other is probably on the line (sad, but true). If the caller is standing erect and staring down at some notes or looking straight ahead in concentration, the call is, most likely, business related.

Don't forget that body language doesn't replace other forms of communication. Body language is part of the big communication package everyone uses all the time. You should evaluate verbal and nonverbal messages within the greater context of the situation. (Read the section "Don't Believe Everything You See," at the end of this chapter.)

Next time you watch a feature film, pay particular attention to the actors when they are not speaking. What are they saying to you with their bodies? Consciously think about the message being communicated. The better the actors, the more they are able to communicate without words. Feature films can provide a wealth of education about body language, especially scenes without dialogue. We watched John Malkovich in a film last night. We saw him walk thoughtfully, stand pensively, realize his wife may be in danger, and race in a panic to save her. The wordless performance was marvelous. Look for such a sequence in the next film you watch.

Making a career of reading body language

During court trials, most people focus on the lawyers, witnesses, defendants, and victims. In high profile cases, however, attorneys often hire consultants who concentrate solely on the members of the jury. Working in the courtroom, jury consultants study the body language of the jurors and interpret their reactions to specific witnesses and pieces of evidence. Based on these skilled observations, the consultants try to determine which way the jury is leaning — which witnesses are winning favor and which evidence is most persuasive.

When you reenter the United States after a trip abroad, you usually have to fill out some forms declaring what items you are bringing into the country. You hand the form to an immigration official, who is trained to look at a traveler's eyes when asking, "Do you have anything to declare?" What the eyes say is much more important than what the form says.

What Our Bodies Can Say

Verbal and written communications are not the only elements of communication in a negotiation — or in life. Good negotiators only get better when they draw meaning and insight from the way a person stands or sits, the way a person dresses, or the panoply of facial expressions that play out during a conversation. That's why, in our negotiation seminars, we say, "Listen with your ears, your eyes, and every pore in between."

Different nonverbal communications are associated with different attitudes. Becoming savvy to these relationships can put you at a great advantage. As a negotiator, you have two distinct tasks:

- ✔ Make sure that *your* body language expresses the message you want to send. Your body language needs to be consistent with your words.

- ✔ Read the nonverbal signals of the person with whom you are negotiating. You need to recognize when someone is sending conflicting words and actions, and when someone's gestures add emphasis to the words.

When you become a student of body language, you quickly realize that gestures come in packs. Rarely does anyone invoke one gesture to the exclusion of all others; doing so makes a person look stiff.

Next time you are at a school variety show, note the nervous singer who points stiffly to match the words of the song. Contrast that with the fluid motions of a successful singer whose gestures tie into the emotional meaning of the lyrics rather than the literal meaning of the words.

Matching your body language with your words

Don't mix and match when it comes to your body language and your spoken words. Even people who have not read this book draw meaning from your body language when you speak. People expect corresponding body language to accompany verbal messages. Inconsistent communications from you will throw your listener off, even if the person has never heard the phrase "body language."

When you are speaking, be sure that your body language matches your words, if you want your words to be believed. If you are enthusiastic about a project, show that enthusiasm in your body. Don't recline relaxed on the sofa. The message of uninterest communicated by your body will be remembered far longer than the words of interest that come out of your mouth.

Several reasons may explain why your body language may not match your words.

✔ **You are having an energy drain.** When you are tired, keeping your body properly expressive takes extra energy. If your energy seems to drain away in the middle of the afternoon, take an energy bar with you. Some of them actually taste good — a little chewy perhaps, but good. Don't lose a deal because your tired body is saying "I don't care one way or another."

✔ **You are not concentrating on the communication of the moment.** As you read about body language, you will notice that many gestures, movements, and mannerisms indicate that a person is actually thinking about a matter other than the current topic of conversation. If this happens to you, ask for a break so that you can make a phone call and clear a concern out of your mind. When you are in a negotiating session, be sure that you are *in* the session with your heart, mind, and soul. Your physical presence may be much less important than your mental presence. Athletes call it "being in the moment."

✔ **You have developed bad communication habits.** Some classic comic sketches illustrate this point: The disgusted spouse utters a terse, "Fine" with a tight little smile that lets a partner know that things are anything but fine. Or the smiling letch leaning in for the kill says, "Why, I wouldn't hurt a fly." If you have any mannerisms that project a different meaning from the words you are uttering, work on breaking the habit.

For one gender to misread the behaviors of the opposite sex is common. This situation doesn't have to involve words at all — just one person looking at another and reading entirely different meanings than those intended. In *Sex For Dummies,* Dr. Ruth Westheimer includes a whole section on mixed signals between the genders in the chapter "Ten Things Men Wish Women Knew about Sex." She gives a great example of a wife simply trying to cool off as she arrives home from a hot afternoon of shopping, and the husband entirely misreading her movements. Learning to read suggestive body language can make you a great negotiator with your partner; misreading it can put you in the doghouse.

Reading someone else's body language

Being able to accurately read the true attitude and feelings of someone across the table can be enormously important. Seldom do you see adults physically clap their hands over their ears to avoid hearing something, but people have other ways of signaling that they aren't listening, such as allowing their eyes to wander or attending to an unrelated task.

Disney released a wonderful film called *Frank and Ollie* about a couple of the world's greatest observers of body language: Two of the original animators of such classics as *Cinderella* and *Bambi*. This film shows the two mimicking various elements of body language to communicate feelings and then making sketches of their own movements. Watch this movie as a primer on body language; it illustrates the points of this chapter better than all the words ever written on the subject.

The ability to read a person's body language enables you to adjust your approach to that person. Based on what you learn about the other person's mood or attitude, you can temper your own words and actions appropriately — for example, you can calm down someone who's agitated or perk up someone who's bored.

Several studies conclude that women are better at reading body language than men. You may think that this gender difference is due to the practice many women get standing over a crib at 2:00 in the morning trying to figure out the exact meaning of the flailing arms and heaving chest of a little bundle of joy. Actually, the discrepancy has to do with the fact that men tend to take in data sequentially (piece by piece), whereas women usually absorb the entire picture at once before focusing on the details. If you're guilty of overlooking the forest for the trees, try taking a moment to size up the next person you meet as a total package before commencing a conversation.

Discover how much fun you can have reading the body language of others. The more you practice this skill, the better you will be at negotiating. The next time you go to an event connected to your work, pause a moment at the door. Instead of looking for someone you know, look over the room. Identify the more influential people. Try to distinguish who wields power. Who are the employers? Who are the employees? What differences in body language make social status apparent? If you're at a social gathering, see if you can spot very outgoing people. Who is shy? Are any of the couples fighting?

Conflicting messages

Reading the body language of another person is not a trick to gain advantage. It is a tool to improve communication. People who are exhibiting incongruous body language are frequently unaware of the fact that their spoken words and their true feelings, as revealed by their body language, are not consistent. By drawing out those differences and reconciling them, you have done a great service to your side and to the person with whom you are negotiating.

If you pick up an incongruity between what a person's body is saying and what that person's mouth is saying, you can assume that something is going on. It is usually one of the following:

- The person is unaware of his or her effect on others.
- The person's body language is expressing a hidden agenda.
- The person is too tired or is confused.

In any case, you want to take a reality check and start asking the person questions about what he or she is thinking and feeling.

One of the most common examples of body language not matching the situation is the *nervous laugh*. A laugh that is not a reaction to anything humorous signals nervousness or discomfort. In fact, it's a dead giveaway. If you hear a nervous laugh, let a few beats go by and then turn directly to the source of the laughter and encourage that person to verbalize his or her feelings. Depending on the situation, you may say: "Ben, how do you feel about the pricing structure?" or "Ben, how do you feel about adding Leslie to this team?" Often, the person won't admit to having any concerns. You know better. Keep probing. You may have to return to the subject a few times, rephrasing your request until the truth comes out.

Many employees complain that their supervisors give mixed messages with body language. The words are positive, but the body language is negative. For example, your boss calls you in for a meeting. She says, "Good morning," and begins to discuss your recent improvement in punctuality. However, her arms are crossed at the waist, and her head is angled away from you so that she's looking at you sideways. You know that these are negative signals. If you have the guts, you may venture, "It looks to me like something else may be bothering you." Your boss may be forthright about her annoyance, or she may pound a fist on the table and deny her true feelings with a sharp reply, "What makes you think anything is bothering me?"

Mi Says • Mimi Says • Mimi Says • Mimi Says • Mimi Says • Mimi Says • Mimi Says • Mimi Says • Mimi Says • Mimi Says • Mimi Says

Reading body language at home

I learned to read Michael's teenager pretty well. Because my office is at home, I was often there when she came home from school. I could tell what kind of day she had by the intensity with which she slammed the door. Then I listened to her footsteps. They were happy, skipping footsteps, or plodding, weight-of-the-world-on-her-shoulders footsteps, depending on what kind of day she'd had.

She called out, "Hi, Meem" when she was in a happy or neutral mood. When she was unhappy, she went directly to her room to unwind or cool down before she came into my office to say hello. If she was seeking her own space to unwind, I left her alone before sharing my day with her. Wendy is thoughtful and quite private. I would never barge in on her in that circumstance. When she was in an "up" mood, I would just holler out an invitation to come on in.

What I was doing was not just being friendly. This sensitivity is actually a negotiating strategy: when you respect a person's feelings and/or need for privacy, he or she is more likely to respect yours. I built trust between us — any negotiator would be wise to do so.

Mimi Says • Mimi Says • Mimi Says • Mimi Says • Mimi Says • Mimi Says • Mimi Says • Mimi Says • Mimi Says • Mimi Says • Mimi Says

If you get conflicting verbal and nonverbal messages from someone, but that person denies that a discrepancy exists, you are witnessing a *blind spot* — something you know about others that they themselves are not conscious of. Blind spots cause miscommunications and resentment.

In a negotiation, if you suspect the other party has a blind spot, you need to take frequent reality checks. Check out your understanding with your counterpart's body language. You may even begin with the statement, "I need a reality check." Then go right into your reading: "I sense I have lost you," or "I sense we should take a break." If you take responsibility for your need, your counterpart is less likely to be defensive, and you are more likely to get truthful information. This way you may get at your opponent's true feelings. Sometimes you even uncover some underlying interests.

Most people have at least one blind spot: one area in which they don't really know how their words or actions are affecting people. Blind spots are like bad breath — everyone knows except the person who has it. The best way to find your blind spot is to invite feedback.

If the blind spot belongs to another, you need to ask the person if he or she wants your feedback. If the response is no, believe it. You may need to find a higher-up to deal with the issue — someone the individual *must* listen to.

Emphasizing with body language

Pound the table. Wave your arms. Jump up and down. These are a few of the classic ways the body emphasizes communication. It is the equivalent of scrawling something in all caps and red letters. However, save these demonstrations until you need them.

If you use loudness throughout a negotiation, the added volume carries no special meaning when you really need it. You just seem bellicose. Johnny Carson used to refer to his lawyer as Bombastic Bushkin. The tag fit, and it stuck. Soon, no one around this particular lawyer paid much attention to the bombasity.

We recently went into a print shop with a rush project. The owner slapped a big red sticker on the order. We felt good. He threw our project on a stack of work. Everything in the stack had the same red sticker. Our hearts sank. The red sticker lost all its meaning. Raising your voice too often has the same result.

The key to emphasis is a change from the norm. Body language always involves a cluster of movements. It should naturally be tied into voice levels, tempo, and loudness. Sometimes, you can create extra emphasis by exhibiting body language that runs counter to the communication. For example, you may lean forward and quietly, slowly say that you are very, very angry. Here the emphasis is created just as powerfully — maybe more so — than if you had been yelling at the top of your lungs.

Surprises can occur in any negotiation. Generally speaking, however, you should know going into a negotiating session what will and won't be important. Hold back your emphasis until you get to the stuff that is really important to you. This strategy is why a good negotiator lets the merely annoying issues slide by and saves the emphasis for the truly important points.

Using Your Knowledge of Body Language in Your Next Negotiation

In Lerner and Lowe's *My Fair Lady,* Professor Henry Higgins notices a lascivious nobleman chasing Eliza Doolittle. Higgins says of the nobleman, "He oiled his way around the floor, oozing charm from every pore." Higgins may exaggerate the body language of his rival, but some men and women do seem to have that *certain something.* They enter a room and immediately draw people's attention. These charmers are not necessarily the best-looking people in the room; they are the ones who have a command of body language. They use this ability to signal their message, "I'm desirable, attractive, and worth getting to know." And when such a person focuses on you, you definitely know that the person is interested; the attention can almost make you blush. The person is employing dozens of nonverbal signals to convey his or her intent.

From the moment you walk into a negotiation, you should observe the body language of everybody in the room. All during the negotiation, keep observing your opponent's body language. Focus on the four channels: face and head, arms and hands, legs and feet, and torso. When you are so focused on the total person who is talking to you, you will listen better. Your observations of body language will help you pick up unstated nuances such as what items are more important, and what items are less important to the other side.

Complete shifts in body language during a negotiation can be more telling than isolated signals. These shifts reveal that an issue is vitally important or is causing stress to the other party. For most of the negotiation, your counterpart will stay in the same general position. Notice any shifts from that position. These movements indicate that the person you are dealing with has changed in attitude in some way. Being aware of this body language can be particularly important if the other party:

- ✔ Feels that you are talking about a sensitive issue
- ✔ Is losing interest
- ✔ Needs a break or a stretch
- ✔ Is turning off to your arguments

Watch that body language! It can be like a traffic signal. The shifts in body language can be yellow caution lights telling you to proceed slowly, look, and listen. In the extreme, they are red lights telling you to stop! Stop now! Don't go further without taking a break. They can also be green lights telling you to go in for the close.

Don't ignore nonverbal signals. You may even want to include your observations in your written notes just as you include spoken words. This record helps build familiarity with the other person's unspoken vocabulary. Everybody uses body language differently.

Knowing where to stand

The most important single observation you can make about a room full of people is the personal space each person commands. During conversation, for example, people don't lean closely into the space of an important person they think has greater standing than they do (either in wealth, influence, power, or social status). In studies of personal space, rooms of unsuspecting subjects are photographed and later identified. Without fail, the more powerful people are accorded greater personal space by the other people in the room. Figure 11-1 illustrates how your use of space communicates certain signals to others.

Mimi Says • Mimi Says • Mimi Says • Mimi Says • Mimi Says • Mimi Says • Mimi Says • Mimi Says • Mimi Says • Mimi Says • Mimi Says

Human instincts

Animals are instinctive about personal distance. My nephews, aged three, six, and ten, took me on a walk around their neighborhood bordering on the mountains in Boulder, Colorado. When we rounded one corner, we saw several deer: two does and three fawns. Matthew, the six-year-old, whispered, "Shhh, Auntie Mimi, I'll show you how we can get close." All three boys started tiptoeing, forefingers to lips, creeping toward the deer. I could tell that my nephews had done this before. When we got about 25 feet from the deer, the deer moved away slightly.

With every few steps of ours, the deer moved a few steps away correspondingly.

"Why are the deer afraid? We won't hurt them," whispered Mark, the three-year-old.

"They always move away," whispered ten-year-old Adam, knowingly.

Adam suspected the basis of formal public distance — animal instinct. We kept creeping forward, but the deer never let the distance between us shrink to less than 25 feet.

Mimi Says • Mimi Says • Mimi Says • Mimi Says • Mimi Says • Mimi Says • Mimi Says • Mimi Says • Mimi Says • Mimi Says • Mimi Says

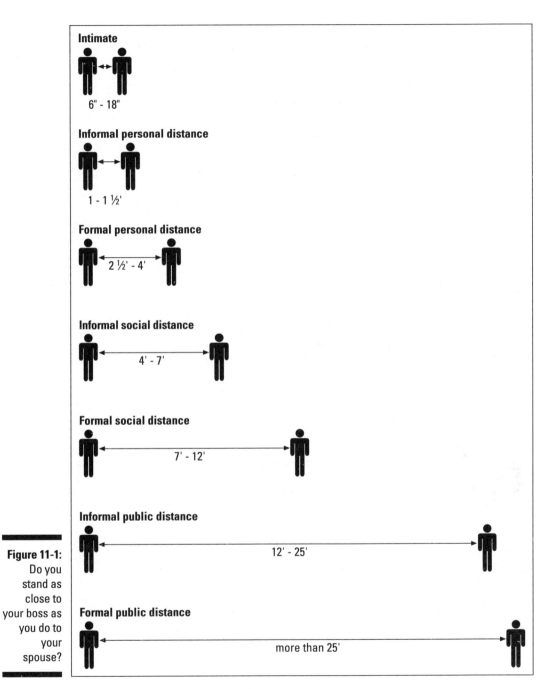

Figure 11-1:
Do you
stand as
close to
your boss as
you do to
your
spouse?

Spatial relationships come into play when you set up a room for a meeting. Almost intuitively, people know that an important negotiation warrants a table large enough to keep a formal distance between people.

If someone must dominate a meeting, that person is seated at the head of the table. Control over the dominant chair may be the most obvious and enduring sign of power both in the workplace and at home. Remember Archie Bunker from television's *All in the Family?* Archie didn't control a clear position of power at work, so his chair became a very important symbol of his status at home.

Seating in a meeting is important, because once the spatial relationships are established, they are not easy to change. Take a moment before your next meeting and think about what relationship you want to establish with the other attendees. Arrange the seating accordingly.

Making the first contact

One of the best ways you can begin a meeting is with great body language. Let your enthusiasm and energy show. Stick out your hand. Meet the other person's eyes and give a good, firm handshake. If you don't own a good handshake, develop one now. This skill is not difficult, but we are amazed at how many people don't shake hands well. Let the flesh between your thumb and forefinger meet the other person's flesh between the thumb and forefinger. Press — do not squeeze — the hand. One pump accompanied by eye contact is plenty. One or two more may express great enthusiasm; any more than that can make the person uncomfortable.

Women greeting women in America can touch both hands at the same time as an alternative to a handshake. A hug, even in a business meeting, is appropriate if the relationship between the two women warrants this familiarity. Increasingly (especially in Hollywood), hugs between men who know each other are common. We are glad that this practice is beginning to extend to friendly respectful hugs between men and women.

Handshaking is far from uniform around the world. Germans seem to be a nation of one-pump people. The French often shake hands when entering and when leaving a room. The Japanese forego the whole handshaking business for a bow, but they understand that Americans are handshakers and have embraced the custom.

MEN & WOMEN ♀♂

Touching is different

When women engage in conversations, they often touch each other. When they don't, social status may be a factor. If one woman is higher-up on the social ladder, the subordinate often hesitates to touch first. If the higher-up touches the subordinate's arm or hand for emphasis, this overture is generally perceived as okay.

Men touch each other, too, in the form of playful elbowing or little light punching jabs to the arms. In the workplace, women used to be able to touch men on the arm for emphasis; men were generally not allowed to touch women in this way. Now, corporate customs and policies are much more strict, given the raised consciousness about sexual harassment. If you are wondering whether to touch *anybody* in the workplace of the '90s, our advice is this: If you are in doubt, don't touch.

How comfortable you feel touching the person you're negotiating with depends, in part, on your cultural background. When we conducted a seminar in Milan, Italy, on negotiating, we suggested not to invade the personal space and not to touch the opposite sex during a negotiation. Hands shot up all around. The Italians let us know that they *do* touch each other, and the custom is considered acceptable by both sexes — it is not a man's domain, and it is not considered sexual harassment by either gender. One woman said that touching each other was a part of conversing and if she told a man not to touch her, she would highly offend him. A man said dramatically, "It would be as if she cut off my hand."

Consider the environment in which you are negotiating and assess the acceptable norms for touching.

Showing that you're receptive (and knowing if your counterpart isn't)

If you pay attention to body language early in a negotiation, you can spot signals of how *receptive* (that is, how ready to listen and how open to your ideas) your counterpart is. Remember to look at all four channels of body language (see "Everybody's Bilingual," earlier in this chapter). Consider eye contact, for example. Research shows that, during conversation, people look at each other between 30 and 60 percent of the time. A listener who meets your eyes less than 30 percent of the time is probably unreceptive. If eye contact is made more than 60 percent of the time, chances are the listener's attitude is positive.

Table 11-1 shows the positive and negative cues associated with being receptive and unreceptive. If you want to look ready and attentive, or if you need to recognize these qualities in your counterpart, look for the positive cues. You probably don't ever want to look unreceptive, but you do want to notice if others are unreceptive, so you should also be familiar with the negative cues in Table 11-1.

Table 11-1 Body Language of Receptive and Unreceptive Listeners

Body Channel	Receptive (Positive Cues)	Unreceptive (Negative Cues)
Facial expressions and eyes	Smiles, much eye contact, more interest in the person than in what is being said	No eye contact or squinted eyes, jaw muscles clenched, cheeks twitching with tension, head turned slightly away from the speaker so the eye contact is a *sidelong* glance
Arms and hands	Arms spread, hands open on the table, relaxed in the lap, or on the arms of a chair, hands touching the face	Hands clenched, arms crossed in front of the chest, hand over the mouth or rubbing the back of the neck
Legs and feet	Sitting: Legs together, or one in front of the other slightly (as if at the starting line of a race). Standing: Weight evenly distributed, hands on hips, body tilted toward the speaker	Standing: Crossed legs, pointing away from the speaker. Sitting or standing: Legs and feet pointing toward the exit
Torso	Sitting on the edge of the chair, unbuttoning suit coat, body tilted toward the speaker	Leaning back in the chair, suit coat remains buttoned

Receptive people look relaxed with open hands, displaying the palms, indicating an openness to discussion. The more of the palm that is visible, the greater the receptivity of the person. They lean forward, whether they are sitting or standing. Receptive negotiators unbutton their coats. Public television's Mr. Rogers always removed his sweater, exemplifying the body language of an open, honest person ready to listen to what you have to say.

By contrast, people who aren't willing to listen may keep their hands on their hips, lean back in the chair, or protectively fold their arms across their chest. People who aren't receptive clench their hands into a fist or tightly grip some other body part. Having one leg up on the arm of the chair often appears to be an open posture, but watch out; more often, this position signals a lack of consideration. Figure 11-2 shows the typical body language of someone who's receptive and someone who definitely is not.

Studies show that parties are more likely to reach an agreement if they begin a negotiation displaying receptive body language (shown on the left in Figure 11-2). This result appears to be true whether the stance was an unconscious

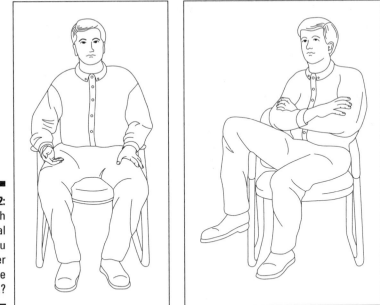

Figure 11-2:
Which
individual
would you
rather
negotiate
with?

decision or a contrived strategy for beginning a meeting in a positive manner. In addition, the defensive postures are also contagious. If one person assumes a defensive posture and holds that position for any period of time, you can actually watch others in the room adopting the same position.

Seeing a change of heart

Observing how someone is sitting or standing (as in Table 11-1) is only the first step in reading body language — after all, people aren't frozen in time like statues. They move; their positions and gestures change with their attitudes and emotions. Notice these shifts. They are important. They may mean that the person is getting restless, or they may mean a shift up or down in the person's acceptance level.

As someone's acceptance of your ideas grows, you may notice the following indicators:

- Cocking the head
- Squinting the eyes slightly
- Taking off or otherwise playing with eyeglasses
- Pinching the bridge of the nose

✔ Leaning forward, uncrossing legs, and scooting to the edge of the chair

✔ Increasing eye contact

✔ Putting hands to chest

✔ Touching the forehead or chin, as in the statue *The Thinker*

✔ Touching you (if the movement is to reassure, and not to interrupt)

Figure 11-3 shows someone who's receptive to the other party's position in a negotiation.

Figure 11-3:
This woman is listening to what you have to say.

Just as you can gauge increasing acceptance to your ideas by watching body language, you can also notice signs of increasing resistance to your ideas. For example, if someone clutches the back of his neck with his palm, you can interpret this gesture quite literally as, "This message is a pain in the neck." Here are some other gestures of resistance:

✔ Fidgeting nervously (cannot accept what is being said with stillness)

✔ Reducing eye contact (cannot accept what is being said with eye contact)

✔ Placing hands behind one's back (indicates an attempt to stay in control of one's own self — resisting the urge to act out verbally or physically)

- ✔ Placing a hand over one's mouth (may indicate an attempt to hold back a negative comment)
- ✔ Locking ankles
- ✔ Gripping one's arm or wrist
- ✔ Crossing arms in front of chest
- ✔ Squinting eyes dramatically
- ✔ Making fistlike gestures
- ✔ Twisting the feet or the entire body so that they point to the door

Ferreting out boredom

One of the most important body language messages to look for during any conversation, but especially a negotiation, is an indication of boredom. Looking out the window, holding the head up with one hand, doodling in a way that seems to absorb the doodler's complete attention, drumming fingers on the table — all these indicate that the listener is no longer paying attention.

What should you do if you notice that the other party in your negotiation is showing signs of boredom? People who are losing interest may be shifting in their seats, fidgeting, or pointing their feet toward the exit. Don't start speaking louder or faster, as you may be tempted to do. Instead, say, "Wait. I need a *reality check.* I'm sensing that I'm losing you. What's happening?" And then listen. You may find out what's really keeping this person or group from accepting your idea. Doing a reality check can save a great deal of time and win you respect as a person who is perceptive and willing to risk hearing the truth. This fact alone makes huge points in your favor during any negotiation.

Negotiating charades

You can modify the familiar game of charades to sensitize you to the importance and meaning of body language. These two formats seem to work best:

- ✔ Someone can mime an emotion and the other players must identify it. This game is simple and fun, and it demonstrates the

variety of nonverbal communications available in face-to face-communications.

- ✔ Players can mime an entire negotiation — either individually or as teams. The other team or player is required to figure out specifically what the negotiation is about and what positions are represented.

Wearing your confidence on your sleeve

During a negotiation, projecting confidence is important. A lack of self-confidence can result in nervousness. If your body language reveals that you are nervous, your counterpart may deem that you are not secure enough to maintain a strong position in the negotiation. This person may be less inclined to compromise on the terms in an effort to reach an agreement.

In addition to making sure that your own body language expresses self-assurance, you can also benefit from being able to gauge your counterpart's confidence level. This awareness of the other party's strength as a negotiator can help you determine your own goals, limits, opening offers, and attempts to close the deal. Watching body language is the key to assessing your counterpart's degree of comfort during the negotiation.

Just like children, adults who get nervous tend to fidget in their chairs (although this behavior can also indicate boredom or preoccupation with other matters.) Nervous fidgeting can also include putting hands into the mouth, tugging at clothing, jingling change, fiddling with items in a purse, or fondling any personal object. When people are nervous, they often increase their distance from those they are negotiating with. Nervous people frequently verbalize their condition without using words through throat clearing, oral pauses, or guttural sounds.

Confident people may place their hands in a steeple position (touching the fingertips of both hands together to form what looks like a church steeple). Sitting up straight and using frequent eye contact also shows confidence. Someone who is confident physically sits on a level slightly higher than anybody else. Propping your feet up is not just an expression of confidence, but an act of claiming territory. If you can put your feet on something, you own it.

Leaning back with your hands laced behind your head is basically an American gesture — and a male one. In fact, it's hard for us to imagine a woman using this gesture. This position shows confidence and indicates an easing of aggression. It is generally a good sign, showing that barriers are down — a good time to close the deal.

Closing the deal

Often, closing a deal means physically closing in on the person with whom you're negotiating. Consider the insurance salesperson who physically leans into the buyer's space with an assuring nudge for her to sign the application. The agent lowers his voice, softens his tone, leans forward with the completed application, and says, "If all the information is correct, place your name here."

Closing means *closing in*. Intimate distance — touching or being 6 to 18 inches apart — is usually reserved for personal, affectionate interactions. However, you may find yourself or your counterpart naturally moving that close as you reach more agreements and draw nearer to closing the deal. A good salesperson knows that an appropriate touch on the customer's forearm or hand cements the deal.

The body language of acceptance varies widely from one individual to another. The exact point in time at which you get concurrence is more often marked with slight nuances than raucous outbursts. Seldom does someone jump up in joy at the moment of making the decision to close a deal. In our experience, the bigger the deal, the more subtle the display at that magic moment when the other side makes the mental commitment to close the deal. The terms are then generally reviewed by both sides to be sure that the deal is acceptable.

Every culture has a traditional bit of body language to mark the sealing of a deal. Most commonly, a handshake is used. Sometimes a hug, a slap on the back, or a "high-five" marks the event. A physical connection is generally made. Always — in every part of the world — make eye contact and let your appreciation show. Reinforce the body language with words of encouragement, support, and optimism. Each side needs to feel good about the deal.

If you close a deal, don't forget to carry out the terms of the agreement. This follow-up is important. There is no bigger let-down than to shake hands on a deal and then not hear from the other side for days. Be sure that the next step is taken. If it isn't your direct responsibility, keep checking with the person who is responsible. You are the person who closed the deal, so your integrity is on the line.

Don't Believe Everything You See

Body language augments rather than replaces the spoken word. The meanings of certain actions or gestures can vary depending on the circumstances and the individual. Consider these examples:

- ✔ Sitting erect may indicate a stiff bargaining position, or it may indicate a stiff back from too much tennis the day before. Stay alert to the body language, but combine your observations with the spoken words to determine the correct meaning.

- ✔ Gestures of anger are used when a person is genuinely angry; however, these actions can also be employed for effect. In addition, keep in mind that some people are just blustery by nature.

Evaluate body language cautiously, just as you do all the other information that comes to you during a negotiation.

Different strokes for different folks

No matter how much you know about body language in general, don't grow overconfident when applying your knowledge to a specific person — especially someone you don't know very well. Each individual has unique body language. A child can tell when a parent is really angry, even if the body language that parent uses to indicate serious trouble is the opposite of what the general public uses. For example, although silence usually indicates that a person is calm, some parents clam up when they're angry. In such families, the children soon learn that silence means real trouble is looming.

Consider the context

As you become more sensitive to body language, you become more conscious of the differences in the meanings of gestures. A clenched fist usually represents anger. Held firmly above the head, it can be a symbol of quiet rage. Pumped up and down, especially if the person is also jumping and squealing, a clenched fist can be an expression of extreme joy.

The rules of body language differ around the world as dramatically as other social norms. Be sure to acquaint yourself with the language of the body, as well as the spoken language, before you travel too far from home.

Prepare for the bluff

Most adults have the art of "faking it" pretty well perfected. People are prone to hide their real feelings in a business setting. Negotiators may display all the signs of accepting a deal, while their true reaction is quite opposite. When you think the other side is accepting your proposal, try to close the deal. That provides a good check on your reading of the other party's body language. If you can't close, what you observed was something other than acceptance. Don't be fooled the next time you see the same reaction from that person — and keep trying to close.

Smiles are almost always an expression of happiness. However, society sometimes requires a smile when the soul is not happy. The mouth drawn tightly and obligingly back reveals a devotion to duty more than merriment. And a half-smile (one corner of the mouth crooked upward) reveals a wry feeling of superiority — like the smile on the face of the bad guy just before he shoots the good guy in an old Western.

INSIDE SCOOP

Michael Says • Michael Says • Michael Says • Michael Says • Michael Says • Michael Says • Michael Says • Michael Says • Michael Says

Learning the hard way

After providing training and conducting seminars extensively on this subject, I can still make mistakes in reading body language. Just after writing the first draft of this chapter, I had an important negotiation in my office. My counterpart was a well-known financier of independent films, but I had never met him face-to-face. He came into my office and headed right to the corner, which contains two sofas, a large coffee table, and a couple of chairs.

He chose the love seat, put a hand on each armrest, and discussed the project with legs spread apart. "Wow," I thought, "This guy is really open with me. He is not nearly as tough as his reputation." We continued on. Slowly, I realized that he is every bit as tough and closed up as his reputation purports.

I went home very frustrated and described the entire scene to Mimi. Mimi listened carefully and then pointed out that my visitor is also extremely overweight; the sprawled position is the only one that is comfortable for him. Mimi later observed that his body language was also territorial. He came into my office and staked quite a claim. He literally possessed one sofa all to himself for the duration of the meeting.

Eventually, we made a deal. During our next meeting, however, I didn't misread him. I bargained hard. Melting him down took awhile, but I succeeded — partly because I knew that convincing him was necessary. The first meeting produced less progress because I had not been as aggressive. I thought we were already in agreement. I worked harder after Mimi corrected my reading of the body language.

Michael Says • Michael Says • Michael Says • Michael Says • Michael Says • Michael Says • Michael Says • Michael Says • Michael Says

Remember, most of the differences between the body language you see and the intended spirit of the communication is accidental. These differences are generally not the result of a sinister plot. The impact on you will be the same if you are misled. This chapter is to help keep you from being misled by body language that is different from the message of the spoken word. When you make such an observation, don't assume that the other person is intentionally trying to mislead you.

You can read more about body language with the two seminal works: *Body Language,* by Julius Fast, and *How to Read a Person Like a Book,* by Gerard I. Nierenberg and Henry H. Calero. Both books contain very good bibliographies. And, by all means, look into the granddaddy of them all: *The Expression of the Emotions in Man and Animals,* written by Charles Darwin and first published in 1872.

A look that deceived the experts

I recently had a protracted negotiation lasting over five months. My clients and I shared many meals and meetings with the other side. In every meeting, the other party was attentive and interested. The words and body language were supportive and encouraging. My clients and I left every meeting feeling heard and understood. Some meetings were attended by outside consultants on the project. They also shared our perception that the other side was moving towards agreement.

The long negotiations culminated in a phone conference scheduled to confirm the details of the deal. A third-party financier from New York was on the line. My clients were standing by. Several members of the other team were plugged in.

The president of the opposing company began speaking. We were shocked to hear the opposite of what we expected. "I've decided not to go forward with this deal," was the opening sentence. "We have all worked hard on this, so I wanted to give all of you my exact thinking," he continued. He set out four reasons for rejecting the deal. We had heard every objection before. Each objection was systematically answered several times in the proposal. He obviously had not understood our proposal.

My clients were so upset that they didn't go to work. Instead of calling in sick, they called in "disgusted." When they told me what they were going to do so, I pointed out that their contract had sick-day provisions. However, it did not have "disgusted-day" provisions. Nonetheless, they called in "disgusted." That ploy got some attention. The president invited my clients to his house that afternoon. They talked. We arranged another meeting.

I knew I had to gain my counterpart's interest and attention. My clients and I made charts and graphs. We made up some new words to describe the plan we were proposing. We put the results of our efforts into two fancy, leather notebooks with the names of the two managers embossed on the cover.

Watching the body language was fascinating. In the past, my counterpart was earnestly leaning forward, nodding, and saying, "I understand." He demonstrated all the classic signs of approval. This time he acted a bit giddy right in the middle of the presentation. "Oh I got it. I got it," he exclaimed, very animated and excited. He was laughing as though we had just finished some one-on-one basketball. "Very good," he said, "You got me." I thought he was going to give me a high-five.

He knew all about body language. He knew how to *look* attentive, interested, and approving in spite of the fact that he wasn't understanding my words. When we changed some of those words and added pictures, we got through to him. When that happened, he dropped the well-practiced body language of careful listening and took on the joy of a kid with a lollipop. After we got past this hurdle, the rest was easy. We signed agreements within the month.

Part V

Telling It Like It Is

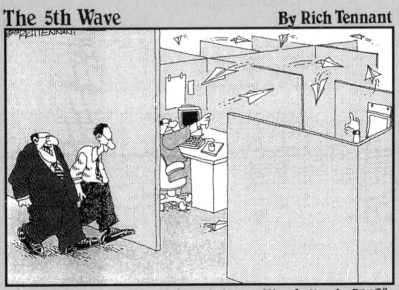

The 5th Wave   By Rich Tennant

"So, Mudnick, you say you've cut down office chatter by 85%?"

In this part . . .

When the time comes for you to speak up in a negotiation, make sure that what you say is clear, concise, and effective. This part is full of practical tips for better communication, and no-nos you should avoid if you want to get your point across. We devote a whole chapter to telephone negotiating, because speaking over the phone requires a special set of skills. If you feel that no one understands you, perhaps this section can show you how to be heard.

Chapter 12

Control through Clarity

*R*aw power flows from the simple ability to be clear and accurate in every step of a negotiation. Unfortunately, no one is born knowing how to express ideas clearly. This chapter is actually a short course in communication skills, showing you how to speak, write, and conduct yourself clearly at every stage of a negotiation.

The ability to communicate clearly is one of the six basic negotiating skills. With practice, you can see how communication skills impact a negotiation. You can tell when your negotiation is faltering because of weak communication.

To improve your ability to communicate clearly, play the games sprinkled throughout this chapter. These activities help build communication skills just as practice improves the chances of making a basket from the free throw line. If you want to be the best at anything, practice the component skills.

What Being Clear Means

In many ways, clear communication is the other side of effective listening. Just as you cannot listen *too* well, there is no such thing as being *too* clear. You can be too blunt, too fast, and too slow. You can't be too clear.

Being clear does not mean that you reveal your position at the earliest opportunity or that you lay out your limits as an opening salvo. Being clear simply means that when you speak, write, or otherwise communicate, your listener understands your intended message. Sounds simple enough. Why aren't more people successful at it?

The reason more people are not good communicators is that most people communicate from this point of view: What do *I* want to tell my listener? Not effective. Your point of view must be from the listener's side of the communication. Ask yourself this question: What do I want my listener to do, think, or feel as a result of my communication?

First, you must be clear with yourself about what your goals are. (See Chapter 5 for more on goal setting.) Then you must have information about who the listener is, what filters are in place, and how to get through those filters so that you can be understood. (See Chapter 2 for more on preparation.)

Present your ideas in an order that the listener can understand. You want the listener to be nodding in agreement with you as you speak. You don't want the listener to feel lost or unsure about where you are going. Be careful to lead the listener from point A to point B.

If this concept is new to you, try a simple technique. Use the P.R.E.P. approach to organize your thoughts and communicate logically. This approach is great because you can use it in an impromptu fashion. P.R.E.P. stands for *point, reason, example, point.* Here's an example:

> ✔ **My point is:** Exercise is energizing.
>
> ✔ **The reason is:** It gets your heart rate up.
>
> ✔ **My example is:** After at least 20 to 30 minutes of increased heart rate, you are more energized when you come out of the gym than when you went in.
>
> ✔ **So, my point is:** Exercise is energizing.

This formula works with any presentation, from a five-minute informal chat, to a thirty-minute formal speech using many examples. The P.R.E.P. approach is a great way to get organized and be clear.

Another strategy is to list and number your points. The following is an example:

I recommend that you hire the new consultant to create a plan that will

1. Increase sales.

2. Improve morale.

3. Generate productivity.

Clear and to-the-point

Harry Truman was so clear with the American people that he became known as "Give 'em hell, Harry." Truman used simple language that everyone could understand.

Truman was equally clear with the Russians. In April of 1945, preparing for the Potsdam Conference, he had his first personal exchange with Vyacheslav M. Molotov, the Soviet foreign minister, in Washington. The President used words of one syllable to convey his view that Poland had to be free and independent.

"I have never been talked to that way in my life," Molotov is reported to have said.

"Carry out your agreements, and you won't get talked to that way again," was Truman's retort.

Truman's blunt style created great successes in international negotiations.

How Clear Are You?

Most people consider themselves to be crystal clear in their communication with others. But if you truly want to know how understandable you are, you should consider taking a *clarity inventory.*

To take a clarity inventory, ask for feedback on how clear you really are from two sources: the members of your immediate family and your personal assistant or coworker. Usually, these members of your inner circle are the most likely people in the world to understand what you are trying to say.

You need only concern yourself with taking a clarity inventory if you seriously want to improve your negotiating skills. If you aren't serious, just skip on. This topic is too sensitive and carries too much of a risk for hurt feelings to bother with unless you are serious in your desire to become a top-notch negotiator.

If, indeed, you want to build a real edge into your negotiations, sit down quietly with someone you trust. Tell that person that you are trying to improve your ability to communicate clearly. Ask for suggestions. Then listen. Don't correct, defend yourself, or explain.

Your goal is not to instruct the other person on how to understand you better. Your goal is to find out how to communicate better with this individual and with the other people in your life. Even if you believe that the entire communication problem is with the other person, don't let on.

Take notes when people give you feedback. The effort flatters them and gives you something to do rather than tell them they are wrong. Hearing how unclear you are is difficult. It hurts. You learn you fail far more often than you ever dreamed. This activity is one of the best ways to find out which areas you need to improve to be easily understood.

Your Clarity Quotient

Another way to take inventory of yourself is to discover your clarity quotient. Think of a recent personal or professional communication you initiated that was ineffective. That is, you did not achieve your desired outcome. With that communication in mind, fill in the survey below.

1. Did you have a clear result in mind prior to the communication?

    Yes   No

    If so, what was it? _____

    _____

    _____

2. Did you plan what you wanted to say?

    Yes   No

    If so, what was it?_____

    _____

    _____

3. Did you communicate your intentions clearly and specifically?

    Yes   No

4. Did you maintain your original intentions in the communication or did you wander into other subject areas?

    Yes   No

5. Was your style of delivery consistent with the results you wanted?

    Yes   No

6.   How did the specific results differ from what you wanted? _____

_____

_____

7.   What might have you done differently? _____

_____

_____

Where did you circle No? Those are the areas requiring improvement.

Tips for Being Clear

A well-turned phrase always involves an element of art. You don't have to be an artist to be clear. The flowery phrase is nice; the clear phrase is a necessity. Part of the beauty of a clear phrase is how accurately it hits the bull's eye; that is, how precisely it conveys your meaning.

If you assign people to complete tasks for you at work, your first task is to *clearly* tell the person what you want them to do. Easier said than done. Getting results in the workplace has less to do with charisma than with clarity. Here are some hints for maximizing clarity.

1. Set the climate.

Be sure you're in a place conducive to concentration at a time when the assistant or coworker is free to pay attention. Listen to your words as you set the tone. A harried manager may unwittingly say, "Now this is a simple, mindless task; that's why I'm giving it to you." Not very motivating.

2. Give the big picture.

Describe the overall objectives. People need to see where their part fits into the whole to feel like they are a part of the loftier goal.

3. Describe the steps of the task.

This is the meat of the delegation discussion. Sometimes these steps are already printed in an instruction or procedures manual. You still need to go over these steps, however briefly, to assure yourself that the employee is familiar with them. If the steps are not already written out, have the person write the list as you speak. This effort increases the probability of retention.

4. Cite resources available.

Point out where to find other references on the task, if any. Resources include people who have completed the task or parts of it before.

5. Invite questions.

Even if you feel that you don't have time to answer questions, the extra attention is worth the effort. Better to spend the time to explain a task up front than be unhappy with the results later. Invite questions with open-ended prompting such as, "What questions do you have?" not "You don't have any questions, do you?"

6. Get the person to summarize his or her strategy for accomplishing the task.

This step takes guts on your part; you risk being answered with a defensive "Do you think I'm stupid?" Use this sentence: "Call me compulsive — I need you to summarize how you will get this done." When you take responsibility, you reduce defensiveness in the other person.

7. Agree on a date to follow up.

The deadline depends on the complexity and value of the task. You may need time and practice to develop the fine art of following up without hovering.

When you speak, ask "Did I make myself clear?" Ross Perot's line during his oh-so-brief presidential campaign was, "Are you with me?"

Such questions often help both parties proceed more productively. "Did I make myself clear?" may remind the other person to listen instead of lazily replying "yes." If the point is critical, you may ask the other party to repeat the information back to you just to be sure that you are communicating effectively. Assure your counterpart that repeating vital information does not constitute an agreement — just clarification.

Know your purpose or goals

When you know exactly what you want to say, communicating clearly is much easier. In the past, you must have had the urge to say, "So, what's your point?" — usually with an exasperated tone. More often than not, a person who is asked that question looks surprised and fumbles for a good, one sentence answer. When the speaker does not know the point, the listener is hopelessly lost.

In any communication, you should know the point and be keenly aware of the overall purpose or goal. Simply saying, "Oh, I just like to talk" is okay for recreational situations. But if you are trying to get someone else to provide some action, approval, or acquiescence (that is, if you are in a negotiation), you need to have your short- and long-range goals in mind.

Cut the mumbo-jumbo

Some concepts are, by nature, just plain difficult to grasp. Sometimes, being clear requires creativity. For example, if you have many numbers to present, try putting them in graphs — bar, pie, or line charts — anything but reams of numbers. Keep the lists of numbers as a backup.

By all means, oversimplify technical points at first — you can explain fully later in the conversation, once you have your listeners hooked. Also, define jargon and spell out acronyms. For example, we say "LAX," and people from outside of Los Angeles may not know that LAX is the airport. Avoid references that may alienate your listener. In written materials, footnotes and appendices serve the purpose of clarity. Do everything you can to make listening easy and enjoyable.

Keep your commitments

Being clear includes being consistent in the words you say and the deeds that follow. If you say one thing and do another, it is confusing. Your inconsistent conduct turns an otherwise clear communication into a real puzzlement. Keep each and every commitment that you make during a negotiation. In life, keeping commitments is important; in a negotiation, it is essential.

Keeping your commitments is the acid test of clarity; it is also the bedrock of trust. A notorious thief can look you in the eye and say, "I will have that assignment on your desk at 2:00 p.m." If the assignment is there, the thief has gained your trust. On the other hand, if an honest person misses the 2:00 p.m. deadline, your trust in that person is diminished.

If you tell the other party that you will call back at 9:00 the next morning, be sure to call at that time. Breaking your promise calls your integrity into question and creates confusion about what exactly you meant when you promised to call back at 9:00 a.m. Failing to keep your word is also upsetting for the other party. Such inattention may be considered, debated, and evaluated by the other side. Their loss of trust may call into question side issues and create tensions counterproductive to a negotiation.

If you are negotiating with someone on behalf of a client or company, failure to keep commitments is harmful to you and the party you are representing. This neglect can damage your relationship with your client or your standing within the company. Word often gets back about your unprofessional behavior. Professional negotiators are often falsely blamed for not returning calls or not providing documentation in a timely fashion. Don't provide grist for that mill.

Write it down

The written word is often more useful than the spoken word when you communicate clearly. When you have something to say, write it down, look at it, edit it, and make it right. When the words are your own, you don't have to release them until they are as near to perfect as possible.

Many people believe they can't or don't know how to write as clearly as they speak. This is rarely true. The simple fact is that when you write instead of speaking the words, you can see more easily whether your message is unclear. You can see in black and white that the words are ambiguous or your thoughts are incomplete.

Also, the written word disallows such conversational crutches as "ya know what I mean?" When used as a rhetorical question, this phrase does not clarify the issues. It moves the conversation deeper into confusion.

The process of putting your thoughts into writing brings you face-to-face with your failure to communicate clearly. Rather than bemoan your lack of writing skills, open your eyes and say honestly — maybe for the first time in your life — "Wow, I didn't realize how poorly I have been communicating my ideas."

Here are some basic tips to get you on the road to clear communication:

- ✔ Use short sentences.
- ✔ Use short words.
- ✔ Avoid jargon and abbreviations — even when you are writing to another professional in your field — unless the other person uses these terms exactly the way that you do.
- ✔ Complete your sentences.
- ✔ Stick to one idea per paragraph.
- ✔ Have a beginning, middle, and end to the overall communication.
- ✔ Be accurate.

Don't be afraid to number paragraphs to cover different points, but don't delude yourself into thinking that numbering paragraphs brings order to a document that otherwise lacks coherence or good sense.

Try being a journalist

When you think of clear writing, the most common reference point is your daily newspaper. From coast to coast, there is a consistency in stories written for the newspaper that seems to cross regional lines, ownership, and size of the newspaper. You may find it odd that so many journalists write in the same style with the same degree of clarity.

Actually, every school of journalism in the country teaches students about the "five horsemen" of journalism: Who?, What?, Where?, When?, and Why? The journalist is supposed to answer these five questions in the first paragraph of a story. The next five paragraphs should each expand on the answer to one of the questions. The least important information appears at the end of the story. That way, if the story is too long for the available space in the newspaper, editors can just delete the end of story and no important information is lost.

Look at a copy of today's newspaper. Pick any story that interests you in the first section. We point you to the first section because that is the section that follows the traditional structure of news stories. Reporters depart from the structure in some of the special interest sections, such as the sports or enter-tainment sections. Read the first paragraph and notice how the reporter explains:

- ✔ *Who* the story is about
- ✔ *What* the person did to land in the news
- ✔ *Where* the event happened
- ✔ *When* the event took place
- ✔ *Why* the event occurred

Read the last paragraph of the article and notice how trivial that information is compared to the first few paragraphs. Notice how the first few paragraphs after the lead paragraph are packed with important material compared with the information later in the story.

Use the same technique, and you can't go wrong. Remember: you're providing the information your listener needs to know to achieve *your* goal. Organize the facts like a newspaper story.

Play Whisper

You may remember this game from your youth. Sometimes called Telephone or Rumor, we use this game to teach listening and clarity skills. It also teaches the dangers of believing a story handed to you through a number of different speakers.

First, we come up with a one- or two-sentence story. We usually pick a sentence right out of the newspaper. Whisper the story into the ear of the person on your left. That person repeats the story exactly to the next person, who then repeats it to the next person, and so on. The last person in the chain repeats the story aloud. Each additional person in the chain seems to add an individual twist to the story. Everyone has a good laugh when comparing the final story to the original.

When we play advanced versions of this game, we add time pressure and distractions to the repetition process. For example, we often stand at the front of the seminar room hurrying the class along.

This game can produce a lot of laughs in a classroom, at a party, or at a dinner table. But at the negotiating table, miscommunication is no laughing matter.

Barriers to Clarity

The biggest barriers to clarity are your own fears and lack of concentration. You fear that if you make yourself clearly understood, an adverse reaction will follow — some vague, unspoken, definitely unwanted reaction. Identify those fears and work to make them less of a roadblock.

Fear of rejection

Everyone has a built-in fear factor. You may be afraid that if you present your ideas clearly, the listener will reject you or your conclusions. The natural inclination is to avoid rejection by blurring lines, being unclear, and failing to state your case accurately.

Instead, you postpone the inevitable. After all, when the listener eventually understands you, he rejects the concept with the added energy that comes from frustration. "Why didn't you say so?" he asks. "Why did you waste my time?" he demands. These are tough questions to answer.

If it is true that an accurate statement of intent would cause the deal to fall apart, being clear is even more important. When you close a deal without being clear, the parties have different understandings and expectations. You are finalizing a bad deal. In fact, you are closing a deal that cannot possibly work.

Fear of hurting someone else

Often, people avoid hurting the feelings of others not out of compassion, but out of self-protection. Everyone wants to be liked; no one wants to be shunned. Toward that legitimate social end, you have probably learned to obfuscate with a vengeance.

As a couple, we have developed some stock phrases to use after a bad play or a weak film when the producers cluster around to hear our praise. "Very interesting" is one of the most damning. "Brave" is good. "Top of the genre" is probably our noncommittal favorite. Sometimes, when a work is a "work in progress," such vague statements are suited to your purpose of encouraging the creators. Such phrases are intended to mask the truth, and they do just that.

Being clear and being confrontational are two different things. If you have bad news to deliver, do so with dignity and respect for the feelings of the person to whom you are speaking. Even if you feel, in every fiber of your being, that the person is overreacting to your news, don't say so. Let the feelings run their course. But don't flinch or amend your statement. Just wait. This, too, shall pass. Being clear in such situations takes strength and confidence. Never sacrifice clarity to avoid confrontation. Your desire to do so generally masks the real motive — which is to spare yourself the discomfort or trauma of delivering bad news.

General distractions

Other barriers to clarity can be fatigue, laziness in preparation, or the clutter of distracting interruptions.

- ✔ **Fatigue:** You may be just plain tired and unable to focus. Pay attention to your body's signals. Sometimes, a brisk walk outdoors revives you. Good nutrition and adequate rest are requirements for a master negotiator. If you eat right and get plenty of sleep, you can eliminate the need for cup after cup of coffee to stay alert. But, in a pinch, an occasional dose of caffeine works, too.

- ✔ **Laziness:** You may not have prepared well enough, and you are dreading being clear on some facts that are unsubstantiated. If this strikes a familiar chord, do your homework.

- ✔ **Interruptions:** Your listener may be doodling or not making eye contact. The room temperature may be extreme. Noise levels may be too high for you to be heard clearly. Hopefully, you are assertive enough to request these changes appropriately.

If the conversation or negotiation is important, be sure that you are well rested, prepared, and in an environment where clear communications can be heard.

When You Have to Say No

Sometimes, you just need to say no. Here's how to do it without alienating a coworker.

Tom knocks on top of your cubicle partition, leans in, and asks "Got a minute?" Instead of glancing at your watch and saying okay with a martyred sigh, you look up and analyze the request. You see his lower lip trembling and his eyes filling with tears. You know he wants to talk about his divorce — again — and you have a report to finish. You recognize that this will not be a 60-second interruption, no matter what he claims. You resist the reflexive *hot button* response, "In your dreams, pal," because you depend on Tom in your job. A rapport with him is a priority for you. Use the following three steps:

- ✔ **Acknowledge:** Tell him that you understand how he feels and what he wants. "Tom, you look upset — it looks as though you need to talk." This statement, which takes only six seconds to say, calms him because now he doesn't have to work to make you understand his feelings. You have said, in essence, "I understand your priority — and it's important" (another sentence that takes six seconds to say). We call this *six-second empathy*.

- ✔ **Advise:** Let him know *your* priority — calmly and confidently. Say, "Tom here's the situation. I have a report to finish for the boss, and it's due in half an hour." You have understood his need, and now you're asking him to understand yours. Many people, when told of your priority, will back off. But not Tom. That's why there's a third step.

- ✔ **Accept or Alter:** Accept the interruption with time limits ("I can give you five minutes") or suggest an alternative option ("I'll come to your cubicle after I finish the report").

This is the best way to say no. Use it as a model. You won't always be able to achieve the ideal outcome described, but try to come as close as you can.

With peers, you can suggest an alternative option, but *what about with your boss?* Tom will actually thank you and go away happy. With the boss, your best option is almost always to accept. The boss's priorities *are* your priorities — it's in the job description. However, don't leave out the second step. Always advise the boss of your activities and priorities. Sometimes, the boss is grateful for the information and withdraws the request or removes some of your existing obligations. Other times, you are expected to do all the work anyway. Advising puts the burden on the boss to say which task is to be done first. Never skip that step.

The High Cost of Not Being Clear

We realize that our clarion call for clarity flies in the face of advice you may receive from some others who are not professionals in the area of negotiating. In fact, some say that ambiguity is the lubricant of negotiations. That saying not only prolongs a bad myth about negotiating, it has spilled blood, cost lives, and wasted millions of dollars, drachmas, and dreams.

The highest cost of all

The Gulf War (Desert Storm) may well have been avoided if the diplomats had been clearer in the days just before the invasion of Kuwait by Iraq. President Saddam Hussein of Iraq wanted to destroy Kuwait for a number of reasons — all of which were good and valid to him. He was not prepared to take on the United States, let alone the entire world. Therefore, he met for several hours with America's Ambassador April Glasbie.

The Ambassador said to Hussein, "We have no opinion on Arab-Arab conflicts, like your border disagreement with Kuwait."

Astonishing.

The Ambassador insists that there was more to the discussion than was printed in the transcript, but she does not deny these comments. A disparity exists between the two parties' renditions. Assume that each party related the events as accurately as possible. Obviously, they were not as clear with each other at the time of the original discussion as they were in the reporting of the discussion afterward.

Even Hussein's telling of the tale indicates some lack of clarity regarding his intentions toward Kuwait. He never said his intention was to eliminate Kuwait from the face of the earth. On the other hand, the United States never even hinted at the kind of response that was ultimately invoked.

Obviously, the communication was not clear. Clear communications may or may not have prevented the Gulf War. A clear message from the United States to Iraq may not have been believed. Perhaps Iraq was willing to wage war against the United States for some mysterious reason. The world will never know. However, documents show that within the month before the invasion, the United States communicated directly to Saddam Hussein in a way that caused him to think Iraq could cross the border into Kuwait without repercussions.

If you ever question the wisdom of being clear, please think a moment of the men and women who died in the Gulf War and their families who still miss them. Every war provides stories of the high human price paid for failed communications. In World War II, Japan actually intended to send us a two-hour warning before the attack on Pearl Harbor on December 7, 1941. The Japanese decoder at the embassy was out sick that day, and his replacement could not type. Consequently, the message wasn't delivered to anybody in authority until after the fact.

Deals that disappear

A common example of lack of clarity occurs when one party intentionally makes an unrealistic opening offer. Early in the negotiation, one person throws out an outrageous opening offer as a trial balloon, floating it up as though it were a reasonable offer. If the offer doesn't get the expected reaction (shock, disbelief, laughter, and ultimately bursting of the balloon), the person who made the offer often recounts, with great animation, that the other person "didn't even bat an eye."

Too much is made of the fact that a counterpart doesn't faint when an unrealistic number is offered. What you don't hear about so often is the follow up. As we were writing this book, we purposely did follow up every time we heard such a story. We tracked the negotiations to see the results. We were not totally surprised to discover that — in a majority of the cases — the deals fell through. In all but one case, the reason was an excuse other than the initial high demand, such as scheduling conflicts, changing concepts, and postponements.

This little study of ours was not scientific in any way, but it provided interesting support for our theory: When you start with an opening offer or a demand that is well outside the reasonable range, the other side will often slink away rather than get involved in a futile negotiation.

It would be difficult to ascertain what percentage of negotiations never get underway because the initial demand was too high. We believe that it happens more often than most people suspect. The person who is turned off may never say a word to the party making the demand. Think of your own behavior. If you think the prices in a boutique are outrageous, do you say so? Or do you smile at the shopkeeper and say, "Just looking"?

The prices you don't even know

Deals that don't close are to be expected if you are not clear during the negotiations. The harder item to assess is how the dynamic of the discussion changes when communications are not clear.

When you are not clear, the other party feels insecure. Rather than confront you on your lack of clarity, the person you're negotiating with often just compensates in one of two ways:

- **Reciprocal obfuscation:** That term simply means that the other party starts to be unclear, too. (We love the irony of using a hard-to-understand phrase to describe things that are hard to understand.) The other party doesn't know where you stand, because you are not being clear. So, they won't feel comfortable in making a clear commitment either. This situation substantially slows down a negotiation and may make productive communication almost impossible.

- **Leaving lots of room to maneuver:** If you are not clear, others won't feel safe enough to tell you specifically what they want. Rather than commit to a position, your counterpart will leave lots of room to maneuver, until you clarify where you want to end up.

These consequences are almost impossible to detect. Instead, you begin blaming the lack of clarity or indecisiveness on the other party. If you run into one of these behaviors, see whether the problem didn't start with you. Even if it didn't — even if you are dealing with someone who is naturally unclear or reluctant to take a position — you can push that person to greater clarity or decisiveness by communicating more clearly yourself.

Worst case: the deal closes

When a lack of clarity is a major factor in a negotiation, the biggest disasters occur when the deal closes and no one realizes that confusion remains. When written contracts are to follow, a lack of clarity is usually caught by the lawyers during the drafting stage, and ambiguity can be worked out.

In a less formal situation, the confusion generally isn't discovered until much later. When that happens, both sides feel cheated and misled. People are rarely neutral about the cause of miscommunications. Blame is never far behind the discovery that the two parties miscommunicated. Each party feels intentionally misled. The acrimony often permanently damages the relationship between the parties. The fallout often damages reputations, too.

The truth of the matter is that the results of an intentional lie and a mere miscommunication are often about the same. Preventing an innocent miscommunication is well worth the extra energy expended.

Play Newspaper

For this game, turn to the editorial section of your newspaper and randomly pick a sentence — any sentence — in the middle of an editorial. Read the sentence out loud. Have each person in your family give his or her version of the probable viewpoint of the author of the editorial. Note carefully all the variations. Now read the opening and closing paragraphs of the editorial. The person with the closest interpretation doesn't have to help with the dishes.

Now, let another family member supply the sentence. Repeat the process with different stakes. The point of this exercise is to discover the ease with which individuals may interpret the same phrase differently. Correct interpretation is necessary for clarity. Usually, the discussion turns to how the idea could have been expressed more clearly.

Speaking to Foreigners

Sometimes, a language barrier can inhibit clear communication. When two parties are having difficulty understanding one another, the first instinct is to say the same thing at the same speed . . . only louder . . . and then LOUDER. This ridiculous escalation never accomplishes anything more than embarrassing, or perhaps, insulting the participants.

If you are trying to negotiate with someone who is having trouble understanding you, try the following instead:

✔ Drop your voice.

✔ Speak more slowly.

✔ Find simpler words to express the same idea you were trying to communicate. One syllable words are best.

✔ Engage your hands. Bring your hands to the level of your shoulders. Keep them out in front and use them to illustrate your points. At the same time, engage your face and your voice. Be as expressive as possible and be consistent; that is, make sure that your hands, face, and words are expressing the same message.

✔ Be patient.

If you are unable to make yourself understood, apologize and then stop trying until you can get some help. If your face and hands are fully engaged, your apology will be understood, even if the words aren't clear. You can usually find someone to help you with the communication problem. If you make the other person feel bad for the communication snafu, no one can help you.

Cultural barriers to understanding

I once did a morning speech to native-born Japanese entrepreneurs who owned businesses here in southern California. They wanted the title to be "How to Manage American Employees." I knew, from my experience in training managers at Honda and Toyota, what they meant. The basic difference is that Americans need to be told *clearly* what to do; otherwise, in some employees' minds, "We don't have to do it." In Japan, high value is placed on anticipating the superior's wants and needs. Being told directly what to do means a loss of face; it means you were not clever enough to read the manager's thoughts and body movements and anticipate the next need.

After a very traditional Japanese breakfast of baked salmon and rice in a black lacquered box, the attendees illustrated my point. As the leader of the group began rising to his feet to introduce me, all 20 men fell silent instantly and turned attentively to him. I made this observation, pointing out that their priorities are group decorum and group purpose. I explained that when a speaker rises to speak during an American meeting, many are so focused on their *individual* conversations and agendas that the speaker needs to rap on a glass with a spoon and yell "quiet." The attendees smiled politely; emitting a little chuckle here and there. I could tell that they were embarrassed for this hypothetical group of "barbaric" Americans about whom I was speaking. They thought it was quite natural to keep one eye on the leader in anticipation of the meeting's next agenda item.

Of course, differences don't automatically mean that one culture is barbaric or another is subservient. Diversity can be pleasant, as long as you know what to expect.

Chapter 13
Verbal Stop Signs

C lear communication is as much about getting rid of bad habits as it is about acquiring any new skills. As you look over this chapter, ask yourself whether you do any of the things that interfere with communications. Getting rid of those habits will serve you better than any new skill.

Nobody wants to be a bad communicator. Most people are insulted if they are accused of being difficult to understand. At the beginning of our seminars, we discuss the six basic skills needed in every negotiation. Then we ask students to rate themselves. We have never had anyone in any seminar describe himself or herself as a poor communicator — even those who say that communication is the area that they need to work on the most.

This chapter is designed to provide tips and techniques to improve your clarity quotient starting today. The truth is, being clear requires periodic checkups like an annual physical. Everyone needs to look at this aspect of home and office life from time to time. Bad habits creep into communications rather easily.

Phrases You Should Never Use during a Negotiation

Certain phrases go "clunk" against the ear every time you hear them. The sections that follow discuss phrases that have little place in life, let alone a negotiation. When you hear these phrases, a yellow caution light should start flashing in your head. These phrases often indicate a situation that needs to be addressed. And if you hear one or more of these utterances come out of your mouth, stop immediately. Laugh about the slip or apologize, but don't assume that the listener doesn't have the same set of yellow caution lights that you do. Maybe the listener doesn't, but you can't take that risk.

"Trust me"

This overused term is now the hallmark phrase in motion pictures for the producer who is not to be trusted. People who must say "trust me" are often the very people who don't deserve to be trusted.

When someone says "trust me" as a substitute for providing the specific details you requested, be very cautious. Ask again for a commitment. If the person balks, explain that it's not a question of trust, but an acknowledgment of the fact that circumstances change. Explain that the agreement must be enforceable, even if the current negotiators are no longer accessible. You want an agreement so clear that you don't have to trust the other person.

"I'm going to be honest with you"

So has this person been dishonest all along? This cliché is the cousin to the phrase, "I'm not going to lie to you." It makes you wonder, "Oh? Would you lie to someone else?"

William Shakespeare's great line delivered by Queen Gertrude in *Hamlet* is, "The lady doth protest too much, methinks." Shakespeare knew a great deal about human nature. When people loudly declare their innocence, they almost always lose credibility. Gertrude says that the Player Queen affirms too insistently to be believed. So those who are always reassuring you about their honesty probably aren't being very honest with you.

"Take it or leave it"

Even when you are making your final offer, presenting the deal as a "take it or leave it" proposition is a mistake. Even if the other side accepts the offer, the deal leaves them feeling bad about the decision. Unbelievably, we have heard of people putting such an unpleasant tag on an offer that was otherwise okay. This label makes the offer sound bad even if the terms are reasonable.

If you hear this phrase, evaluate the offer on the merits, not on the way it was delivered. Especially if you are a professional negotiator, figure out if the offer is acceptable based on what you want out of the negotiation. Go back to the limits you set (see Chapter 4) and the goals you set (see Chapter 5). Don't let a bad negotiating style confuse you. If you are negotiating for yourself, and you must continue working with your counterpart in this deal, you may want to consider whether or not you can maintain an ongoing relationship with a person that is bullying you with "take it or leave it" statements.

If you are making a final offer, say so without using the antagonistic take-it-or-leave-it phrase. If you are feeling frustrated and anticipating a refusal, push the pause button (see Chapter 6). When you are feeling that way, it is hard to calmly explain the reasons that this must be the final offer. You are likely to use this verboten phrase (take it or leave it) or something similar. That approach hurts you in the long run because you look like a bully. And you do not increase the chance of your proposal being accepted.

"You'll never work in this town again"

This is a bully's threat. Everyone has observed this bullying behavior. Once is enough. Threats never win the hearts and minds of the person you are attempting to persuade. In today's litigious society, threats are not smart.

"You'll never work in this town again" used to be a stock phrase in the entertainment industry, uttered furiously by the tirading studio executive dealing with a recalcitrant actor or writer. An executive at Twentieth Century Fox once issued this threat to an actor who refused to accept a lesser credit than his contract guaranteed for work on a television series. The series ultimately failed, and, guess what? The actor was unemployed for several years. The actor sued Twentieth Century Fox, attributing his long period of unemployment to the studio's threat. Who knows, he may have been out of work anyway, but given the threat, the jury sided with the actor and awarded an enormous judgment.

People in positions of power often get frustrated when someone of lesser status refuses what they view as a simple and reasonable request. Usually, the next step is a plea to "play ball." Then some avuncular advice follows, such as "You know, you really would be better off helping us out of this one," or "We'll make it up to you on the next one." When the person isn't persuaded, the power player often pops a cork.

Good manners, common sense, and the growing body of employment law all favor the threatened person. Don't resort to this tactic. You could lose the farm.

A slur of any kind

It is the twilight of the twentieth century and, in the United States at least, negative comments about the race, gender, or national origin of another person are no longer widely tolerated. A concern with being "politically correct" preoccupies many people. There are those who are offended at any inquiry that could even identify these traits, such as "What kind of a name is that?" Unless you know differently for sure, steer clear of the most innocent of references unless they are relevant.

If the information is irrelevant, you should even avoid neutral statements such as, "The person was a woman" or "The man was from China." You may receive an angry response, such as "Just what is that supposed to mean?" "Why did you mention that?" Worse yet, the person you are speaking to may think those thoughts without verbalizing them. This situation raises a barrier to communication that you won't even know exists.

Even if you are with a group that seems to be quite open about expressing whatever it is that they happen to think or feel about another group, don't join in. Be discreet. You never know who may be suffering in silence — feeling outnumbered and helpless.

Oh sure, you may be able to disparage all members of a certain group in the privacy of your own home with impunity. But even there, we urge you to curtail such comments. Those attitudes are too easily passed on to the young, and the slurs have a nasty way of showing up in conversation outside the home.

The last thing you want in a tough negotiation is to let an offensive phrase slip out just when you want to close. You can lose the deal you are working on *and* the trust and confidence of your counterpart in the negotiation. Unwitting slurs can stop a negotiation in its tracks. You may be pegged forever as a bigot; and some people don't negotiate with bigots. If you have some bad habits in this area, work on cleaning up your language.

Steering Others to Clarity

When the other party is not being clear, your job is to steer that person toward concise communication. Don't just toss them this book (although it may make a nice gift). Coax from your counterpart a clear statement of intentions, wants, and needs. Your technique for acquiring this information depends on the type of person you are dealing with. The following sections contain some tips for accomplishing this important task. Each section is devoted to a personality type you may encounter.

Tangent people

Some people are not clear because they ramble; that is, they go off on a tangent.

- ✔ Listen up to a point. You are listening especially for a good break point.

- ✔ Be assertive when you interrupt.

- ✔ Your first statement should be a validation, "Yes, you're right. Now, as to the purpose. . . ." That's how you get people with this type of communication pattern back on track.

Interrupters

These people even interrupt themselves. They lose their train of thought while they are speaking.

- ✔ Take careful notes while an interrupter is talking.
- ✔ Concentrate and stay focused.
- ✔ Keep reminding him or her of the most recent statement before the interruption. Don't leave until you get a specific answer.
- ✔ Be appropriate but keep pressing with your own specific questions.

Unprepared people

Some people may have difficulty getting fully prepared for negotiations.

- ✔ Postpone the meeting.
- ✔ Conduct the meeting at the unprepared party's office. Tactfully invite your counterpart's support people who may know more about the subject.

Too busy to be clear

These important people don't think they can take the time to be clear. They save minutes, but others may spend hours trying to figure out what they want and need.

- ✔ Schedule meetings at the beginning of the day to avoid distractions and ensure everyone's full attention.
- ✔ Guard against interruptions; for example, request they hold their calls for ten minutes in order to get information.
- ✔ Be efficient in meetings — have a written agenda even for a two-person meeting. The agenda shows others how much you value their time.
- ✔ Show you are taking notes and recording comments.
- ✔ Be appropriate but keep pressing for the details you need.

AT WORK

Sometimes, you need to steer your boss to clarity. The next time the boss slams papers on your desk and says, "We need this yesterday," do the following:

1. **Stifle the urge to answer "in your dreams."**

2. **Answer immediately.**

   Respond with a positive, "Yes, absolutely — will do." After all, this *is* the boss. And this reply will relax your employer because it's what any boss wants to hear.

3. **Ask for prioritization.**

   This step is essential: Because you are already *fully aware* of your priorities and the allotted time to accomplish them, answer, "Here's the situation, Boss. I've got these other two priorities you want by 3:00 today. Which of these can be put off until tomorrow?"

By following these steps, you have forced the boss to be clear. Your boss needs to prioritize — that's a boss's job. Sometimes, your boss will go away without making any further demands, realizing that you are already working on important projects.

Four Strategies for Women Who Want Men to Hear Them

Because of early social pressure to be "good girls" and "little ladies," women get the message that being confrontational isn't acceptable. Often in a negotiation, women hear their inner voice say "speak up," but many squelch these messages because of upbringing and the early lesson discouraging complaint. Women have been socialized to avoid verbal confrontation more than men, and to speak more politely.

Everyone is susceptible to these basic differences between men and women. Even if you think you personally don't fit the typical mold for your gender, you're sure to negotiate with men and women who do.

The following sections contain four strategies for women who want men to hear them. If you practice one of these strategies each week, you'll quickly alter the way others perceive you. The prerequisite is to start listening to yourself. Awareness is the first step to any behavioral change. Accept and grow, or be left in the dust in this hardball world of negotiating. These strategies are based on making yourself heard in present-day negotiations, in which the successful role model has been, up to now, a no-nonsense, concise leader.

Strategy #1: Avoid apologies

Women tend to be more apologetic than men. Even assertive women sometimes unwittingly use power-robbing devices in their speech. The words avoid certainties; hence, the speaker avoids risks. If you have something to say, don't apologize for saying it. Here are the specific devices under the general banner of apologies:

Prefacing and tagging

Prefacing and *tagging* refer to those little extra words before and after a statement:

- **Prefacing:** leading into a statement with a phrase that weakens it. For example, "I'm not sure about this, but. . . ."
- **Tagging:** adding a qualifying phrase at the end of a statement. For example, "We should take action, don't you think?" "Don't you think" and "Am I right?" are typical tags.

Questioning tone

A *questioning tone* is intonation that goes up a little at the end of the sentence. This tone takes the power right out of an otherwise declarative sentence. To the listener, the speaker sounds like she is unsure and lacks self-confidence. What the tone communicates is, "Don't you agree?" Or worse: "Please agree quickly, so I know that what I just said has value."

If you don't have confidence in what you say, how can you expect anybody else to have faith in you? Listen to yourself or ask a trusted friend. If you find that you have this damaging habit, start practicing today to get rid of it. Remember, awareness is the first step to behavioral change, and you are now aware.

Hedges or qualifiers

Women tend to use many little words like "kind of" and "sort of" that rob their statements of power. If you use these phrases, it is a habit. You can break this habit and bring more power into your speech right now. A few examples are:

- "I kind of think that. . . . "
- "We probably should really. . . . "
- "It seems like a fairly good way to. . . . "
- "Kind of/sort of. . . . "
- "You maybe need to. . . ."

These phrases don't just contain extra words, they contain *unsure* words. Using these weak words may make *you* seem weak.

Perhaps you developed these speech patterns to cover your rear end. They are non-risktaking and may indicate that you're reluctant to state issues definitively. Beware of sounding indecisive and hesitant when you want to convey certainty. You don't need to banish these words from your repertoire. You can use these words when you desire to hedge your bets. The point is to *have* a repertoire and be able to *choose* the words to achieve your goals.

Nonwords and nonphrases

Nonwords are all those little extras that get plugged into speech — those words or syllables that take the place of silence by giving you a pause to pull together your next thought. Nonwords show up in the darndest places, and they always slow up or divert an otherwise fine presentation. Here are just a few examples:

- **Really:** As in, "Really, I really want this to go forward."

- **Like:** As in, "Do you want this to go like, forward?"

- **Um:** As in, "ummmmm," or "uhhhhhh"

Use the silence to give power to your statements and opinions. Practice the power of the pause in your very next negotiation.

Strategy #2: Be brief

For women, talk is relationships. Men use talk to exchange information. Men and women bond differently. Men bond through competitive mind games with their knowledge banks. They test each other with questions. "Who pitched the last game of the World Series?" one may ask. If the other guy knows, he gets a point. And if he doesn't, that's fine, too, because now the other guy is one up. And then the other guy will have to get him back. That's how men bond.

Women don't bond that way. They don't bond through test questions. In fact, if a woman asks another woman who pitched the last game of the World Series in 1954, the listener may extend both arms and say, "Do you need a hug?" And she probably would, because that behavior isn't normal. Women don't bond through competition.

Women bond through stories. You walk up to a woman you hardly know. You say, "Gee, I love that pin. It's beautiful." And she says, "Thank you," and proceeds to tell you the story behind the pin, because *there is one*. Women have a story for every piece of clothing and jewelry on their bodies. They have a story for their haircut. Some of them have stories about their hair color. You find something in her story you can relate to and tell her a story back. If you have enough stories in common, you will bond. Men may arm wrestle to build a relationship. Women talk to build a relationship.

The whole story or just the bottom line?

Men don't use a lot of words. For over 20 years, I've been observing men going to lunch on breaks from my training courses. One guy turns to the other, and says, "Lunch?" The other guy says, "Sure." That's it. They don't say, "Wanna go to lunch?" "Yeah, it sounds like a great idea. Where shall we go?" "I don't know — where shall we go?" No. "Lunch?" "Sure."

This pattern starts in childhood. My friend has twins. The twins returned from their first day in school. My friend asked each of them how the first day of school went. The little boy said, "Fine. Can I go play ball?" The little girl said, "Well, I got on the bus and there was Suzie, so I sat next to her and . . . and then . . . and then . . ." She took 15 minutes to answer the question.

Each child was communicating in his or her own style. This style comes naturally. Studies show that women use an average of 25,000 words in a typical day. Men use about 15,000 words in the same day. I always quip, "The problem is that by the time men come home from work, they've used all 15,000 up. We haven't even started on our 25,000 because we've had to be concise all day long."

When we were courting, my jaded memory is that Michael would hang on every word of my stories. Then we got married. I started a story, and he stopped me, saying, "Mim, wait. Are you going to do, 'he said, she said, he said, she said'?" That's his code for the way I tell stories from the beginning with the details, chronologically to the end. (Men are wincing just reading this.) And I remember my response, "Tsk (sigh)." Men hate that response because it's a sneaky way of saying "You stupid idiot," without actually saying it. I said, "Tsk (sigh), yes, honey. That's how the story is enjoyed the best." and he said, "Not by me. Can you just skip to the bottom line?" I remember feeling offended — I thought he was going to miss the good part. Then I discovered that the story is not the good part for him. He really does want the bottom line. So I give him the bottom line. Now, he has to *beg* me to tell him the whole story.

Women generally use more details in their conversations than men. The information you want the male listener to hear may be lost in all those details. Watch for signs that a male listener is glazing over and cut down on the number of words immediately. In fact, tell men right at the start how long the story will take and stay within the allotted time. Men feel they are responsible for the energy they allot to a certain activity. So they feel they need to "set their energy clocks" so they don't run out of energy. Running out of energy makes them feel out of control — a feeling they hate.

Strategy #3: Be direct — don't hint

Make sure that you are direct — even to the point of spelling something out. Men, more so than women, require clear messages as well as brief ones.

mi Says • Mimi Says • Mimi Says • Mimi Says • Mimi Says • Mimi Says • Mimi Says • Mimi Says • Mimi Says • Mimi Says • Mimi Says

Hinting is futile

Men and women are different regarding hinting. Don't give men hints. A woman may give a man big hints over and over, such as, "I love flowers." And no flowers arrive. So she gives him *huge* hints next, such as (upon seeing a person give another person flowers) saying to him, "Oh look. I love flowers." She waits and no flowers arrive. Finally, she decides to be direct. "Honey," she says one day, "Do you know what I would really love you to do?"

He looks up attentively. That is a focusing statement. It gives him *hope* that the next thing out of her mouth will be specific. "What?" he asks.

She says, "I would love you to bring me flowers sometime, when I least expect it, like on my birthday."

He gets the message. She can tell! It clicks. She gets gorgeous flowers on her birthday. She is so happy. Her women friends are livid. "You had to *tell* him," they say. "It's not romantic," they say. "He should have known," they say.

"Right!" she answers back, "On the one hand, I could have said 'He should have known.' On the other hand, I could have flowers. And I went for the flowers, and I am so glad that I did."

When she debriefs him on this incident, she may say, "What were you thinking for two years when I said I loved flowers?" And he loves that question; it's analytical. He says, "I remember I had a warm feeling, because it was so feminine; and I also thought you should probably plant some." "I love flowers" means "I love flowers" to men. They don't search for hidden meanings. They listen literally.

And it all has to do with the definition of romance. Here is romance for women: "He read my mind. He knew what I wanted before I asked for it." You know what that response means for men? Work. Hard, energy draining, hit-or-miss work. If they are wrong, they hate it. They lose face. Here is romance for a man: A woman tells him exactly what she wants. He gets it for her; she rewards him profusely. That's romance for a man.

Mimi Says • Mimi Says • Mimi Says • Mimi Says • Mimi Says • Mimi Says • Mimi Says • Mimi Says • Mimi Says • Mimi Says • Mimi Says

Strategy #4: Avoid emotional displays

Crying or other emotional displays in a negotiation can be more distracting than a low-cut dress. It can be just as ruinous to a woman's position in a negotiation. Men have been socialized to be less emotionally demonstrative. In fact, men have probably gone too far in the other direction, but that's another discussion. Women have not been socialized in the same way as men. In fact, women cry four times more frequently than men, according to a Minnesota-based study.

The place to start curtailing emotional displays is on the job. The crying person seems to demand a sympathetic response from the listener. Someone who is sobbing also signals to the listener and observers that — for the moment at least — this person is not capable of handling a situation. Crying also annoys and angers people who have shut off their own feelings. If they don't want to deal with their own feelings, they don't want to deal with anyone else's. Men may feel a woman who cries is being manipulative.

If you feel a cry coming on, excuse yourself, go to the bathroom, cry your eyes out, take a deep breath, and go back to the meeting without risking that particular mistake. If you are prone to crying, be sure you carry eyedrops to remove the redness from your eyes.

Four Strategies for Men Who Want Women to Hear Them

Some speech mannerisms, common among men, are so off-putting to women that they rob men of the opportunity to be heard no matter how valuable the words are. This concept is not just theory. Because women have become a major force in the workplace, men need to alter their style to communicate successfully with women. Everyone is somewhat susceptible to these basic differences. Some people are more susceptible, some people less. A rare few are not at all. But even for those few, the differences are not irrelevant — because they negotiate with men and women who do communicate differently.

The following sections contain four strategies for men who want women to hear them. If you can practice one of these strategies each week, you'll quickly advance the way in which you are perceived. The prerequisite is to start listening to yourself. Awareness is the first step to any behavioral change. It isn't right or wrong — it's just true. Accept and grow or be left in the dust in this ever-changing world of negotiating.

Strategy #1: Don't be condescending: "honey," "baby," "sweetie," and other malaprops

It is the '90s! That any American male can still be using these words in the workplace is shocking. Forget that some women still address customers in this fashion! Those phrases don't give them power either. For a man to use these phrases when talking to a woman is entirely inappropriate. Think respect. When your words flow from that place, they don't contain such verbal pats on the head.

Strategy #2: Share before deciding

Sharing does not come naturally to most men. They have been socialized in the "strong, silent" stereotype. They must have things all figured out before they say anything about a subject. If you are negotiating with a woman, she may want to know your thoughts part way through the process. The natural way for a man to express his conclusions is at the very end of the process — to announce his decision after he makes it.

If you are totally silent while you are going through the decision-making process, she may think you are shut down. It may be hard for her to stay interested, and she may become frustrated with the lack of feedback.

Strategy #3: Share something personal

This is not a suggestion to be intrusive or sexual. This approach is essentially humanizing. Share stories of humankind with the woman on the other side of the negotiating table. This approach may not seem natural for you at first. Mention something about your family or what you did over the weekend. The topic doesn't have to relate to the negotiation. Provide some of the detail. Most women love details.

Men are better off making personal comments about their own life, not about a woman's personal life or appearance. Because of the history of sexual harassment in this country, men do not have the same freedom that a woman has to comment on the clothing of the opposite sex. Not fair, but true. If a man thinks a dress is attractive, he should keep that to himself. If he likes an item that is personal, but not quite as personal as a dress, he can go ahead and comment on it. A beautiful fountain pen or an attractive briefcase are acceptable areas for compliments. Dresses and perfumes are dangerous. Necklaces and necklines are absolutely verboten to mention in the workplace environment today. The smart advice is "When in doubt, don't."

The inhibiting and somewhat artificial restraint in today's American workplace is not worldwide. In Italy, women employees told us they receive compliments and bearhugs from appreciative bosses without sexual overtones.

Michael Says • Michael Says • Michael Says • Michael Says • Michael Says • Michael Says • Michael Says • Michael Says • Michael Says

Finding common ground

In business, I sometimes let a woman know that I raised my three daughters. Working mothers usually love to know that. Only one of my daughters was living at home and still in high school on Mimi's and my wedding day. I often share perils-and-joys-of-raising-a-teenager stories, because most women who negotiate these days have teenagers or children who will be teens.

I need to emphasize that I share this information only at appropriate times. Forcing these asides into a conversation is hazardous.

Michael Says • Michael Says • Michael Says • Michael Says • Michael Says • Michael Says • Michael Says • Michael Says • Michael Says

Strategy #4: Avoid emotional displays

Yelling and other emotional displays in a negotiation can be more distracting than a wrecking ball through the wall of the negotiating room. It can be just as ruinous to a man's position in a negotiation. Men have been socialized to be less demonstrative with all of their emotions, except anger. Many men still think yelling when they are frustrated or angry is acceptable behavior. In fact, men yell much more frequently than women in the office, according to a recent study. Not surprising?

The place to start curtailing that activity is on the job. The yelling person seems to demand a sympathetic response from the listener. The person who is yelling signals to the listener and observers that — for the moment at least — this individual is not capable of handling a situation. Yelling also creates shame and resentment in those subjected to the outburst. If they are not able to yell back, they may get even in other ways. Not only women feel that a man who yells with hostility is being dominating and controlling.

If you feel a yell coming on, excuse yourself, go to the bathroom, yell your lungs out, take a deep breath, and go back to the meeting without risking a public outburst. A man who yells is seen as a flawed individual. Many people know that anger is a cover for fear or sadness, and hostility can mask vulnerability. Nobody has trouble shouting down the chain of command. Most people have trouble shouting up the chain of command. Women and men can learn from each other. Respect the differences and alter your style to be heard. Remember: you can be the world's best negotiator, but if your words are not heard, your message doesn't matter.

How to Really Garble Communications

Sometimes, we can talk all day about how to improve communications and people never get it. In the spirit of fun, here are some handy tongue-in-cheek tips for people who strive to be bad communicators, to stay unclear, and to keep creating quagmires and confusion in their lives.

Use these six little secrets to keep your life in chaos. Use them in business and at home to keep things in turmoil. These are also handy ways to ensure a high employee turnover.

Raise your voice

If you really don't want to get your point across, just begin shouting or scolding. Either response prevents any further intelligent discourse. This rule is particularly important when a language barrier is preventing someone from understanding you. When someone doesn't understand your language, just talk louder. *Loud* communicates the same message to people all around the world. *Loud* is disrespectful. *Loud* characterizes someone you don't want to do business with.

Leave out details

Details let the other person know exactly what you want or need. Leave the message fuzzy if you want to continue having bad communications. Details take time. You can shave valuable minutes off the average communication by leaving out the details. After all, it only takes a few *hours* to clean up most messes created by such an omission.

Don't check to see if you were understood

This rule is very important for would-be bad communicators. If you spend time checking to see whether you were understood, all the other efforts you make to be a bad communicator can be thrown out the window. Don't give the other person a chance to say, "I didn't understand xyz." Otherwise, you'll *have* to clarify. If you want to be unclear, do your deed and skedaddle before anybody can ask any questions.

Walk away and talk at the same time

Toss your request, instruction, or demand flippantly over your shoulder as you are walking away from the person to whom you are speaking. Preferably, avoid looking at the other person during conversation. This denies virtually any possibility of being understood. And you haven't wasted those precious seconds required to face the person you are talking to and make eye contact.

Assume that everyone understands you

If you are a bad communicator, you already know about the dangers of assuming information, but we thought we would remind you anyway about the most popular tool of the unclarity trade.

Don't permit any objections or questions

Heck, don't permit *any* response. The other person may be taking up your time to understand the niggling information. Toss out whatever you have to say and cut off the discussion. Anything further would just help clarify what you are saying.

Chapter 14

Telephone Negotiating

. . . .

In This Chapter

▶ Getting through to the right person

▶ Negotiating tips especially for the phone

▶ Choosing the best equipment for your telephone

. . . .

*N*egotiating over the telephone is never as good as negotiating face-to-face, because of the increased difficulty of listening effectively. Unless you are very careful and very clever, telephone conversations rob you of much of the data that comes to you almost automatically during a face-to-face meeting. The gestures, the facial expressions, the sidelong glances between members of the other party — all these are lost in the telephone negotiation.

This chapter covers the special considerations necessary when you use the telephone to negotiate. All the other aspects of negotiation are still in play, so don't ignore the rest of the book just because you are on the telephone. If anything, those other parts become more important.

Reaching Out and Touching Someone

The higher up a person is on the corporate ladder, the more his or her time is protected. You may have to get past various staff members who screen calls. Sometimes, all the skills of negotiating the deal are necessary to get a *screener* to put you at the top of the priority list.

Getting past the gatekeeper

Often, you are unable to get through to the right person on the first call. If you want to enjoy maximum success on the phone, you should treat *gatekeepers* — the assistants who take your calls — with respect.

...ael Says • Michael Says • Michael Says • Michael Says • Michael Says • Michael Says • Michael Says • Michael Says • Michael Says

Getting through

Many people get really frustrated with the gatekeepers of the world. This attitude puzzled me a great deal because I never had that problem. Then I stumbled on the answer accidentally. A well-known writer client of mine was trying to reach Steven Bochco. My client was frustrated and railing about Bochco's failure to call him back. "Does he know why you are calling?" I asked. "No" was the impatient reply. "I have not been able to talk to him."

"But what did you tell his assistant?" I could hear my client's impatience rising steadily as he said, "I don't want to talk about this to his assistant, I want to talk to Bochco. Could you call him?"

"Sure. I'll be glad to do that for you." Then I had to pick my words carefully. We had already discussed the advantages of my client pitching his idea himself. "Okay. Here's my theory. If you want to talk to Steve Bochco, you have to talk to the assistant. Tell him who you are, who your dad was, why Steve knows you, and the general nature of your call. Bochco is busy. You had better give him a darn good reason to call you back."

An hour later, my client called to tell me that he had just had a half-hour conversation with Steven Bochco. He was very happy. Interestingly, my client's career has taken off since he learned how to get past the gatekeepers with respect.

Michael Says • Michael Says • Michael Says • Michael Says • Michael Says • Michael Says • Michael Says • Michael Says • Michael Says

By and large, after the switchboard operator or receptionist, the assistant you talk to first has the support and confidence of the person you want to contact. Give the assistant the same respect and confidence you would give the person you're trying to reach. You get through the screening process more often, and you can make progress even when you speak only to the support staff. You don't always have to talk to the boss to get things done.

- ✔ **Don't wear out your welcome.** You find that you get much more accomplished by working as much as possible with assistants and support personnel. Always recognize that until you have established your relationship with the boss and the gatekeeper, the gatekeeper is unable to respond to any of your requests without approval from the boss.

- ✔ **Don't get cute, coy, or flirtatious with the gatekeeper.** This sleazy approach demeans both parties in the conversation. Respect carries you further in the work-a-day world than all the sexual charm you may exude over the phone.

- ✔ **Be businesslike in all your dealings.** Using the name of the assistant, especially to the assistant, is very positive. Always write down the names of key support staff.

One of the best movies in recent times about turning the gatekeeper into an ally is *Wall Street*. Charlie Sheen's character successfully gets through to an executive many levels above him. Watch the first ten minutes of the movie for everything you need to know about how to get past a gatekeeper: persistence (he called 59 days in a row), preparation (he knew about family, birthdays, and preferences), and most of all respect for the gatekeeper. If you want to get the respect of the boss, you need to give respect to the boss's choice of assistants. If you want to watch the whole movie, be warned of the R rating.

Leaving a message

If you can't reach the person you're after, you often have to leave a message. If someone is taking down the message for you, make your comments brief. If you are recording the message on a machine, you can include more detail, but still be concise. Pack in the information in as few words as possible and be logical.

To add importance to your message and avoid playing phone tag, you may inquire when you can call back. If that doesn't work, give two or three times when you can be reached. One of these approaches is almost certain to work. Arranging a time for the next call elevates your importance and engages the assistant in making the next call the one that connects with the boss. Remember, no one can be more helpful or harmful to you than a seasoned gatekeeper.

When traveling, the ability to leave and get messages is still important. In the U.S., having voice mail on individual phones in upscale hotels is increasingly common. In hotels that are not so up-to-date — ski lodges and such places — the likelihood of having a suitable answering service or voice mail system is slim. We own and carry with us a small digital answering machine. The machine records better messages than any desk clerk and makes the caller feel comfortable leaving a more complete message. Often the message is so complete, the call doesn't have to be returned. Most people are more confident that we will receive a message when they speak to an answering machine.

Assembling the Participants

Deciding who participates in a telephone negotiation is as important as choosing whom to invite to a live-and-in-person meeting. Conference calling no longer reduces you to one-on-one negotiations over the phone. Check out the section, "Who to Invite" in Chapter 3 — the same rules apply.

After you decide on the participants, choose the best way to gather these people together. The following sections describe the three basic choices.

Gathering in front of the telephonic campfire

If one or two other people within your organization need to be included in the conference, invite them into your office and use the speakerphone. That way, at least the two or three of you who are together don't lose the benefit of sharing gestures, documents, and facial expressions. Be sure to read the section in this chapter on equipment, although we can summarize our advice here: get the best.

For a very important meeting, you can even set up a video telephonic conference. Remember the television Jetsons of the '60s with their futuristic phones that had a television screen attached? Thanks to video conferencing, sending your image along with your voice is no longer science fiction. Desktop video-conferencing is fine for some applications, but the small picture size and the jerky quality of PC-based video-conferencing is a very poor substitute for face-to-face meetings. Room-based video-conference centers provide the large-screen images that show subtle communication clues contained in body language. These systems are really helpful when groups of executives are assembled for a meeting.

You need not go to the expense of building your own room-based video-conferencing system. In the United States and the United Kingdom, for example, video-conferencing rooms can be rented by the hour. AT&T's Global Business Video Services, for example, has more than 500 publicly available video-conference rooms across the United States and plans to add more. AT&T has linked them with high-speed fiber optic communication lines that can carry high-resolution video images. Don't automatically assume this choice is out of your reach.

Conferencing with your own equipment

These days, most office phones have conferencing capabilities. Don't miss out on your phone's conference feature just because the procedure seems like too much trouble. See the technological tips at the end of this chapter. This is one feature you should know how to use.

Using conference calling saves you the time of having one conversation and then calling someone else to repeat the message. Conferencing also maximizes accuracy of communications and prevents delays. Because all parties are hearing the same thing, everyone's confidence level in the negotiation is at its highest.

Conference calling works when you have at least two phone lines. On a single line, you pay the local telephone company for this feature.

Asking Ma Bell for help

Hooking up four people to a private conversation using standard equipment is possible, if you are willing to pay a little extra for a phone with this feature. Arranging a conference call through the telephone company is usually a better approach, if you want more than three people on the line at the same time. This is especially important if they are to be on the line the entire time rather than just a small portion of the conversation.

The charges are quite nominal. The phone companies are glad to get the long distance business and charge very little for the convenience of coordinating all the callers, taking a roll call at the beginning of the phone meeting, and providing the best possible voice quality.

Elevate the Occasion

The biggest disadvantage of telephone negotiation is that the convenience of the telephone can cause people to devalue the importance of the negotiating session. In a face to face meeting, the parties gather together all the materials they could possibly need during the conversation, drive across town, battle the parking problem, find their way to a particular office or conference room, take time to pour a cup of coffee, find a seat, and commence the conversation. After this effort, everyone knows the meeting is important.

Frequently, when negotiators save time by using the telephone, instead of putting some of that time back into the actual discussion, they hurry through the conversation as if it were less important than if they had spent unproductive time commuting and getting settled in.

Never lose sight of the fact that every communication is important during a negotiation, whether by telephone, letter, or face-to-face discussion. Take care of the conversational niceties and then some, even if you don't have to drive all over kingdom come to have the meeting.

Crisp beginnings

Before you go into an important meeting, you take a beat to be sure that you look your best. You automatically check your hair, your collar, or your teeth (especially if you had spinach for lunch). Do the same on the phone. If all you do is take a deep breath and put a smile on your face, you feel more prepared, and the telephone session begins much better.

Always put your best foot forward, even if no one can see your feet. When you start a telephone negotiation, give the same attention to a good first impression that you give to a face-to-face meeting. How you answer the phone or initiate the call is important. Too many people just pick the phone up and say "Yeah?" or some other perfunctory greeting. Don't be rude. Start with a positive greeting, "Good morning," "Good afternoon," or "Thanks for calling." It sets a positive tone. If you don't have time to talk, ask the caller if you can arrange another convenient time. If you are the caller, ask if the time is convenient. Arranging another time shows respect. And you must give it to get it.

When the meeting starts

If time or circumstances force you to conduct important negotiations over the telephone, try your best to compensate for the lack of face-to-face interaction with careful listening and pointed questions. By keeping in mind the disadvantage of having less feedback inherent on the phone, you turn the telephone into a negotiating instrument almost as effective as the face-to-face meeting. This awareness gives you a powerful advantage in a day in which the telephone is probably used more frequently than face-to-face meetings in business negotiations.

Remember the person on the other end of the line can't see you either, so give lots of auditory feedback. In a face-to-face meeting, looking out the window and contemplating your next thought is perfectly acceptable. But the people on the other end of the line can't see what you're doing. They're likely to think that you've been disconnected or that you are distracted.

Speaking with authority

Because you only get one chance to make a first impression, develop your *vocal personality*. The first impression you make over the phone depends entirely on how you speak. Begin to listen to yourself by working with an audio tape and tape recorder. Pay attention to these characteristics:

- ✔ **Volume:** Others must be able to hear you clearly. You don't want the listener straining to hear your soft voice or holding the phone away because you are irritatingly loud.

- ✔ **Pronunciation:** Others must be able to understand you. The word "five" cannot sound like the word "fine." Mumbling can be corrected by putting energy and lip motion into your voice. If you're not excited or enthusiastic about what you are saying, fake it.

✔ **Rate:** Speak at a moderate pace — not too fast or too slow.

✔ **Intonation:** Avoid a monotone by letting your voice rise on important words and lower on the not-so-important ones.

✔ **Nonwords:** Look out for the "ums" and "uhs." These fill silence, but a short pause is so much better.

✔ **Emotion or tone:** This element is hard to define, but you know it when you hear it. It's the emotion or attitude in your voice — the edge you put on certain words. When you say "I've told you before," your tone can convey that you are angry, condescending, or defensive. Saying the words differently ("*I've* told you before") can convey that you are friendly, happy, or nonjudgmental. Put a smile in your voice.

Never mumble — especially not over the telephone. Speak clearly. Speak slowly. Just think of all the time you saved not having to drive somewhere for a face-to-face meeting.

Women have distinct advantages and disadvantages in telephone negotiations. Women are wildly successful in sales and marketing, and they are breaking sales records and glass ceilings all over the place. They tell us some reasons for this success. These are areas where men are learning from women, even though some have already caught on:

✔ Many women say developing a warm telephone personality is easier for women than men.

✔ Making small talk and developing relationships is easier for women than men. For example: A woman calling Los Angeles from Chicago may ask the administrative assistant about the weather or comment about having visited Los Angeles. Small talk breaks the ice and establishes a relationship; then the assistant is motivated to help the saleswoman meet with her boss.

✔ Today, thanks to years of effort to raise consciousness of gender equality, a woman caller is no longer assumed to be a man's assistant. People who answer the phone are more likely to listen carefully, so they don't make that mistake.

Women tell us they also have some disadvantages:

✔ Although male secretaries are on the increase, some people still assume that female callers are secretaries. This is a common mistake even when female secretaries receive a call from another woman. If a woman is mistaken for a secretary calling on behalf of a male employer, the wisest response is to correct the error with a diplomatic chuckle. A good-natured correction avoids embarrassing the offending person and gains an ally.

✔ Some men still resent being told what to do by a female voice. To prevent a conflict, women must be firm and friendly at the same time — charming without being suggestive.

✔ Some people are still suspicious of a female voice calling an important male executive. One would think those days would be over by now. More and more women are gaining stature and power and are treated as fellow professionals. Some industries are slower than others, but progress is occurring.

Shaking hands over the phone

At the end of a negotiating session, you wrap it up. If the deal has not closed, you walk the person to the door and arrange the next session. Finally, you look the person in the eye, say good-bye, and shake hands.

You cannot shake hands on the phone, but you can use words as though you are shaking hands. Recall the walk to the door at the end of your last face-to-face session. You almost always have a mini-conversation about something other than the business you were discussing. Do the same thing on the phone.

Too often, the efficiency of the phone works against using closing pleasantries. Fight that instinct. Take the extra moment. Try to end on a personal, positive, or forward-looking note. The specific communication is a function of your personality and your relationship with the other person. Whatever closure you use face-to-face at the end of a negotiating session, you should use at the end of a telephone negotiation.

Questions to Ask on the Telephone

Some good questions are designed to close the sensory gap imposed by the phone. The questions are easy; you have probably heard them before. If you thought they were polite inquiries, you were only partly correct.

Add these questions to your telephone routine:

✔ "How are you doing today?" and "Is this a good time to talk?"

These two classic inquiries serve one purpose: Taking the temperature of the person with whom you are speaking. Don't rush right into a negotiation — find out whether the person you want to negotiate with is ready. If you poke your head into someone else's office, you can see if the person is on the phone or otherwise preoccupied. Do the same when you initiate a discussion on the phone.

✔ "Do you have a half hour or should we schedule a phone appointment?"

This inquiry is a more sophisticated version of the first two questions. If you know the phone session is going to be long, check with the other person's schedule first. Don't draw someone unwittingly into a long session. Also, scheduling a phone appointment elevates the importance of the conversation.

✔ "Do you have the file on your desk?" and "Do you need to get anything else before we go ahead?"

If you refer to a document, find out whether the other party has the document in hand. Be sure that you are both working with the same version of the document. If a question exists, try to fax the version under discussion during the conversation. Faxing documents while you are on the phone is good not only for clarity, the practice gives you authority and power.

✔ "I hear a change of tone. Is everything okay?" and "You sound down today."

These are two classic ways to articulate what you suspect is true. Go ahead and put words to what you hear. Do the same if you hear that someone has become distracted, started munching a late lunch, or lit a cigarette. Noting such a distraction permits the person on the other end of the line to ask you to repeat whatever was missed — and surely something was missed. It acts as a bridge back into the negotiation. These comments also dissuade such conduct. People aren't likely to turn away from the conversation if they know that you are aware each time they do so.

As your listening skills improve, you may find that you can hear some of the facial expressions you don't see. Our friend Tom Sullivan — who is a speaker, composer, writer, actor, and anchorman — has been blind since birth. His listening skills are extraordinary. Sometimes, when we are talking, he stops and says to one of us, "You sound a little stressed out." He has never been wrong. If you are that good at listening, let the other person know. Your insight is flattering to them and helps confirm the information you are receiving.

To Be the Best, Own the Best

If you negotiate frequently on the phone, don't shortchange yourself. Your phone is simply too important. Don't be left in the technological dust; use the information in this section as a departure point. Whatever you purchase, do additional research to be sure that you have the latest and best equipment on the market.

Keep current by paying attention to advertisements and networking with your colleagues. Find out how your industry is benefiting from new technologies.

An excellent resource is Consumer Reports. They have a fax service through which you can order a report completely by touch-tone phone. To access that service, dial 800-999-2793 and follow the instructions. If they have not prepared a report on the item you are buying, they can often direct you to another resource.

We recommend consulting Consumer Reports because they do the research for you. Recently, they tested 26 different telephones — including basic models, speakerphones, and two-line phones. Almost three phones in four failed one or more durability tests — an extraordinarily high failure rate. Failures occurred in expensive phones and cheap phones, and across brand lines. The Consumer Reports tests answered these questions:

- Will the phone survive a fall?
- Can it handle a thunderstorm?
- Can it withstand static electricity?
- How is the voice quality?
- Is your voice or your caller's voice distorted?
- Are the voice levels too low?
- Does it have a volume control on the receiver?
- Are the keypad options easy to use?
- Does it have redial or speed dial?
- Does it have a speakerphone?
- Does it have two-line capability?
- Does it come with caller ID?

The top-rated phones change from year to year. As of February, 1996, Radio Shack ET-206, AT&T Trimline Memory 230, and General Electric 2-9267 are the top-rated phones. The only full-featured phone to survive all the durability testing was the AT&T 822.

When you begin owning equipment that gives you certain advantages, you may want to take some of it with you when you travel out of the country. Don't forget that almost every nation has its own form of plug for phones and other electronic do-dads. Strangely, these common connective devices are not uniform, nor are the adapters you may need for them uniformly available. Plan ahead to avoid disappointment.

Automated phone systems

These days, when you call an office to negotiate, the first voice you hear will probably not be a live person. A recorded voice greets you and directs you to your options. These automated phone systems are becoming more and more common. Private providers, and now your local phone company, can install these systems for you.

The newest innovation has been *voice response.* This system directs you to the right extension with an automated instruction to "push one" or "say one." Your voice activates the response. Voice response is very convenient if you have a hand-held portable phone; you won't need to remove the phone from your ear to press the buttons.

Voice mail and other automated phone systems are the wave of the future, but they can be frustrating with the interminable list of instructions. You don't want to frustrate your clients or create negative public relations. A good voice mail system keeps things moving. Contact your telephone company or a private provider such as AT&T or Nortel. At a minimum, you want voice mail capability. The hallmarks of a good automatic system are

- ✔ Simplicity
- ✔ Brief instructions
- ✔ Absolute guarantee that the caller can reach a human being

Many people still prefer a live operator, despite the fact that messages are occasionally lost or garbled and that phone numbers are occasionally scrambled. They yearn for that personal contact and become anxious if they are not able to reach a live voice. Even though an automated system is more reliable, you cannot ignore the feelings of the people who call you.

The telephone instrument

Whether you lease or buy your phone system, be sure that your system has all the features you want and then some. Be sure that the instrument on your desk has enough buttons to automatically access all the convenient features you may want now or in the future. When your instruction booklet arrives, read it over immediately. Note the features you will use most frequently. Program your buttons so that you can do the following things with a single stroke:

- ✔ Create a conference call
- ✔ Disconnect one party from the conference call
- ✔ Redial the last number
- ✔ Put a number temporarily in memory

Your phone should include an easy-to-use conference feature. Conference and conference drop should have specially marked buttons. If your phone doesn't have easy access to these features, see if you can specially program the unit to include such buttons. You should never have to say, "wait for me to figure this out." One punch is all it should take to create a three-party conference call or to drop a person from a conference call.

Local telephone companies offer a wide range of services: call waiting, voice mail, conference calling, and caller ID. New automated phone systems are updated every year by companies such as AT&T. The new AT&T Two-Line Personal Information Center 882, with speakerphone, a keyboard-like computer, and a large integrated display screen enables you to store up to 200 names and associated personal information, including telephone numbers, addresses, and birthdates. The names are automatically alphabetized in up to six separate directories for easy access, and all street numbers can be auto-dialed from the display.

This model is targeted at the small-office and home-office market. You can have two telephone lines, including distinctive rings for each line; three-way call conferencing; ringing line auto-select, which allows you to answer the ringing line without manually selecting it; and idle line auto-select, which lets customers make a call when the other line is in use, without manually selecting it.

Speakerphones

Speakerphones are just telephones that enable you to fill the whole room, rather than just your ear, with the other person's voice. Speakerphones can be a great tool but also a great distraction. Just remember that there's a time and a place for everything.

- ✔ The disadvantages show up most acutely during extended conversations. These disadvantages include the following: the speakerphone may create an in-a-tunnel sound; occasionally the sound cuts out, creating interruptions in conversation; if you have a speakerphone, the person on the other end often feels distanced or not important enough to merit your picking up the phone.

- ✔ The advantages are that you are not a prisoner when you are put on hold. You also have your hands free to write. If you intend to take notes while you talk, tell the other person. Let the person know exactly who is in the room. This disclosure is courteous and respectful. The prime advantage of a speakerphone is that it enables more than one person in your office to participate in the conversation.

hael Says • Michael Says • Michael Says • Michael Says • Michael Says • Michael Says • Michael Says • Michael Says • Michael Says

Extension cords — a priceless piece of equipment

I have a cord on the headset of my phone that stretches 18 feet. That long cord cost a few extra dollars, but the extra length gives me access to every paper and file in my office. I have the freedom to exit my office without leaving the line and hand things to my secretary who can modify documents, fax documents, and otherwise silently assist in the negotiation process.

I remember being in an associate's office for an important conference call. The phone cord could not reach the middle of the table, and all the people in the room could not be heard through the speakerphone. When I complained, the host commenced with a tirade about supplies. He mentioned the cord twice.

When we gathered the following week, the same problem ensued. As my friend started his tirade, I reached into my pocket, brought out a new cord, opened the package, and plugged it in. This was a million dollar deal; I wasn't going to stand on ceremony for $1.98! I said so when he tried to pay me. Everyone else in the room got the point. I don't know if he did or not.

Don't be penny-wise and pound-foolish regarding telephone equipment. Get the best; use the best.

Michael Says • Michael Says • Michael Says • Michael Says • Michael Says • Michael Says • Michael Says • Michael Says • Michael Says

You definitely want this feature. It adds about $30 to the cost of the instrument depending on your locale. Just don't overuse it. We suggest an enhanced speakerphone with improved sound quality and simultaneous conversation without the annoying sound cut off distraction often experienced with other speakerphones.

The AT&T Speakerphone 870 is equipped with the patented Bell Labs Clearspeak technology, so it really is advantageous to business speakerphone conversations. This model has a directional microphone that improves the speakerphone sound quality, digital signal processing technology that eliminates the choppiness in conversation when both parties talk at the same time, and an improved loudspeaker for a warmer, more natural sound. This particular speakerphone with a three-line system sells for under $200.00.

All modern phones have a *silencer* or mute feature for speaker phones. Learn to use it. You press a button, and then you can speak to someone in your office without the person on the phone hearing what you say.

Never assume that silencers are flawless. Don't use them while you discuss top-secret information. But they can be very handy for giving directions, "Joe, go get that file and bring it in." No interruption disrupts the flow of the conversation, and Joe is dispatched with specificity.

Headsets

Headsets are hard to get used to but well worth it. At first, the freedom may drive you crazy. For some reason, not having to be a contortionist during a long telephone session feels strange. It is amazing how liberating these gadgets can be. Currently, the good ones are priced between $100 and $250. We use the AT&T Plantronics SOH1858.

As helpful as the headset is for long calls, for short conversations, messing with all the wires doesn't seem worth the effort. Enter the *cordless headset.* Don't wander too far from the base, and this device is enormously liberating. The key is to obtain the very best. At the time of this writing, the sound quality is inferior to the headsets with a cord. However, by the time you read this, the technology will likely be vastly improved.

Car phones

Car phones are great for keeping a link to the office and letting people know that you're running late, but the car is not the best place for a real negotiation. You can't concentrate on negotiating a fee and negotiate for the left lane at the same time.

Again, you want the very best hands-free car phone kit you can afford. Be careful. The best car phone often means the best antenna and hook-ups. The phone is no better than the antenna system. A small differential in the cost of the systems ($25) can create a huge difference in the performance of the phone.

Cellular phones

A cellular phone is a portable wireless phone that can fit into your purse or the lapel pocket of your suit coat. It can snap into your car phone set up, which allows the car battery to power the phone while the cell-phone battery is being charged. No longer is this an ostentatious symbol of self-importance. Soon fifty million people will own cell phones. Cellular phones can be flip-style or not. The newest features include message service, caller ID, message waiting indicating, and anti-fraud devices where available from cellular service providers.

Many tests exist for determining the best cellular phone. Obtain the latest Consumer Report information by calling 800-999-2793. Get the latest test data and then get the best phone.

Beware of the free phone. If that free phone costs you one garbled negotiation, the unit could be the most expensive item you ever purchased.

Mimi Says • Mimi Says • Mimi Says • Mimi Says • Mimi Says • Mimi Says • Mimi Says • Mimi Says • Mimi Says • Mimi Says • Mimi Says

My favorite bumper sticker: "Hang up and drive!"

I bought my first car phone in 1985, one year after starting my business. Many of my female business-owner friends had them, too. My first reason for the purchase was to return calls before 5:00 p.m. as I was driving home or to the gym. 3:00 or 4:00 in the afternoon is usually car time for me, after an appointment or teaching a class. Few things were as satisfying to me as getting home at 6:00 or 7:00 p.m. and seeing that "0" on the phone message monitor in my office. It meant I could really be home, not back in my home office. I invariably let out a sigh of relief.

When I met Michael in 1989, he proudly told me that he was probably the only person in Hollywood without a car phone. He knew the car was not the place for a negotiation. He gave negotiations his full attention. But soon he started using my car phone for checking in with his office or his daughters and answering calls that required brief responses. Then he started asking to borrow my car. He was discovering that he could use the 45-minute drive downtown to court. I lent him my car several times. I was so used to my phone, I found myself at roadside phone booths yelling into telephones. The next time Michael asked to borrow my car, I said no. The next day, Michael bought a phone for his car. Now, he even has a separate cellular bike phone so he can check in with me (on my car phone!) during long bike rides.

Mimi Says • Mimi Says • Mimi Says • Mimi Says • Mimi Says • Mimi Says • Mimi Says • Mimi Says • Mimi Says • Mimi Says • Mimi Says

When you use a cellular telephone, you are, in effect, having conversations in public. Appropriate uses include: calling for help, making or accepting urgent calls with family and business partners, or getting directions when you're lost. You can also pick up messages — silently on your end. Communications too confidential to be splashed across the headlines in the tabloids are inappropriate. Also, turn off your cell phone before going into theaters, places of worship, club meetings, or court trials.

Part VI
Closing the Deal

The 5th Wave — By Rich Tennant

"I'm not actually buying this stuff, I've just got to have something to negotiate with when we reach the candy counter at the check out register."

In this part . . .

This is the glory moment when you close the deal. Some people believe that closing the deal is the automatic end point to every negotiation. Not so. You must keep closing the negotiation constantly in mind as a separate step. Negotiations can drag on interminably when this simple fact is forgotten. Closing the deal also means beginning the performance of the agreement. Make sure that both sides can perform the agreement — and that your side does — or the agreement won't be worth the paper it is written on.

Chapter 15
Win-Win Negotiating

*Y*ou are about to end the negotiation, either by closing a deal or walking away from it. Take a moment — push the pause button (see Chapter 6): If you are going to close the deal, be sure that the deal is positive for both parties. If you are thinking about walking away from the negotiation, be sure that you aren't overlooking some way to achieve a mutually satisfying outcome. This may be the most valuable moment in the entire negotiation.

Up to the point when a deal is about to close, look out for yourself. With style, respect, and intelligence, passionately pursue your goals. Hopefully, your opponent is doing the same thing. Nobody can figure out what is best for you better than you can. Nobody can figure out what is best for the other party better than the other party. Before you close the deal, however, step back to be sure that you have a win-win solution.

In the commonly used sense of the phrase, a *win-win negotiation* is a deal that satisfies both sides. In an ideal world, a win-win agreement is the only kind of deal that would ever close. Even in today's world, the vast majority of negotiations end in win-win situations.

The term "win-win" became the battle cry for the successful negotiation after the publication of the best-selling book, *The Win-Win Negotiator: How to Negotiate Favorable Agreements that Last* by Ross R. Reck and Brian G. Long. That book tells a parable about a young man seeking success. The young man learns that effectively dealing with others is the common thread among successful people. He learns that this requires negotiating with integrity, working with people in a positive manner, and keeping the agreements you make. He learns that you can't use tricks or gimmicks, and you must be your own natural self. The moral of the story is that negotiation is not a game with a single objective, but one step in building effective long-term relationships based on agreements that work.

Win-win negotiating does *not* mean that you must give up your goals or worry about the other person getting what they want in a negotiation. You have your hands full looking out for your own interests. Let others bear the primary responsibility for achieving their goals. We aren't telling you to run rough-shod over your opponents. Practice honesty and respect in all of your negotiations. But looking out for the other side just isn't your job — it's theirs.

Good Deal/Bad Deal

Finding a win-win solution is difficult if you don't even know when your own team is winning. We are continually astounded that so many people can't tell the difference between a good deal and a bad deal. That situation should never be the case if you use this book. Usually, we hear the lament about a deal long past. When we hear an associate complain about a deal he or she made, we are immediately curious. We ask. We explore. We coax out the details. More often than not, we find that the speaker either forgot why the deal was made in the first place, or the other party breached the agreement.

A *good deal* is one that is fair under all circumstances at the time the agreement is made. It provides for various contingencies before problems arise. A good deal is workable in the real world.

What is and isn't fair is very subjective. The parties must decide for themselves whether an agreement is fair based on their own criteria. Make sure that everyone is in agreement. Draw the other side out on this basic point before closing the deal. You don't want to sign a deal with someone who is harboring resentments over some aspect of the agreement. Be sure that the other side agrees that the deal is a good one.

A *bad deal* is not fair under all the circumstances. It allows foreseeable events to create problems in the relationship after the deal is struck. Some aspect of the agreement looks great on paper but simply doesn't work out in the real world — for reasons that were predictable during the deal-making process.

Each party should assess whether the deal is good or bad. You determine whether a deal is good or bad for you; the other party determines whether that same deal is good or bad for him or her.

To be sure that you have a good deal and a win-win situation, take a break just before closing (push the pause button — see Chapter 6). Ask yourself the following six questions:

✔ Does this agreement further your personal long-range goals? Does the outcome of the negotiation fit into your own vision statement? (See Chapter 1.)

✔ Does this agreement fall comfortably within the goals and the limits you set for this particular negotiation?

✔ Can you perform your side of the agreement to the fullest?

✔ Do you intend to meet your commitment?

✔ Based on all the information, can the other side perform the agreement to your expectations?

✔ Based on what you know, does the other side intend to carry out the terms of the agreement?

In the ideal situation, the answer to all six questions is a resounding *yes*. If you are unsure about any one of them, take some extra time. Review the entire situation. Assess how the agreement could be changed in order to create a *yes* answer to each question. Try your best to make the change needed to get a firm *yes* to each question.

When you have a yes response to each of the above questions, close the deal. Don't go for any more changes even if you think that the other person wouldn't mind — you never know! As Solomon wrote many years ago: "There is a time to reap and a time to sow." When it's time to close a deal, close it. Don't risk the deal by bringing up a new point, no matter how inconsequential the idea may seem.

If you can't alter the deal so that you can answer yes to each question above, be very thoughtful before closing. If you decide to go forward, write down exactly why you are closing the deal anyway. For example, you may have a project or piece of property that no one wants except the person you are talking to right now. Your choice is to wait or accept less favorable terms. Your choice. Just write down why you are making the choice so that you don't become part of that army of people with tales of exploitation. This exercise is particularly helpful to your state of mind if the results don't work out — you have a record as to why you took the deal. You won't be so hard on yourself.

If you have a question about the answer to either of the last two questions, get more information either from the other side or from another source. Ask people who may know about the other person. You would be amazed at how much people like to talk when you ask for an opinion and wait.

Remember that the people you are dealing with are more important than the paperwork you draft. Know your counterpart very well before you enter into a long-term relationship. No lawyer can protect you from a crook. Lawyers can just put you in a position to win your lawsuit. People do bad things all the time.

Checking out references is one of the most overlooked resources. Many people look at a list of references and assume that the referral would be positive or the source wouldn't be on the list. So they don't check the references. You can learn a great deal from checking out references, even from the most obviously biased sources. Relatives who serve as references are going to say good things, of course. But they can also provide valuable, factual information. For example, a relative may volunteer the names of other people with whom the other side has worked, reveal the other party's experience in the field, or offer information on the other side's financial strength.

Myths Surrounding Win-Win Negotiating

Often, participants in our seminars are familiar with the phrase win-win. Many attendees have used this buzzword to justify caring too much and too early about a counterpart's feelings and sacrificing their own needs and goals on the altar of conciliation.

No book or informed advocate promotes giving up or subordinating your goals in the name of taking care of the other person. Always assume that there are two equal adults in the negotiation — unless of course, you are negotiating with a child. Then you really want to hang on to your objectives. Let the child set the agenda, and you lose before you ever begin.

Women are frequently far too concerned about the other party's welfare in a negotiation. Sometimes, their own goals are smothered in the process. (Of course, not all women do this, and some men do.) A woman engaged in a negotiation must allow other people to take care of themselves. She doesn't have to make things "nice" for everyone. That's not a negotiator's job. Her job is to get what she wants. Remaining true to that objective may involve upsetting someone. Part of negotiating well is having the strength to take that risk. Some moms taught women not to "beat the boys all the time," because "they won't like you." Today, most men don't expect women to be lesser opponents. So give the negotiation your best shot, ladies. Successful women have long ago gotten over feeling bad about being called pushy.

If you are one of those people who thinks win-win means skipping over any of the steps in this book, now is the time to adjust your thinking. Use all your negotiating skills for every deal you negotiate. Pursue your dreams with passion and with respect for others. There are no shortcuts.

MEN & WOMEN

mi Says • Mimi Says • Mimi Says • Mimi Says • Mimi Says • Mimi Says • Mimi Says • Mimi Says • Mimi Says • Mimi Says • Mimi Says

The truth at last

Over the years, during my seminars and lectures, I've told women not to believe the myth that "men are good losers." Men claim that they are. They made up the phrase, "It's not whether you win or lose; it's how you play the game." That principle hangs over every Olympic game and is, allegedly, an American ideal.

Don't believe it. Even at the Olympics, gracious losing is not in vogue. Winning is the only goal worth pursuing. Defeat causes men to lose face, and they hate that most of all.

When you negotiate with anybody, but especially with men, closing is a time to emphasize what both parties are gaining — not what they're losing.

Creating Win-Win Negotiating

Some negotiations are pretty straightforward in terms of the interests of each party. When you are buying a car from someone who wants to sell a car, the negotiation is win-win if you find a price that works for each of you. In more complicated negotiations, the answers are not always so easy to find. Sometimes, some head-scratching and imagination are required.

Because creative thought is often necessary to arrive at win-win solutions, we have found that the best negotiators in a tight spot are also people who enjoy games or riddles — people who enjoy figuring things out. This is not to say that the only good negotiators are those with a Rubik's Cube lying around the house somewhere. But it does help if you enjoy the challenge of figuring out what serves both sides — and the solutions are not always easy.

In our seminars, we like to follow up the discussion about thinking creatively with a negotiating problem. This problem is adapted from a story we learned from Anne Miller, a skilled teacher of negotiation based in New York. She calls it the "Story of the 19th Pig."

A wealthy Australian died, leaving all his pigs to his three sons. To the oldest, he left half of his pigs. To the middle son, he left a third. To the youngest, he left a sixth. Unfortunately, he had 19 pigs when he died. Nineteen does not divide by any of the fractions without carving up at least one pig.

The three sons quarreled long into the night. (*Quarreling* is unartful negotiating.) Finally, they consulted with the wise woman of the village. What did she tell them?

Before reading any further, pick up a pencil and try to come up with a solution. Play the role of the wise woman of the village. If you don't reach a conclusion, here is a hint: This wise woman is smart enough to know that she ought to charge these three lads for solving their problem.

The Solution: The wise woman told the three young men to give her one pig, and the payment would solve the problem. Then she wished the sons well. Each of the sons thought long and hard, and then agreed to give up the pig. This decision left them with 18 pigs. The oldest son took his half of the pigs (9), the middle son took his third (6), and the youngest took his sixth (3). The wise old woman, to whom they gave the 19th pig, also received their enduring gratitude.

This is a great story, but it comes with a caution: The wise woman's solution only worked because the brothers wanted to close the deal in any way that was fair among them, even if the deal meant making a substantial donation to the local shaman. If any one of them was seeking an exact, legal interpretation of the father's will, this solution was nothing more than a mathematical trick. If the participants were fooled, each son was merely tricked into thinking he received his exact share.

Here, the solution was objectively sound. The answer provided fairness among the brothers, which is what they sought. But an exact division of the 19 pigs, according to the father's formula, would have carved up the single pig which went to the wise woman of the village. This deal worked because all three brothers wanted to accept the expedient solution of giving away one pig.

Note also that the brothers could have fought another night or more over which pigs they each received. Or they could have argued about the crazy formula their father used or some other real or imagined affront. But instead, the brothers pushed the pause button and agreed to defer to the wise woman. She used a little sleight of hand, but she solved the problem and received legitimate compensation for her very valuable services. Each of the sons got what he wanted: a good feeling about the father's will . . . and some pigs. Sometimes, even substantial real-life situations are settled with such simple win-win solutions.

When you work in a culture other than your own, being sure that you have a win-win solution takes a little extra effort. During a cross-cultural negotiation, be thorough in your investigation of what is and isn't acceptable. In Japan, for example, achieving the suggested result in the preceding paragraph would be easier because people are accustomed to the team approach used in the workplace. Concern for the company's good overrides individual interests. In Japan, you are less likely to hear, "That's not my job." Sometimes, however, the cross-cultural aspect of a negotiation makes a solution harder to find.

INSIDE SCOOP

ael Says • Michael Says • Michael Says • Michael Says • Michael Says • Michael Says • Michael Says • Michael Says • Michael Says

Win-win on the airwaves

In my own practice, I recently negotiated the contract for John and Ken, who are the number-one talk show hosts in Los Angeles. They were brought to Los Angeles from New Jersey at a mere 10 percent over the minimum union scale. They were glad to take the job because of the opportunity to work in a much larger market. After two years, they thought that they had proven themselves, and they wanted a very substantial increase in salary. The station manager agreed that they were well received by the listeners, but pointed out that their ratings had been up and down. The station executive thought that the team had pretty much reached a plateau in ratings. He was happy with that outcome but could do no more than double the hosts' salaries. I was seeking much, much more.

We finally settled on a base salary with bonuses. A modest improvement in the ratings would slightly increase the bonuses. At the high ratings levels that the station didn't think were achievable, the station manager agreed to very high bonuses. When the ratings spiked upwards and John and Ken beat all the competition, the station was ecstatic and did not begrudge paying the talented John and Ken much more money than they had originally requested.

Our arrangement protected the station from taking a high risk, which would have been very burdensome if the team had not performed as I

predicted. John and Ken were happy because they earned their compensation. This was a true win-win result.

When we started the negotiation, we were so far apart on salary points that it seemed we would never get together. Even as the bonus concept was put on the table as an approach, we remained far apart. The negotiation was a real struggle. The answer came when we made the bonus structure start with small increases at the beginning. An additional 100,000 listeners didn't add much to the salaries. But as the size of the audience grew, 100,000 additional listeners were very valuable to my clients.

This solution gave great comfort to the station manager, who didn't really mind paying heavily for spectacular results. The agreement gave my clients hope and incentive. Today, everybody is as happy with the results as we were on the day we signed the agreement.

Both sides were sensitive to the needs and desires of the other. We spent a great deal of time educating each other about our needs and hopes. What we didn't do is spend time worrying about the people on the opposite side of the table. That is how we got to our win-win result.

Michael Says • Michael Says • Michael Says • Michael Says • Michael Says • Michael Says • Michael Says • Michael Says • Michael Says

AT WORK

Creating win-win negotiations at work usually means resolving conflict arising from the different needs or values of the opposing parties. Thinking of manager and employee as opposing parties may seem strange, but often the relationship sure feels that way. The boss's need is to get the job done, no matter how long it takes, and the employee's need is to leave at 5:00 each Wednesday, no matter what. A conflict results. The boss's work must get done (that's why he or she is called boss).

In this kind of workplace stalemate, getting more data is almost always step one. If the work must be on someone's desk at 8:00 a.m. Thursday, there are two solutions. The employee could come back later that evening or arrive early the next morning. If the situation is more of a pattern than a true emergency, the employee also should anticipate a conflict and ask the boss on Tuesday what needs to be done by Wednesday at 5:00. Then, the employee could stay late on Tuesday or come into work early on Wednesday. If the situation is a true unanticipated emergency, the employee could recruit a coworker to cover for this exceptional event.

AT HOME

Michael Says • Michael Says • Michael Says • Michael Says • Michael Says • Michael Says • Michael Says • Michael Says • Michael Says

Honey, please put the seat down

The example of putting the toilet seat down started as a jocular way to describe the seemingly trivial, but potentially explosive, situations to which the basics of negotiation apply. In our own house, putting the seat down after I used the facilities was an issue only at nighttime, and the conflict turned into a stalemate. Mimi and I had both been single for many years, and now we were forced to think about this issue. One Sunday, we were having brunch with friends — a local judge and his wife. We talked about the book and this particular situation.

They were totally nonplussed. They looked quizzically at each other and said, "That's not a problem with us." Then the judge revealed their compromise, which he said came "with aging" — the exact moment had been long lost in the history of their successful marriage. "Why don't men just sit down and be done with it?" he asked. "That's what I do at night, and the seat thing is just not an issue for us."

With this wonderful suggestion, the toilet seat controversy is no longer an issue in our house, either. That is a win-win solution to a situation in which repeated requests had not worked consistently. Both parties must be motivated to use the win-win basics in this kind of situation. Both parties have to want to negotiate. Agreement is not something you can do alone. Repeating the same request over and over to someone who isn't interested in negotiating quickly becomes nagging.

Michael Says • Michael Says • Michael Says • Michael Says • Michael Says • Michael Says • Michael Says • Michael Says • Michael Says

Chapter 16
Getting Past the Glitches

· ·

In This Chapter
▶ Handling bullies and other difficult types
▶ Solving problems
▶ Walking away

· ·

Sometimes, you feel that you've done everything right in a negotiation, and the deal still won't close. The other side is not interested, or gets angry, or goes off on tangents, or is not available, or is making unreasonable or unrealistic demands, or, or, or. . . . This chapter looks at mishaps that occur in a negotiation to keep a deal from closing.

Many circumstances and events can send the best of negotiations skidding off track. In chess, these moves are called gambits. In track, such barriers are hurdles. In steeple chasing, they are hedgerows. In a crime chase, they are roadblocks. In the military, they are Catch 22s. In a negotiation, they are glitches — from the German word, *glitchen,* meaning a slippery spot in the road.

Overcoming the Glitches

Glitches happen. You cannot ignore them or be overly frustrated by them. You can't avoid them. They are part of the life of any negotiator. Heck, they are part of *life.* If you are prepared for them, you actually derive a certain pleasure from dealing with glitches when they come up in a negotiation.

We could write 22 volumes describing all the different glitches you may encounter, and sure enough, your next negotiation would uncover a new variation, a new slippery spot for you to maneuver. But the secret to successfully negotiating through any glitch is the same — keep your ultimate goal in mind. You are trying to reach an agreement — don't get sidetracked by glitches.

The best way to get through your next glitch is to push the pause button (see Chapter 6). Take a mental break from the negotiation. Check your own performance on each of the essential skills of any negotiation. Use that pause button with a vengeance. Find the problem and fix it. Then you can get back to the substance of the negotiation and close the deal. Always keep the negotiation moving toward the desired end.

The following sections provide both general guidelines and some easy steps for getting past the glitches.

Personality Types That Block Closing

Certain types of people always seem to get what they want and leave a destructive wake of bad feelings behind them. When you negotiate with such people, you feel that the only thing that would get through to them is a sharp jab to the chin. You walk away feeling angry and inadequate. This is the kind of person who makes you say horrible things like, "I coulda' killed 'em."

Before you spend one more moment of thought deciding how to beat these people at their own game, understand one thing: People with this type of personality are not nearly as good at negotiating as you are. The fact that you are even thinking about this problem, when you could be out playing tennis, is proof positive that you are in the lead. You can be sure that not one of those difficult types thinks about the impact on you. Ultimately, such people are the big losers in life. They usually fail to gain as much as they could in specific negotiations, too.

Noted psychiatrist Dr. Ellis Schwied states the concept another way: "When dealing with troublesome personalities, calm yourself. Find your own inner strength and relax into it, rather than trying to overpower the apparent strengths of the other person."

In his poem *If,* Rudyard Kipling said, "If you can keep your head when all about you are losing theirs . . . you'll be a man, my son." Old Rudyard knew a thing or two about negotiating.

You possess the tools to deal with difficult people. Unfortunately, in the heat of the moment, forgetting that fact is easy. The following are some helpful tips.

The bully

Bullies come in all sizes, shapes, and colors. They use a variety of techniques, such as making take-it-or-leave-it offers, screaming, needling, and making their counterparts the butt of a joke. You may remember such a person from the schoolyard. A bully is anybody who tries to intimidate someone who is perceived as weaker.

No matter what you do, negotiating with a bully is not going to be a pleasant experience. If you are negotiating on your own account, you may be wise to call the whole thing off at this point, because someone who bullies you during the negotiation will probably try to bully you after you reach an agreement. Unfortunately, sometimes walking away is not an option.

Whatever you do, don't try to outbully a bully. Instead, rely on the six basic skills in this book:

- **Prepare (Part I):** Be sure that you know everything you need to know about your counterpart before you begin the negotiation. To be forewarned is to be forearmed. Knowing ahead of time that you are dealing with a bully somehow takes much of the sting out of the bullying remarks.

- **Set limits (Part II):** Be sure that you are very clear about the limits you have set. Never accept from a bully a deal that you would not accept otherwise.

- **Maintain emotional distance (Part III):** Keep a tight grip on your pause button. Responding in kind is easy when someone is trying to bully you. Take a few minutes to cool off, if necessary.

- **Listen (Part IV):** You must work hard to listen to a bully. First, bullies mask their message in a melange of language that is hurtful in some way or another. Second, your own animosity is building, so empathetic listening is virtually impossible. Finally, if the bully's purpose is to achieve a desired outcome by using intimidation rather than sharing information and reaching a common solution, the bully may never give you the information you need.

- **Communicate Clearly (Part V):** This is very important. Don't speak often . . . but when you do make it count. With as little emotion as possible, let the other party and everyone else in the room know exactly what you are after. Even if you don't persuade the bully, someone else may later bully the bully for you.

- **Close (Part VI):** Try to close the deal at every opportunity. After all, if the negotiation isn't fun, you don't want it to last any longer than it has to. After the deal is done, you are done. Fight the impulse to spread the word about the new Biggest Jerk in Your Life.

If you have followed these steps, and closure still seems unachievable, try telling your counterpart that you are feeling bullied. This may not do any good, but sometimes a bit of candor can diffuse a situation. Yelling back at a bully does no good, but telling the bully that the behavior is having the intended result may just change that behavior. It's crazy but true: Even bullies don't want to be known as bullies. Your simple, unemotional assessment of the situation will go a long way toward turning things around — especially if other people are around when you make your statement. Use nonaccusatory words and "I" phrases, such as "I really feel beaten up when you talk like that."

Frequently, bullies act from a perceived threat to their position of power. A landlord may be a bully, but a landlord is sharply restricted in every jurisdiction by strict laws governing the rights of the tenants. The same is true of persons to whom you may owe money. Harassing tactics used to be stock in trade for creditors. No more. Consumer protection laws exist in every state in the union. If you face off with a bully, find out what your legal rights are. Then speak softly and carry a big stick.

Inside every bully is a real wimp that can't bear the thought of anyone finding out about that weakness. The bullies of the world don't have any confidence in their inner strength, their true stature, so they create false strength by bullying people. This compensating behavior doesn't work in the long run. It doesn't even work in the short run if a counterpart realizes what is going on and walks away from the deal.

Remember, the more bluster you hear, the more frightened and scared the bully is. This knowledge is not all that comforting when you are being yelled at, but push your pause button, figure out your next move, and then present it calmly. Sometimes, talking about the other person's fears at the beginning of the next negotiating session can be very helpful. The other person generally denies any fear but often settles down because you have made fearful feelings acceptable. Once that mask is removed, you can get on to the substance of the conversation.

The screamer

The screamer is anybody who does a great deal of yelling or screaming. This personality type is a variation on the bully, but we deal with screamers separately because three distinct types of screamers exist. Each type requires a very different response:

- The screamer is truly angry, upset, or scared. That is the subspecies this section is about.

- ✔ The screamer is a habitual screamer. Like Old Faithful in Yellowstone Park, this person just pops off every now and again. These types are annoying, but harmless — if you know you are dealing with such a person, just don't respond.

- ✔ The screamer is a bully. If the person is just trying to bully you, read the preceding section.

The worst thing you can do is sink to the level of someone else's negative behavior pattern. If you are not normally a screamer, don't start just because the person sitting across from you starts screaming.

A chilly, "Are you through?" works well in the movies but is probably little more than an unimaginative insult in most real life situations. A better, if more difficult, approach is to be sympathetic. Empathizing with someone who is yelling at you runs against every instinct in your body, but it may be the best way to take the fire out of an angry screamer. The next time someone is yelling at you, try one of these phrases:

- ✔ "I hear from your voice that you're upset."

- ✔ "Let me be sure that I understand you . . ."

- ✔ "Tell me more about that."

All these phrases are surprisingly calming. It's not that you're agreeing with the screamer, but you're using empathy, telling your counterpart that you want to understand what he or she is saying and feeling. Let others know that you are not upset by their hysterics and deal with the behavior independently of the substance of the conversation.

The emotional blast and the content are two different things. If you are able to draw a distinction between the two in your mind, the other person may also be able to establish the distinction. If the blast is more than a style — if it is born out of true emotional outrage — take a break. A situation is seldom so urgent that you can't take a breather and come back at a later time. Even a short break is helpful to clear the air after an outburst.

If you encounter a personality clash that seems too serious to resolve with any of the preceding methods, you may be able to substitute one or both of the negotiating parties. Another member of the team may be fresher and perhaps better able to deal with the bellicose negotiator.

If your boss is a screamer, the result can be very damaging to your health and your mood, if the screaming is personally insulting, blaming, or shaming. This person's anger is most likely not confined to the office, and unless you are a psychologist on the side, you should not attempt to treat the emotional problem. You can attempt to modify the behavior toward you in several ways. When the screaming begins, use an "I" phrase such as, "I feel belittled when you raise your voice this way. Can you speak more calmly?" If the boss yells back and refuses, say, "I can't listen to this. I'll be back in a few minutes." And leave the room. The screamer will either be calmed down when you come back, or it will be time to dust off the old résumé. . . .

We have heard many success stories using this approach, and many stories of dusting off the old résumé, which is a success as well. You determine your own limits for how you will be treated.

The star or the boss

Everybody is awestruck by someone. The problem may even be worse in the United States, where we make so much of our heroes. Negotiating with anybody in whose presence you feel helplessly speechless is difficult at best. You cannot negotiate effectively if you can't even get the cotton out of your mouth to speak.

How do you handle these situations when you have business to transact? Perhaps you have to negotiate with a celebrity. Even having to speak to your boss's boss's boss can give you that same sort of feeling. What can you do?

Prepare yourself. Make sure that you know well what you want, why you want it, and what the justification is for your request. Also, find out about the human being under the image. Inside every famous, powerful, or wealthy person is a person. Find out about the individual. Is he or she married or single? Are there children? What hobbies interest the person? The best way to diffuse the situation is to go back to Chapter 2 and work on gathering information.

The best piece of film on this subject is *The Wizard of Oz.* Poor Dorothy has quite a job getting an interview with the Wizard. The importance of the meeting is of gigantic proportions in her mind. Emerald City has all the trappings of power, money, and influence. She follows the Wizard's instructions exactly and returns to collect her trip back to Kansas. She doesn't have any luck with this distant, powerful presence until her little dog, Toto, pulls back the curtain to reveal the real person. That's when Dorothy begins to make progress.

If you negotiate with someone who has you quaking in your boots because of star power, do what Toto did — pull back the curtain. Find the real person. If you talk to the real human being rather than the image on the pedestal, you make good progress. Otherwise, things are pretty hopeless.

Going ape over the Ape Lady

My own example of speechlessness in the presence of a hero was the evening I met Jane Goodall, who devoted her life to the study of the silver-back gorillas in Rwanda in West Africa. Mimi and I were at the Governors' Ball after the Academy Awards ceremony. Ms. Goodall attended because a documentary about her work had been nominated for an Oscar. Obviously, the place was packed with the biggest names in Hollywood.

There, standing in a shaft of light that bathed her in the look of soft talcum, was Jane Goodall. I grew up reading *National Geographic* magazine and fantasizing about doing such important work.

There she was. I introduced myself. All I could do was blurt out the facts I just shared with you, and then my knees turned to butter. Fortunately, there was no need to negotiate anything. But if negotiation was necessary, I'm sure I could find the gentle, modest human inside my idol, who would admire some of my own skills and abilities. If you are worried about your own ability to negotiate with a star, keep this in mind: Being struck speechless can happen to anyone who has no connection with a person other than absolute awe. If you need to negotiate with a star, just take care to be well prepared and have your own purpose firmly in mind.

The biased buyer

Even though society is approaching the 21st century, some negotiators still occasionally suspect that they are about to lose a deal simply because they belong to a particular group. Not fair. Not right. Yet it happens. And dealing with this phenomenon is particularly difficult because this subtle discrimination is never verbalized.

If you have substantive evidence that bias exists against you, facing it head on is best, in a matter-of-fact manner, calmly and with dignity. A well-rehearsed phrase, delivered without accusation or emotion, is very helpful. "Are you open to granting this contract to a woman?", " . . . to an African American man?", " . . . to a Chinese paraplegic?"

You almost always receive a torrent of assurances. This is the '90s. Basing decisions on anything but merit is not politically correct. Today, being politically correct is very important, especially in the business community.

Accepting that assurance is in your best interest, whether the sentiments are true or not. The mere fact that the assurance was offered benefits your position, even if it doesn't change societal behavior in general. But after you acknowledge and accept the assurance, don't drop the matter too quickly. Ask this important follow-up question: "Exactly what is your criteria for making a decision about the terms of this deal?"

If the answer is price, press on. "What price must be beaten?"

If you are told the price level, ask whether your price will be *shopped.* Shopping means that one of the good old boys retains the contract by matching or minimally beating your price. This is important data to obtain in any event. The information is absolutely essential if you suspect bias. The earlier you obtain the detailed, specific data upon which the decision will be made and the more thorough you are, the less room the other side has to manufacture objective data later. Keep good notes.

You must be vigilant not to jump too quickly to the conclusion that bias is the basis for a particular result. In the workplace, discouraged workers often complain about the boss and sometimes jump to the conclusion that they are being picked on because of race, creed, or religion. Actually, a large number of jerks in the work-a-day world are equal-opportunity oppressors. They savage any underling who happens along, regardless of race, religion, nationality, gender, or sexual orientation.

Could it be you?

It is hard to admit and hard to face, but consider the possibility that the difficult personality in the room may be your own. What a revelation. No one likes to think this, but if you hear people yell often, you may have a negotiating style that is particularly frustrating. If your negotiations seem unnecessarily contentious, consider what *you* can do to change that pattern.

One difficulty is *position negotiating.* If you get stuck on one position, you are not well prepared. You don't have adequate information to understand where other safe areas for agreement may exist. You have not identified your own goals and limits sufficiently enough to define your range of movement. If you have done your homework, you can have the flexibility to reach agreements. In your next negotiation, grab your pause button (see Chapter 6) and listen twice as much as you usually listen. These two simple changes give you an opportunity to observe yourself. If you really want to become a first-class negotiator, you have to take a hard look at yourself.

Let us be more blunt. If two different people got upset with you in two of your last three negotiations, chances are very good that the fault lies with you. No matter how strong a case you can make that the situation wasn't your fault, it probably was. Your version of the facts isn't relevant. The only important fact is that people frequently get upset with you. Try to figure out what element of your style of presentation makes dealing with you frustrating, upsetting, or annoying. Ask someone who loves you point blank. Don't defend yourself. Sit quietly and listen to the whole awful truth. Then, try to fix whatever is wrong.

Tactics That Torment

Most glitches in a negotiation are something the other person says or does. If you make a mistake, the error is easy enough to correct. The frustrations — the glitches — arise from something the *other* party does. It's easy enough to take care of your own goofs. Figuring out your counterpart's goofs and how to get around them takes special talent. Some of the more common, maddening moments in a negotiation are listed in this section.

A constant change of position

Any negotiation involves concessions. Each side makes these concessions based on the information the two sides exchange about the factual matters and the priorities of the parties. Barring unusual circumstances, priorities should not change. Keep a consistent position about those items that are important to you and what your goals are.

If the other side changes its position concerning what is and what is not important, stop everything until you find out what happened. Don't ignore the issue. One of the following situations occurs:

- ✔ Maybe the other party experienced a significant change of circumstances. Get the new situation firmly in mind. Then revisit the point on which you thought there was agreement. Maybe the new situation calls for a new solution.

- ✔ Perhaps the other side is trying to pull a fast one.

- ✔ Maybe the other side is not as prepared as they should be. If that is the case, take a break. Your negotiation will go better for both sides, if both sides have prepared. Just say, "Maybe we should take this up tomorrow. That will give you time to meet and sort out any last minute items. No rush. We want you to be ready for this."

Written memos are useful tools in this situation, but a caveat is in order. If a constant change of position is part of a person's negotiating style, expect the person to constantly lose your documentation, not have time to read it, to misplace it, or simply to ignore it.

If you suspect that your counterpart may conveniently lose your written documentation, be sure to use firm and clear language in your memo: "If you disagree with any portion of this memo, please advise by such-and-such a date." This helps more than "as soon as possible" or "immediately," which mean different time frames to different people. Even more helpful is to distribute your memos to everyone the negotiator wants to impress. This way, the negotiator's peers, superiors, and colleagues can monitor the progress of the proceedings.

Good cop, bad cop

A less obvious but equally dangerous glitch is the good-cop/bad-cop ploy. This label grows out of the police interrogation technique of having one officer question a suspect harshly and another, gentler cop be the relief questioner. The gentler cop — the *good cop* — pretends to befriend the suspect. The theory is that the suspect will spill the beans to the good cop.

Don't fall in love with the good cop. The good cop, more often than the bad cop, does you in. If you doubt that, remember that the good cop is the knowing partner of the bad cop. One does not exist without the other. They don't wander unknowingly down different paths. They do what they do deliberately. The good cop is usually the more pleasant personality of the two, but in a negotiating context, they are in cahoots.

Mimi Says • Mimi Says • Mimi Says • Mimi Says • Mimi Says • Mimi Says • Mimi Says • Mimi Says • Mimi Says • Mimi Says • Mimi Says

Falling for the good cop

The great negotiator — as Michael likes to describe me — *always* fell for the good cop, until Michael pointed out this pattern.

The event that got Michael's attention happened several years ago. I found myself being denied normal side benefits in a deal that was otherwise acceptable to me. The denial was a first for me, so I called the good cop and complained. The good cop agreed wholeheartedly: "Of course, a professional speaker who *donates* her services for a good cause should be provided with appropriate space to sell audio and video tapes and an assistant, free of charge. That's standard. Anything else would be unheard of." The good cop ended with a question that still rings in my ears, "Who suggested that you pay for this? I'm going to take care of this and get right back to you."

I felt reassured. I put the matter out of my mind. Weeks went by and I finally called to check in with the good cop just to be sure everything had been straightened out. I was informed that all the display spaces had been taken. Paid or not, no more display tables were available. Too bad. Maybe next year. "You and I should have talked sooner," said the good cop, charm oozing from her voice.

Yikes!

I should have treated the good cop not as a savior from heaven, but with the same firmness and clarity I always use on the less receptive bad cop. I should have given her a deadline and let her know I would not speak without this courtesy.

Mimi Says • Mimi Says • Mimi Says • Mimi Says • Mimi Says • Mimi Says • Mimi Says • Mimi Says • Mimi Says • Mimi Says • Mimi Says

What's the solution? Use their little game against them. Go ahead and confide in the good cop. *Confide* to the good cop that the bad cop has just about blown the deal. *Confide* about your other opportunities. But never drop your guard. Set deadlines. Be clear. Don't lose focus. Your discussion with the good cop is an extension of your discussion with the bad cop. Don't forget that for one minute.

The invisible partner

One of the more frustrating glitches you can run into in a negotiation is to discover — usually late in the game — that the other side can't agree to anything without consulting some invisible or unavailable partner or boss. Overcoming this glitch can be like shadow-boxing.

If you run into the invisible-partner glitch, you may not have gathered enough information about the other party (see Chapter 2). You should have determined the decision-making authority of your counterpart early in the negotiation. To a large extent, good preparation avoids the problem of the invisible partner.

The invisible partner is quite similar to the good cop-bad cop tactic, and a bit more frustrating. An unnamed, unseen bad cop is off in the wings continually vetoing the progress made in the discussions. This situation usually arises in small business transactions or real estate deals, although a variation of it can exist in large organizations. Banks often use the so-called loan committee in this way.

If you sense a silent-partner excuse coming, ask for the opportunity to pay your respects to that silent partner—no negotiating. Heavens no, wouldn't think of it. You just want to introduce yourself and pay a courtesy call.

Keep your word. Don't use the first meeting to negotiate, if you promised not to pursue a business discussion. Once you have made a courtesy contact, however, you always have the option of making direct contact for the purpose of breaking a logjam. Someone else in your organization can contact the silent partner as well. Frequently, these folks in the wings work behind the scenes because they are really softies and have a hard time saying no themselves. You can use this vulnerability to your advantage.

There is a very helpful, non-negotiating, procedural question that you can ask of the invisible partner, even in the initial meeting. Upon meeting Ivan the Invisible, express your gratitude for having the opportunity to meet him; then assure him that you're delighted to be working with the Designated Negotiator. After the small talk, innocently ask Ivan whether they have had sufficient time to discuss the negotiating parameters. Can you close a deal with the Designated Negotiator? Does Ivan need to be alone with the Designated Negotiator to talk out any more limitations before you and he go further?

You may not be negotiating, but the more you can do to close off this frustrating technique of an invisible authority figure doing you in at every turn, the happier you are and the more smoothly the negotiation goes.

If you are not successful in meeting Ivan the Invisible, try insisting that the invisible partner be in a nearby room or available by telephone during the next negotiation session. Then, if a question arises that requires his or her approval, the other side can't use the absence as an excuse for prolonging the negotiation. You need to prevent delays during the negotiation when you reach the point of conclusion.

The double message

Always stay in step with yourself. By this, we mean that your words and your actions are consistent. Nothing, but nothing, is a bigger barrier to communication than the double message. Here are some common double messages you may have received in your negotiating experience:

- ✔ The threat to break off a negotiation, but the negotiation continues uninterrupted. This behavior baffles the listener.

  This inconsistency will throw into question every future statement the person makes.

- ✔ Not mentioning an issue at all during the first negotiating sessions and then making it the most important item on the table.

  This double message is a quite common syndrome we call the "Wimp/ Monster." Sometimes people are afraid or don't have time to raise an issue, so they "wimp out" and fail to bring the issue to the table. Then when they finally raise the concern and this addition to the agenda is received with less than enthusiasm, they get very upset and turn into a "monster." The better practice is to get all the issues on the table as early as possible.

A common double message occurs when the boss negotiates a task to be done on an immediate, high priority basis. The job is completed on time and is on the boss's desk at the requested moment — where it sits untouched for the next two weeks. Whoever pulled off the miracle must be acknowledged immediately. Otherwise, the person may be turned off the next time they are told that a similar miracle is needed. After all, the last time a big deal was made about a rush job, the project was not important enough to warrant a comment, even though it was accomplished at breakneck speed. More bosses should recognize these workplace situations for the negotiations they are. This common mistake made with a subordinate would probably not be made with an opponent in an important negotiation.

Children are taught this concept early in life when they are told "not to cry wolf." There is a fairy tale about a boy who kept crying out that a wolf was in the area. He had fun because he got a great deal of attention each time he shouted the warning. But when a wolf was really coming and he tried to warn the village, no one listened to him because he had falsely cried wolf too often. We're not sure what happens when these children grow into executives, but some secretaries wish that someone would tell them that story again.

"Let's split the difference and be done"

The concept of splitting the difference is one of the most seductive negotiating ploys, but if someone suggests it to you, measure the result. Sometimes, people begin a negotiation with a number that is unrealistically high just to impress a counterpart with the size of the subsequent discounts as the bargaining proceeds. If you have been more than fair in your approach, splitting the difference is not necessarily equitable. If the result is unsatisfactory, you need to say so. Don't be afraid of being called a *spoiler* by the other side.

Here's what you do:

- Push the pause button (covered in Chapter 6).
- Take time to evaluate the proposed compromise based on all the other basics, and
- Explain why this seemingly fair approach doesn't work.

If you are in a situation where splitting the difference seems fair, suggest doing so and explain why it is fair. If the number is fair, point out why it is fair. Make sure that you specify that the number is about midway between your two positions. If you merely state the phrase, "Let's split the difference" and nothing more, you invite the other side to come back with another split between the compromise you offered, and their original position. This process can keep going until you are far away from where you want to be.

A bad environment

A whole cluster of problems that are not caused by a counterpart can throw a negotiation off track. More often than not, these environmental glitches are as frustrating to the opposing party as they are to you. You can often engage the other side in the solution, unless the problem is bigger than both of you.

Sometimes glitches are not individuals but barriers that are characteristic of certain businesses.

✔ **Too much paper:** So many completed forms are necessary that your buyer turns off. Too many demands for duplicate information may irritate the person to the point where he or she gets frustrated and wants to deal with someone else.

Solution: Fill out as much of the paperwork as possible before you arrive. Have the paperwork well organized. Carry a clipboard so that signing is as convenient as possible. Don't solve the problem by having someone sign a blank form.

✔ **Hidden policies:** These directives are hidden from you — not from the other person. What you don't know can kill you — or at least kill your deal. If the company's policies are against you, all the persuasion in the world won't change things.

Solution: Do your homework. Ask questions. Don't ignore the situation. You can spot this problem when you simply aren't making any headway.

✔ **Poorly designed tools and resources:** If you reach for the contract to close the negotiation and the document isn't there, the delay may halt the negotiation. Even if you do have the contract but it's full of typographical errors or is outdated, the situation spells unprofessional, and the negotiation is a no-go.

Solution: Check over all the materials you plan to use in your presentation in advance. Make sure that they are the best they can be, even if you have to reach into your own pocket to improve them. Your commission or the advancement of your career is at stake. If the document is a form that the company supplies, make the necessary corrections before you start your negotiating session.

The Ultimate Glitch — Someone Walks Away

To our minds, no glitch presents quite the challenge as when someone walks away from the negotiation. This ultimate glitch has the potential to be final. The sensitive situation also raises questions about how to get things going again. Walking away includes such modern equivalents as slamming the phone down or sending a searing fax stating emphatically that the negotiations are over. Obviously, the negotiation won't close if the parties don't start talking again.

This section deals with the three variations on the theme of walking away:

- ✔ The other party walks away.
- ✔ Someone else who is negotiating with the other party (in competition with you) walks away from that negotiation with the other party.
- ✔ You walk away.

If the other party walks away

If you believe that the other party is walking away impetuously or for effect, don't be afraid to make a lunge and pull them back. Shopkeepers have held onto marginal sales for centuries by grabbing the arm of a departing customer.

If your counterpart abruptly severs all contact with you by making a hasty exit from the office, slamming down the telephone receiver, or refusing to answer telephone calls, you may be unable to reestablish communications immediately. If the person you're negotiating with gets out of range, use the time to your advantage. Consider the limits you set (see Part II). Go over all the new information gathered since the start of the negotiation. If, upon reflection, you believe that reopening the negotiation makes sense, do so. Don't stand on pride.

The important thing is to keep your eye on your own goals, needs, and limits. If you didn't prepare thoroughly (see Chapter 2) or you skipped setting limits (see Chapter 4), it's easy for pride or panic to rear its ugly head at this point. Use this unplanned break like a pause button (see Chapter 6). Use it to evaluate and regroup.

The breakdown of a negotiation is no time for emotion; it's a time for enlightened self-interest. DeToqueville, the French observer of American life, identified enlightened self-interest as one of the hallmarks of social and business structure in America. Don't let it fail you now. Keep a steely eye on what you want in life. And never be too proud to pick up the phone and get things back on track, if that's what it takes to achieve your personal goals.

If the other party comes crawling back

If the other party calls, be open to finding new ground. If the other person comes back to you, be sure to respect the opening comment, whatever it is. Even if the other party doesn't come as far as you want, be sure to acknowledge the willingness to make a first step. Under such circumstances, the smallest step may involve a major effort — and may be the key to a final settlement.

When negotiations begin again in earnest, don't dwell on the fact that you went to extremes to enable it to happen. This is not a time for hard feelings or for self-congratulations. Just go forward with the business at hand. Be glad you managed your way through the rough waters.

If one of your competitors walks away

If one of your competitors for a project walks away from the negotiation, move swiftly to close your own deal. Usually, the party on the other side of the negotiation is a bit vulnerable at this time, so you have a good opportunity to obtain a favorable result.

Try to find out all you can about the recent events. Usually the opposing party is your best source. "What the heck happened?" usually brings out more information than you need. Listen. Be sympathetic, even if the person speaking acted a bit unreasonably. Being a strong supporter of your counterpart is one of the best ways to close your own deal.

In the course of listening, try to find out exactly what your counterpart needed that your competitor didn't provide. Find out what both parties had on the table when things blew up. Be sure that the party you are courting is willing to deal with you and won't just use your offer as a club to close the other deal. All of these things are better learned by sympathetic listening as opposed to direct questions. Direct questions can feel too much like cross examination.

Another good source of information is the party that walked away, although this strategy holds several risks. Most importantly, your call may just cause that party to try and get back into the game. At this point, that person is more your competition than the person across the table from you. In addition, the person you are now negotiating with may not like your getting too cozy with the person who just walked away. Be careful about trying this tactic.

Remember, speed is often as important as thorough preparation in this situation. Move quickly to establish communications. Try to listen lots and speak little until you are ready. You already know what you are willing to do in the situation. If you can do so comfortably, make an offer within the range that the other side wants. Close your deal as quickly as possible.

If you're the one walking away

If you decide (based on your solid preparation and honest judgment) to terminate a negotiation, don't send a conflicting message. State clearly the conditions under which negotiations can resume. Then walk. Don't look back or otherwise communicate hesitation.

Looking back is not natural. The human body doesn't work that way. Your feet and your face should point in the same direction. Besides, looking back is confusing — to you and to your counterpart.

Walking away in a negotiation

Never terminate a negotiation when you are angry. We know that when you are angry is just the time you want to storm out of the room or slam down the phone. Fight the instinct.

Before you walk away, give yourself some breathing room. If, after some thought, you want to terminate the negotiations, end the discussion in a way that doesn't damage your own reputation in the community — whether the community is your family, your firm, or your city. Do it in a way that allows you to do business with those who like or respect your current counterpart.

Before you walk away from the negotiation, write a wrap-up letter. We recommend a letter because this process gives you time to edit and correct yourself. It memorializes your view of the situation. If you are mistaken about some aspect of the discussion, your view is clearly stated and easy to correct. A letter puts things in perspective in case the other side is mistaken about some aspect of the situation. Your letter should cover each of the following:

1. **Summarize the final position of the other side.**

   Be painfully accurate. Introduce this section with hedge words, such as "I understand . . . ," or "To the best of my memory . . . ," or "If I understood you correctly. . . ." Close this section with "If that does not correctly state your position, please advise." Such phrases enable the other side to change position or make a correction without losing face or being argumentative.

2. **Summarize your own position.**

   Be painfully accurate. Here again, hedge words let the other side reenter gracefully. Examples include: "In case it was not clear during our discussions . . . ," or "I'm sorry if this was not presented as clearly in our discussions as it is in this letter."

3. **Explain about square pegs in round holes.**

   If you simply don't believe that a deal can be made, because the needs and desires are so different, say so. No one is blameworthy. The parties can work together on another project when the fit is better.

4. **Never, ever blame the other person.**

   Even if you are walking away because you have decided the other person is a sleazebag, hog breath, scumbag, nothing is to be gained by putting that assessment in writing. The sleazebag may have a brother-in-law or cousin that you may want to do business with in the future. Never burn a bridge — a bridge serves an entire village, not just one person.

5. **Send a thank-you note.**

   Always include in your letter a thank you sentence for the time and attention you did receive. This final touch is the classy thing to do.

6. **Telegraph your next move.**

   This feature is optional. A sentence such as, "We will try to sell the script elsewhere," or "Next spring, we will try such a launch again," tells the other side that you have other options, and you will be exercising them. Of course, the sensitivity of the situation may limit you to a statement such as "We will be moving on," or "We will be examining our options over the next few weeks."

Walking away in a relationship

In a long-term relationship, walking away is more difficult. Walking out of a parent-child relationship is impossible. The great search for the natural family, even after years of separation, is a constant in modern life. You can, however, walk out of *specific negotiations* temporarily and decide when to take the matter up again. Make clear what you are doing by stating that you are not walking out on the negotiation.

We end this chapter with *our* story, because it is a story of which we are proud, and it emphasizes the importance of all the skills of negotiating. The following sidebar is a summary of the various skills discussed in this book.

Michael Says • Michael Says • Michael Says • Michael Says • Michael Says • Michael Says • Michael Says • Michael Says • Michael Says

Walking away to come together

My wife is a master negotiator. She also provides the best example I know of walking away.

We had known each other eight months. We had a wonderful time together. We enjoyed all the same things. My friends liked her. Her friends liked me. I had offered no ring, no *specific* talk of marriage, and no invitation to move in. I still wanted my freedom.

Mimi said she needed a commitment. I gave her my well-practiced soft-shoe on the subject. She said it again. I assured her that we could talk about it when I got back from my annual trip to the Cannes Film Festival in southern France.

With a tear in her eye she said, "Michael, if you can't make a commitment, I cannot see you anymore. It is just too painful." She walked away. She didn't waver. She didn't call. She didn't write. She didn't look back.

For my part, I only had a few days to get ready for the trip. I don't know to this day what she was going through at the time. I took her at her word and left on my annual visit to the Cote d' Azure.

Everyone with a television set knows that the Cannes International Film Festival is a real circus. The world entertainment press and those hungry for attention clog the Croisette. The crowd gets so thick by late afternoon that this wide boulevard curving along the Azure Sea must be closed to all but celebrity limousines and foot traffic. I found myself in my tuxedo, sitting on the railing by the wide sidewalk, looking out past the beach, past the photographers, past the topless beauties, out to the horizon — contemplating a life without Mimi. For the entire festival, I contemplated the twelve years since my divorce. I contemplated the next twelve years without Mimi. I thought about every woman I had ever dated, or could have dated, or dreamed about dating during that time span.

All my contemplation had resulted in the conclusion that I was ready to commit. When my plane landed in New York, I called Mimi from the first pay phone I saw. We were married a year later.

Some people hear that story and wish that they could walk away from an unacceptable situation just like Mimi did. It sounds so easy. First, walking away isn't easy. Second, it isn't even possible — not unless you have used the basic principles in this book.

Mimi had prepared (see Part I). She had been dating for 25 years. She knew what was out there. She knew that a number of attractive, decent, single men were available. She knew she was an interesting, appealing woman. She was so well prepared that she was able to set her limits (see Chapter 4) and she had made her goals (see Chapter 5)—she wanted to be married. She would not waste time on a man with whom that was not a possibility. She pushed the pause button (see Chapter 6).

Mimi had listened to what I had to say on this subject before (see Part IV). She had raised the issue of commitment at the three-month stage and the six-month stage. She had heard me profess my love. She had heard me express a general interest in settling down. She had also heard all the lame excuses and substitutes I had created to avoid commitment at that time.

She had communicated clearly about her intentions (see Chapter 12) and had tried to close the deal on acceptable terms (see Part VI). She knew what she wanted out of a relationship and was prepared to (and *did*) walk away if I would not comply.

Everyone likes this story because it has a happy ending. We had a unique and beautiful wedding and winged off to Hong Kong and Indonesia for a honeymoon trip we had won in a charity raffle.

It is important to note that, because Mimi covered all the basic negotiating steps, the story could have had a very different ending and still be a successful story on walking away. I may not have called. I may not have been ready to commit. Had she not put her cards flat on the table and said "This is what I am looking for — period," I may not have felt so compelled to follow through on my inner journey and resolved to make the commitment. Mimi would have been free to go on with her life, and she would have. Knowing her as I do, I feel sure that Mimi would be happily married to someone else today if I had not given her the commitment she sought.

Michael Says • Michael Says • Michael Says • Michael Says • Michael Says • Michael Says • Michael Says • Michael Says • Michael Says

Chapter 17

Closing the Deal: The Big Payoff

. . . .

In This Chapter

▶ Bringing closure to a deal

▶ Recognizing when to close

▶ Understanding how to close

. . . .

*T*his chapter is about the glory moment when it all comes together — when you close the deal. Most people think of closing the deal as the only satisfactory resolution of a negotiation. However, it's critical to figure out *whether* the deal should close and, if so, how to close it to ensure smooth performance throughout the life of the agreement. That's why we investigate win-win negotiating in Chapter 15 and walking away from a deal in Chapter 16. This chapter covers the skills and techniques of actually closing the deal.

Closing is a skill that you must develop separately — and keep in mind every step of the way — if you are to become a successful negotiator. We all know people who don't seem to care whether they ever close the deals they are working on. They are delightful at dinner parties. They can be frustrating at the negotiating table. Don't be one of those people. Use your closing skills from the first moment of the negotiation.

What It Means to Close a Deal

A deal closes when the parties agree on enough terms that they can move forward with the performance of the deal. For example, if you agree to pay someone $500 to paint your house green on Saturday using a certain brand of paint, that may well close the deal for the two of you. If you have some trust or history between the two of you, the other details could remain unexpressed. Without history or trust, you would need to specify the specific shade of green, the quality of the paint, and the amount of scraping and sanding that would take place. For yet other people, the deal would not be closed until everything was committed to writing.

This chapter is designed to get you and your opponent to the point where you both feel the deal is closed and that you are ready to perform under the agreement. It is designed to help you recognize when it is time to stop negotiating the deal and to start living the deal.

Any deal you make is more likely to hold together when you have allowed yourself to push the pause button (see Chapter 6) just before declaring the negotiation officially closed. Take a breather, look over the entire agreement. Make sure it works for you and the other side in the real world. Don't agree to a house-painting contract on Saturday when it has been raining for two weeks, and there is no let-up in sight. In fact, when you use the six essential skills listed on the card in front of this book, somebody at the negotiating table almost certainly figures out how to close up the deal. If everyone at the table is using these basics, you are likely to close the deal much more quickly.

Understanding the letter of the law

A short course on contract law is well beyond the scope of this book, but you should understand a few key points if you ever negotiate a deal in the business world.

Legal definition of a closed deal

Unless you have a specific arrangement to the contrary, no deal is closed until the parties reach an agreement on all the points under negotiation. This truth applies to the way U.S. law works and has given rise to various catch phrases you may have heard:

> "It ain't over till it's over."

> "It ain't over till the fat lady sings."

> "I'll trust it when the check clears the bank."

Nevertheless, students of negotiation are often upset when only one point remains in contention in a deal, and then the other party begins backing off on some of the points where agreement was reached.

In order to have an enforceable contract you need agreement on four elements:

- ✔ What you are getting
- ✔ What you are paying for what you are getting
- ✔ How long will the contract last
- ✔ Who are the parties in the contract

Everything else, you can work out along the way.

Offers and counteroffers

A wide misconception is that you can always accept an offer. When a party makes an offer and you make a counteroffer, the law looks at the transaction in a very particular way. The law breaks that simple process into two steps, one of which is implied. Legally, you rejected the initial offer and put a new offer on the table. If you receive a written offer, you can write "accepted" across the document and the deal is done, but be careful when you counteroffer. The other party may *let* you accept a previous offer, but is not bound to do so. You do not have a legal right to demand that the old offer from the other side stay on the table.

Written versus oral contracts

Samuel Goldwyn once boomed: "An oral agreement isn't worth the paper it is written on." Actually, oral agreements are generally enforceable. The law requires a few contracts to be in writing: Some examples are contracts that sell land, employment contracts for one year or longer, and contracts that convey an interest in a copyright. Generally, contracts do not have to be in writing. The problem is with enforcement of an oral agreement. If you get into a dispute, be assured that you and the other side will remember the agreement differently.

The paper does not fulfill the agreement — people do. No contract can protect you against bad people who are determined to do bad things to you.

Legal protection before the contract

So what happens if one or both parties begins to carry out the terms of the deal before a fully enforceable contract is signed? That's okay. On the basis of a technicality, the courts won't abandon someone who acted in good faith. Worst case: the party who performed — that is, the party who painted the house or delivered the goods — will receive the fair market value for the service or product provided. This concept is called *quantum meriut.* (There — I did it. I got a Latin phrase in the book. Our fabulous editor will probably take it out, but I figured out a way to get it in the book. What good is my law degree if I can't speak a little Latin?)

Closing around the world

English has become the language of international commerce to such a great extent that picking the language of the contract should not be a serious issue in a negotiation. Intergovernmental negotiators must deal with the language issue, but the average American doesn't — except in very unusual circumstances. English is the common business language around the world.

Occasionally, a party in a negotiation suggests a *dual language approach*: One copy of the contract appears in English, and one copy is prepared in the other side's native language. Don't fall for the dual-language approach to the written contract. The idea sounds simple enough, but translations are often so different that disputes can develop over the meaning of the two versions. Interpretation disputes are common enough without having two languages to consider.

The notion of closing a deal varies in different parts of the world. If you aren't familiar with the negotiating customs of another culture, your ignorance can create hard feelings. Most people refuse to acknowledge that any way except their own way of closing a deal makes sense. We discuss three examples of closing around the world to demonstrate three very different traditions of closing. Each one works for the culture that created the particular closing tradition. When you are negotiating across cultures, be sure that you understand their tradition of closing.

Good ol' U.S. of A.

In the United States, closing a deal is a very formal occasion. A handshake or some other ceremonial moment ends the discussion. Then come the contracts. People in the United States write long contracts in an attempt to anticipate every possible scenario, setting out each party's rights, duties, and obligations.

In the United States, people close even common sense matters with enough detail and formality to boggle the mind. Whether this practice is caused by or has produced more lawyers per capita here than anywhere else in the world is a chicken-and-egg discussion. Citizens of the United States and their lawyers are writing longer and more detailed contracts than anywhere else on the planet.

A commercial lease for a simple office can run 30 pages and includes obvious matters, such as the fact that the tenant does not have to pay rent if the landlord shuts the building down for a week. The lease also covers exactly what happens if another tenant is moving in and blocks access for an hour, or if construction is going on that is inconvenient for the tenants.

In part, such detailed contracts are a response to another feature of life in the United States that has the rest of the world shaking its collective head — the rush to sue. Americans face the likelihood of long and expensive litigation over just about any issue. Most of these lawsuits can be initiated without risk to the plaintiff. A new crop of contingent-fee lawyers hits the streets each year. When an attorney renders services on a *contingency fee* basis, that means that the attorney is not billing the client at an hourly rate. Instead, the attorney will take a percentage of the amount the court awards to the client — the plaintiff — if and when the case is won. Because filing a lawsuit on this basis means the plaintiff has nothing to lose, you are probably better off not leaving the interpretation of any legal point to goodwill or common sense if you want to avoid future court battles.

INTERNATIONAL

Closing across cultures

When I sold my last house, the real estate agent wanted to market the house directly to the Arab community because of the growing influx of Arabs into our particular neighborhood. I knew of the custom in the Middle East to adjust agreements as new facts surfaced. I also was well aware of the new American custom of using a home inspection service to look over a house for any problem areas. Mine was a great little house, but it was old. I figured that after the home inspection, the buyer would want to reopen negotiations — which I didn't want to do.

When my real estate agent brought me a quick offer from a Middle Eastern buyer, I used a technique that would be helpful in any negotiation. I thought it would be particularly useful in avoiding a renegotiation of the price. I obtained a back-up offer. That is, I accepted the original offer, provided that title transferred within 45 days. If the closing didn't occur on or before this date, the house would go to the back-up buyer, as opposed to extending the deadline as usually happens. To the back-up buyer, I provided a document stating that by accepting a deposit — to be returned if he didn't buy the house — I was bound to sell the house to him if the first buyer failed to complete the title transfer within the specified time.

As soon as the buyer received the inspection report with its inevitable observations, he wanted to renegotiate. This was not upsetting to me, because I expected it. This custom was part of the cultural tradition of the people I had chosen to sell to. I felt really good when my technique of having a back-up worked, and I didn't have to make a major concession at that point. He was unhappy and felt a bit cheated by my hard-line unwillingness to reconsider the terms of the agreement. He was used to a certain custom. Fortunately for me, I was experienced in those customs, so I was able to come up with a plan that helped me avoid the parts that didn't serve my interests.

He was finally able to make up his loss on the eve of the day escrow was to close. There was a minor, last minute problem with the termite report. I did not have enough time to fix the problem before close of escrow, so I had to make a generous settlement on that point. I felt that I had some room to bargain from the previous round, and the buyer felt that he had made up some of the ground he lost, so we were both happy. Knowing the traditions of both of our cultures really helped to avoid a major cultural clash. The more you know about where the other party is coming from, the easier it is to get where you want to go.

In the United States, the rules are very strict for changing the deal after a contract is signed. You need to change written contracts in writing. You must carry out oral modifications before they are binding.

Middle East

Across the spectrum from the United States is the tradition of the desert. The spoken word and the handshake are the centuries-old traditions of the Middle East. You make a deal in principle, and people start to carry out the terms of the agreement. Changed circumstances allow for further discussions.

To an American, this custom can be very upsetting. The American thinks that the deal has closed; the Arab thinks that the parties can revisit the deal if circumstances change or new information is acquired.

In the Middle East, almost any change in circumstances justifies looking again at a deal. Think of the caravans, and you may understand better. A deal is made for a caravan leader to provide a specific number of carpets to a buyer. The caravan leader goes to the source of the carpets, buys them, and transports them back. But one of the camels died on the way, and the carpets cost more than the caravan leader originally anticipated, so the price is subject to renegotiation. An American becomes irate. A fellow Arab engages in yet another negotiation based on the changed circumstances. Not all the terms are open for discussion; a basic price was already decided. Now the negotiation is over the adjustment.

Japan

Closings in Japan are somewhere in between Arab and American tradition. The Japanese have a history of negotiating written contracts containing the basic terms of a deal, but their contracts are not as detailed as in the United States. Room exists for the relationship of the parties to provide for adjustments as circumstances change.

Because the Japanese leave room for adjustment to the events that occur after a contract is signed, getting to know someone before talking business is important to the Japanese. In the United States, the relationship between negotiators is less important because the contract as written at the time of closing is final.

Recognizing When to Close

The *when* of closing is easy: Early and often. Some people don't seem to want or need to close the deal. They are like cows chewing their cud. They just go on and on enjoying the process, burning up time, and never bringing discussions to a close. But you know that closing is a separate skill.

Keep the closing in mind as you prepare for your negotiation, as you listen to the other side, and every time you speak. A little piece of your mind should always focus on the closing — on bringing the negotiation to a mutually acceptable solution. When you view closing as a separate step in a negotiation, you aren't likely to miss an opportunity to close.

Sitting across the table from someone can be very frustrating. Be alert to the possibility of closing the deal at every appropriate moment. Here are some moments that are more obvious than others. Don't miss these!

> ✔ An acceptable solution is on the table.
>
> ✔ The other side wants to close.
>
> ✔ A real-world deadline is approaching.
>
> ✔ All of the negotiation goals are met.
>
> ✔ You have better alternatives.

The only problem with printing up such a list is that you may wait for *the proper moment.* This is especially true if you have a problem with closing in the first place. The proper moment to make your first effort at closing a deal is when you first sit down.

Remember your mantra for closing: Early and often. A recent study of sales people revealed that a very small percentage of sales close after the first effort. Most sales close after at least three efforts to get the order. Try to close any negotiation as early as possible and keep trying until you prevail.

If you have trouble closing deals, intentionally try to close your next negotiation earlier than you think is possible. You find that no harm is done and that the other side actually becomes sensitized to the need to conclude matters. Make a game of it. Chart your efforts to close. Your rate of successful closings rises as you become more and more aware of closing as a separate skill to bring out early and often.

Knowing How to Close

The purpose of this section is to take the mystique out of closing and to provide the mechanics.

 With a friend or family member, rehearse the various approaches for closing. The more naturally they role off your tongue, the easier the attempt will be for you in a real situation. Role play. Describe a typical negotiation situation to a friend and then have your friend challenge you with the objections in this section.

The good closer

Most used car lots have one person who is paid to close deals. You may have encountered a salesperson who, rather than close the deal, introduces you to "the manager." People in the auto industry call this person *the closer.*

Close it with a no — but close it!

I learned a long time ago that I hated rejection. I held a phone sales job only once in my life. With every rejection, I would go to the vending machine down the hall and buy a candy bar. Two weeks and eight pounds later, I could no longer button my skirts. I quit the job.

Years later, selling my own training courses on the telephone, I felt the same resistance to hearing "no" as a close to the deal. I found myself more satisfied with "I want to think it over." I preferred to accept their indecision rather than close the deal with "no." I had a whole stack (about six inches high) of incomplete files on potential clients for my services as a management trainer. I was spending many dollars following up on these people, only to hear "Maybe — call me in a couple of months," and I would be so happy. Now, a few of these leads were worth it; they came through. But most of them cost me money. I was calling some people for over two years!

It was time to call my mentor. I believe in mentors. Everyone should have one and be one. A mentor is someone you respect who knows more than you do and is willing to take a moment out of their busy schedule and share the lessons they have learned in the school of experience and hard knocks. Anne Miller, a New York-based sales and communication speaker and seminar leader, has been in business a few years longer than I have. She is enormously successful and was one of the people who told me to start my own business. I called her.

Here was her suggestion: Call the prospects in your file *one last time* and tell them that this is your final call. After the initial small talk, say, "I'm cleaning up my files and closing some of them. We've been talking for over a year, and I've yet to arrange a training program for your staff. This will be my last call to you. *Really,* what are the chances of getting to work for you and train your people?"

And then I listened. The results were amazing. About a third of the prospects said they didn't think there was much chance — no budget, the top executive didn't believe in training, all facts I *needed* to know to stop wasting my time and money calling unqualified buyers! Another third made appointments on the spot, to further the negotiation to hire me. And the other third managed to convince me to hang on and keep following up, which I was willing to do, now that my unclosed stack was less than an inch high. What a great feeling closure is, even when the closure is "no."

So be proactive. Ask for a decision.

People who are constantly resolving conflict and solving problems in their personal lives are thought of as agreeable and cooperative. At the negotiating table, they are considered brilliant. When a negotiator finds a solution to what appears to be a difficult negotiation, the feat brings the problem solver praise all around.

> ✔ Weak closers tend to get stuck on a position. Strong closers always seem to find a solution. The approach may not be the original one, but it gets to the desired result.

✔ Strong closers are generally people who accomplish tasks on time. Weak closers often are consummate procrastinators.

✔ Grand closers rejoice when a deal closes. Weak closers feel a sense of loss when the project comes to an end.

Good closers are often witty or clever, but they don't have to be. They just need to have the confidence to follow through with the goals and limits they set when they started planning the negotiation. They consider themselves to be effective people. Creating consensus where none exists is a fun activity for the good closer and a struggle for the weak closer. Each one of these qualities is a result of the learned skills set out throughout this book. People are all born negotiating successfully: For food, for dry diapers, even for a good burp. Over time, life beats up on some people. Take back your life. Methodically set out to get what you want using the step-by-step techniques in this book.

The only three closing strategies you'll ever need

The entire country seems to be in a search of the perfect close — the one that won't fail. When we get to this point in our seminars, pencils are poised. Fresh paper is found. The class is alert. Here is the big secret: The three ways to make the sale or to successfully close the negotiation are ask, ask, ask.

Students always write "Ask" on their papers as we announce the first closing strategy. When we announce the second strategy, some students get a little smile on their face and quit writing. Very few write the third "Ask." But they do get it. A smile spreads across the faces in the room as they realize the wisdom of the ages and not some new high-tech secret.

No matter how powerful your PC is, what the range of your mobile phone is, or how clever your tracking system is, you still have just one way to get the order or close the deal: Ask whether your counterpart will agree to the current terms. If you have trouble asking for commitments, address that issue.

Fortunately for the army of people who give seminars, the nation continues to search for an easy answer to the problem of closing the deal. Meanwhile, earn your success the old-fashioned way: Ask for it. Heck, you should insist on it. Nothing short of persistent, organized inquiry is going to close any negotiation. It just won't happen by itself.

At work, closing a deal is not always something you do just once. A variation on "ask, ask, ask" is "close again and again and again." Suppose that you are assigned a terrific project and then your project gets shelved due to a management change, a reconsideration of priorities, or *rightsizing* (a new, nicer word for downsizing). You are disappointed: All your hard work is down the drain, and you won't get the recognition you deserve. To try to keep the project alive, resell the plan to the powers that be. Treat the project as a brand-new task. Remember all the reasons you were able to get the project in the first place and start from scratch with those points. Self-employed people need to resell major projects to the client all the time, especially if the client is being asked to invest money on the front end. If a project is shelved anyway, make sure that you haven't put all your eggs in one basket. This priority should be only one of several balanced in your business life, so that you won't go into an emotional or a financial tailspin.

Using linkage to close

Linkage is a great concept to help close a deal when no compromise is in sight on the last point in contention. *Linkage* simply means that you hook a re-quested concession to something you want so that the deal can close.

Here is the kind of situation which cries out for a linkage strategy:

- ✔ The parties on the other side are making a final demand. They can't go any further. They can't give any more than they already have.
- ✔ You don't want to cave in on this point, because the deal won't work for you. If you concede, you will not have enough incentive to close the deal.

Here is what you do:

1. **Take a pause.**

   Be sure that the other side is not just bluffing, that they really can't go any further on this point.

2. **Look over the entire transaction; find an area where you didn't get everything you wanted or find a item that can be changed in your favor to bring balance back to the deal.**

3. **Link this issue with the concession that the other side is asking you to make.**

   Agree to concede on the point in contention if they will meet the demand you decided on in Step 2. The item you hook to their request may never have been discussed before, but linkage is always acceptable.

Here are some examples of linkage in response to specific objections:

> OBJECTION: "We can't pay this person more than $100,000 next year."
>
> LINKAGE: "If you could go to $110,000, maybe my client will agree to a two-year contract."
>
> OBJECTION: "There's no way we are going to quit using Joe as our supplier for lead pipe."
>
> LINKAGE: "Maybe we could sell you half-lots of lead pipe so that you could continue to buy from Joe while trying out our company."
>
> OBJECTION: "Your daily fee is too high for just a one-hour speech, even if the conference site is out of town."
>
> LINKAGE: "Maybe I can also give a seminar in the afternoon, so you feel like you are getting your money's worth."

Linkage is a powerful tool that you can use to help close a deadlocked negotiation. Here are some phrases that are often used to introduce the linkage concept:

> "Well, maybe we could look at some of the issues again."
>
> "Well, we may be able to work something out here."
>
> "Tell ya what ahm gonna do."

Linkage is one of those tools that makes you feel like a real top-notch negotiator, because it helps you solve a real problem. Neither side can give on the point under discussion, so you find something to trade. Use linkage to find your way out of a tough spot, the next time you find yourself in one.

Barriers to Closing

If you find it difficult to close, the real question is probably not "How do I do this?" but rather "Why do I hesitate instead of going for it?" Merely stating the question helps you to start thinking about the answer.

Each person who has a barrier to closing a negotiation or a sale probably has some fears or apprehensions about the process. The most common fears are listed here:

- ✔ Closing is the one specific time in the negotiation that your inner critic can say, "You screwed up when you asked for the order."
- ✔ Closing is also scary because it is a commitment. American society has an endemic fear of commitment.
- ✔ Closing brings this phase of the activity to an end.

The real key to success for you may not be an elusive strategy. It may be your own personal, mental blocks to closing a deal. Many people have them. Do your best to deal with your own. Be sure to keep the possibility in mind that the other party has some mental blocks to closing that lie unmentioned behind the stated objections to the deal.

Overcoming Objections

The term *objection* is more commonly used in the specialized negotiation of sales. Salespeople around the world want to know how to get over, past, and through objections. They are looking for simple answers to the two most common objections: Price and product.

When someone directly states an objection to whatever you are proposing, an opportunity is at hand. You have the opportunity to clear away one more barrier. Every objection you get past puts you closer to your goal of closing the negotiation. An objection — honestly stated — is just another way of inviting you to satisfy some concern or to meet a need that you didn't address earlier in your presentation.

Answering objections is the fun part of a negotiation. You get to use your imagination. You get to reach into your information bank and come up with the answer. Countering objections is the part where you get to show your stuff, and your preparation really pays off.

Using questions to get where you want to go

When you try to close a negotiation and you get an objection, a question is your best friend. Gently probe to find the answers to the following:

- ✔ Is the stated objection really the thing that is bothering the other party?
- ✔ What will the other party do if this deal doesn't close? What is their *or else?*
- ✔ Can you meet or beat that alternative?

The frustrating dilemma is that you cannot state these questions in a direct manner. You must ask for the information indirectly. You must tease the answer out. For example, look at the first question in the preceding list. You usually can't say, "Come on, tell me what's really bugging you." You have to relax yourself and the other party so that you can get to the source of the concern. Here are some ways to tickle out the information (each question is a variation on the theme):

✔ If we can find agreement on that one item (price, for example) can we close this deal today? (If not, you know something else is bothering the other person.)

✔ How about if we . . . ? Suggest a whole new approach. Use linkage to make the deal work for the other party. (When that works, you know that you've stumbled on what is really bothering the other side.)

✔ In a perfect world, what would this deal look like to you?

You are inside the negotiation, so you have made some progress. The answers to the last three questions can turn up all sorts of information you need to know — information you can't ask about directly.

Going back to square one

People usually use the phrase "back to square one" to express the loss of a goal or objective. If you run into a blank wall, you may be inclined to shrug your shoulders and say dejectedly, "Well, I guess we're back at square one." Next time that happens, listen to yourself and think of this book. You have just given yourself some great advice. Trouble is, most people don't know great advice when they hear it, even if they hear this wisdom from themselves!

Square one in negotiating is preparation. Part I of this book deals exclusively with preparation. When you have a hard time with an objection or can't close the negotiation, the answer is almost always lurking in Part I. One of the following needs work:

✔ You need more information about the person you are negotiating with — maybe you're not talking to the right person.

✔ You need more information about your own company or product. For example, you may be unaware of performance features worth emphasizing.

✔ You need to know more about the competition. What exactly are the alternatives available to the other party.

✔ Maybe, just maybe, you should not be in this negotiation at all because the deal doesn't contribute to your overall life or business objectives.

The difference between the very successful negotiator and everyone else is in the foundational work he or she does before the negotiation ever begins. We wish that there really were a quick fix, a magic wand, or a sure way to get ahead in life. Unfortunately, no single factor is as directly responsible for success in individual negotiations and success in life as preparation.

In seminar after seminar, we find that our closing question-and-answer session deals with the opening topic of good preparation. This fact is especially true with sales groups where some people are looking for the fast close, that special phrase that saves the day. Nothing saves the day like a good night's rest — after you burn the midnight oil getting ready.

Closing When It's All in the Family

Parents have an important calling and a rewarding challenge. Mothers and fathers teach values, morals, and appropriate behavior by being positive role models, creating consistent and fair standards of discipline, and enforcing the rules with love and kindness.

These qualities are easy to define, but good parenting really takes all the negotiating steps in this book. To reach closing with children means to be explicit about consequences for breaking from expected rules or standards of behavior. First, the standards must be clearly established.

It's a good idea when deciding on rules and standards of behavior to have regular family meetings. As problems and conflicts arise during the week, post them on a meeting agenda sheet on the refrigerator or nearby bulletin board.

The purpose of the meeting is problem solving. Everyone attends and has a voice in suggesting solutions. Decide together on procedures and standards of behavior. These decisions can be posted as Family Rules.

Closing is a necessary skill for you to practice consistently with your children. Adults are more equipped to handle uncertainty. Children need to know where they stand — the young live in the here and now. When you have completed all the other skills, and children are clear about your expectations, closing the deal means checking out the child's understanding of the resolution. Encourage the child to say in his or her own words how they feel after a conflict is resolved, or after something they want is either given or denied.

Beware that you don't set up a situation where a family member *assumes* a conclusion that has not been reached. For example, the teenager *really* wants to stay out all night on prom night. The parents are undecided. Dad says, "Sounds like fun. I remember doing that when I was in high school." The teen takes that as a yes and runs with it — straight to Mom who says "we'll see." The teen goes ahead and makes all the plans, planning a stop to change clothes at someone's house, committing to drive, offering to pitch in with breakfast plans at another's house.

The teen, deep into joyful expectations, assumes that all these plans will definitely close the negotiation with the parental units. When the parents finally research the planned activities and find a lack of adult supervision, Mom says no, and Dad backs her up. Emotional upheaval results. Many teen friends are now inconvenienced, and Mom and Dad are in a weak position — they could be accused of breaching the agreement (which was never really made). Parents need to follow up very carefully when closing a deal with teenagers, so no false closure results. Always be clear about what state of decision you are in, even if you say clearly, "I'm not sure yet; don't make any plans."

When the Deal Is Done

The negotiation is over. The contract is signed. The client is happy. You are being roundly congratulated. Administrative details have yet to be set up, but your job is over — almost.

You have two things left to do for the good of the deal and for your own growth:

✔ Review the process. After a little time has gone by, think back over the negotiation and consider what you may have done differently. Consider the consequences of the various choices you made. We're not talking about self-flagellation; we're talking about calm review of the entire negotiating history, mentally playing out various options you had along the way. This process is one final review after you have time and distance from the completed negotiation. This is particularly useful for the successful negotiation, because you don't have any self-doubt or blame.

✔ Do everything you can to be sure that the agreement is carried out in an ethical, timely, and honest manner. If you were negotiating for someone else, this control is not always in your hands. If you were a principal, your personal duty is to live up to the spirit and letter of the agreement. We consider this a sacred trust. Your word is your bond. Don't ever forget that.

Setting up systems for checking the system

Regardless of whether you are a part of a large organization or you are negotiating on your own behalf, don't close up the file and consider a negotiation over until you have taken steps to ensure that the agreement will be carried out. These precautions include such items as marking a calendar with the dates that various items are due, checking that the people who must carry out the agreement are on board and understand the terms, and making sure that the progress is being reported to the other side.

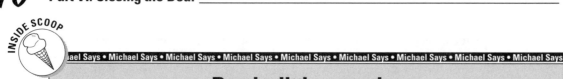

Bend a little, get a lot

I had a client who was about to produce a feature film. We wanted to close fast, but be fair. I offered a relatively short three-page definition of net profits to a young lawyer for his writer client. I made it relatively simple and straightforward, because I did not want an extensive negotiation. This definition was vastly better (in addition to being shorter) than the average studio definition of how profits are determined. The document contained a minimum amount of accounting detail.

"My client insists on a piece of the gross," the young lawyer kept stating loudly and to the exclusion of any comment on details of the definition.

"Okay," I said. "I can't give him actual gross profits, but maybe we can provide adjusted gross profits. Would that be acceptable?"

"Yes," was the eager answer.

I changed the title of the three-page document from "Net Profit Definition" to "Adjusted Gross Profit Definition." I also changed the word "net" to the words "adjusted gross" throughout the document and sent the revision over to the young lawyer. I braced for a tirade. The document was signed without comment.

Not one penny more went into the writer's pocket, but he could say around town that he had received a piece of the adjusted gross profits. He could avoid all those bad jokes about net profits. They are called monkey points, because net profits notoriously translate into no money for the writer. He felt good.

We had made a match. The young attorney had stated what he needed and he got it — even though the victory was largely symbolic. And the outcome didn't cost my client a dime.

Most large organizations have a separate department for just that purpose. The department is often called Contract Administration or something very close. Even when departmental staff handle these details, you should call the department after an appropriate amount of time has passed (usually a week or two) and satisfy yourself that the servicing system is in place. If you are a salesperson, you want to be sure that the order is being or has been processed.

You check because if something goes wrong in servicing a contract, the problem reflects badly on you. This is true regardless of how far such matters are from your responsibility. You negotiated the deal. If the terms are not carried out in a professional and timely manner, the other party will remember that the deal they made with *you* went sour. Unfair, but true.

Make it your personal responsibility to be sure that the other party is happy. The effort may take a few extra moments and involve following up with people who should be taking care of business without prompting. But the benefits of repeat business for you and the preservation of your own good reputation will benefit you many times over.

Remembering to celebrate!

New beginnings and final endings are celebrated in every culture, even though the events may look very different. The signing ceremony to mark the end of the negotiation and the beginning of the life of the agreement looms large in the United States, probably because reopening the discussion on the terms is difficult. Americans shake hands even over the smallest agreements and pop champagne corks for the big ones. No matter where you are in the world, people celebrate reaching important agreements. Some go to church, others throw a party, and some light a candle. A parade occurs almost spontaneously when a surrender is signed in war.

It is also important to celebrate when you decide not to close a deal and to walk away from it. Close only a good deal. Avoid the bad deals. Be happy when you do not close a bad deal. Walking away from bad deals is like avoiding a collision in traffic. You breathe a huge sigh of relief and thank goodness that you avoided the accident. When you are successful in avoiding a bad deal, celebrate whatever way you know and love best — but celebrate. Celebrate with all the joy and verve that you bring to closing a good deal.

Every culture that uses liquor has a special toast to say, "Congratulations, job well done." These cultures also share the custom of raising a glass in celebration of a completed deal. If you don't know any other words besides "hello," "good-bye," and "thank you," you should also learn how to recite the toast that is appropriate for the cultures involved in the deal. Do you know which countries use the following?

Kompai, Nasdorovia, Ma Zdrowie, Cheers, Brost, Salud, Cin Cin, Sköl, Skaal, L'Chaim

Japan, Russia, Poland, United Kingdom, Germany, Spain, Italy, Sweden, Denmark, Israel

Part VII
The Part of Tens

The 5th Wave   By Rich Tennant

"Excuse me, but you've had me on hold for so long I've forgotten who you are."

In this part . . .

Every . . .*For Dummies* book ends with one of these handy collections of lists. Our Part of Tens contains hallmarks of great negotiators, common negotiating pitfalls, samples of specific ngotiations, and fun stuff like books to read, movies to rent, and Internet sites to visit. Turn to this part whenever you want to brush up on your negotiating technique as a whole — even as you work on the six individual skills covered in the preceding parts.

Chapter 18

Ten Ways to Become a Master Negotiator

*W*hen you were born, you were already a great negotiator. The first thing you did was develop your own cries for everything you wanted. And you usually got what you wanted. Over time, your instincts were tempered and controlled in the name of education, order in the classroom, good manners, and a hundred other good and noble social purposes. As a result, you, the individual, may have lost some of the gumption to use the valuable instincts you were born with.

This book is designed to help you recapture your birthright. You can have what you want in life. Review the table of contents and see where you can make the most effort for the most effective return. If you don't have a life plan, perhaps Chapter 1 needs some of your time right now. Whatever area you need to work on, start today. The process is fun and rewarding. You are the most worthwhile project you could possibly undertake.

Commit to the Process

You can commit to any process that may help you meet your individual goals for improving your communication and negotiation skills. We offer a whole laundry list of approaches in this chapter. Figure out today the best process for you personally and go for it.

As you work on your negotiating skills — on getting what you want in life, adapt a new personal mantra:

> I am a great negotiator.
>
> I Am A Great Negotiator.
>
> I AM A GREAT NEGOTIATOR.

This is the first of our ten suggestions because the vast majority of students in our seminars have the opposite mantra. The two most common self-evaluations we hear at the beginning of the negotiating seminars are

- ✔ I'm not a very good negotiator.
- ✔ I avoid negotiating altogether.

The second comment simply isn't true and provides a great excuse to the person for not developing negotiation skills. Obviously, if you don't think you negotiate anything, you won't prepare for negotiation. You won't set goals. You won't set limits. In short, you may unwittingly set yourself up to botch the negotiation almost every time.

The first self-evaluation is a self-fulfilling prophecy. How you perceive yourself and what you say about yourself greatly impacts how others judge you and your performance. This fact is especially true if you see yourself in a negative light. Adopting the new mantra immediately starts changing others' perceptions as well as your own. As you see yourself as a good negotiator, you begin acting like a good negotiator. You eventually begin reaping the rewards of a good negotiator. For the time being, don't study your results, enjoy the process. Enjoy the growth.

Build a Temple

Take care of yourself. Nobody else can take care of your mind and your body and your soul as you can. Each element of your total self needs to be cared for, or your individual efforts in life will not achieve the results you want and deserve. You can't be a great negotiator if you allow the other elements of your life to run amok. Some people can successfully "compartmentalize" their lives for a period of time. For example, they may ignore a physical malady in order to complete a specific, important job. But no one can keep that up for long. Eventually, a problem in one important area of your life affects the other areas of your life.

You may brush off this advice at first, but it does tend to catch up with you. If you want to be a great negotiator, you have to eat right, sleep well, and get some exercise. "Some exercise" does not mean that you have to compete in the Olympics or go on 100-mile bicycle rides. It does mean that you have to move your body in ways that stretch it and keep it flexible. Walking is great. Swimming is a good low-impact activity. Do whatever is appropriate to your situation.

Your soul also needs tending as surely as your physical self. Quiet time by yourself and with those who love you unconditionally is important to replenish the spirit. Beautiful surroundings are important. Whether it is the beach or the mountains or some nice local park, take yourself somewhere you can relax and rejuvenate your spirit. Do it for yourself.

Take care of your mind. Have a hobby: Some activity you thoroughly enjoy for its own sake without any hope or plan to make a profit or a business connection or an ounce of notoriety from it. The rewards will come back a thousandfold.

Finally, continue your mental growth. You are obviously the type of person who already practices this advice, or you would not be reading this book. Books are the hallmark of the educated person. Keep them. Mark them. Treasure them. Pass them on.

Tending to your mental, physical, and emotional health is what we refer to when we talk about *building a temple*. The name of the temple is your name. The care of that temple is solely your responsibility.

Pick Two People and Study Their Negotiating Techniques

The process of observing what any two people do and don't do in a negotiation sensitizes you to the importance of each of the six basic skills in this book. By tracking how someone else does and doesn't perform in each of the skill areas, you realize that consistently positive results only come from a consistently positive application of sound negotiating principles. You may also observe some exceptions: Occasionally good results spring from hopelessly muddled negotiations, and sometimes the negotiator doesn't achieve the desired results regardless of being at the most advanced skill level.

We suggest studying two people because doing so gives you an opportunity to observe different styles. Specifically,

- Pick someone who has a reputation as a great negotiator, but with whom you don't have a personal relationship.

- Pick someone close to you that you can observe close up and question while negotiations are ongoing.

For example, for the first category, you may pick someone like Henry Kissinger. Movies and books about him abound. He currently has a private consulting firm representing international interests on a much larger scale than most of us. Former President Jimmy Carter is still in the news and may provide a better opportunity for study — even if you watch through the filtered lens of the media.

Alternatively, you may want to think back to the best negotiator you have dealt with during the past year. This is not necessarily a person who got the best of you. Sometimes an unskilled jerk can obtain a great result under the right circumstances. For this purpose, identify the person who best exemplified the principles in this book as the negotiation proceeded.

Now try to identify how that negotiator prepared for the negotiation. What limits were set? You may never know for sure, but maybe you pushed the envelope enough so that you were told when you were at or near the limits on a particular issue. Write down two examples of when your point of view was really listened to by this respected negotiator. Write down two examples of clear communication. Can you identify at least one use of the pause button during the negotiation process? Maybe you heard a phrase such as "Let's go back over that to be sure we understand each other." Think about the negotiation and see if you can identify an element that you are aware of before reading this book.

You may decide to study someone you don't even like or respect as a negotiator. Analyze the performance of that person. What specifically could that person do to become a better negotiator? Which of the six skills does that person do well, in spite of your overall low opinion of him or her?

The second category can be a business partner, associate, or even one of your children — the younger the better. The younger the child, the more pure you will find the approach. Watching a child negotiate is fascinating, and you can be a great help to the child as you teach about the importance of honesty and keeping commitments. Many people think we are kidding when we suggest that you study your children until they actually try it.

Adopt a Hero

Pick at least one person, living or dead, near or far, whom you really admire. Follow that person's career. Watch the person rise or fall. If the person is deceased, you can become an expert on that person by reading everything you can get your hands on about him or her. Choose someone who genuinely interests you. Successful people are always successful negotiators. Match this person's escapades with the negotiating lessons of this book

Successful people have the same personal and financial problems you have. Sometimes, the problems are on a grander scale, but more often than not, their problems are similar to yours. You can learn a great deal about your own life by keeping your eyes firmly on someone you admire (be it a sports figure, a business titan, an entertainer, a politician, or your local pastor).

Involve Your Support Group

The human beings you count on most for love, support, and understanding are your support group. These are the people you care about the most and who care about you. For most of us this intimate circle includes parents, a spouse, and friends. You can also bond with people in the pursuit of a common goal and create a support group for self-improvement.

Dieters and those who have tried to quit smoking have known the value of regular meetings with a formal support group to finally achieve their goals.

The film *The Firm* contains a great line of dialogue we will always remember. Tom Cruise plays a young lawyer who enters a large and corrupt law firm. His ambitions keep him from facing the truth for a while, but he finally shares what he knows with a friend and confesses, "When I tell my wife, *then* I know it's real."

Share the following sections of this chapter with a support group. You may be able to get others to join in the fun work of becoming a world-class negotiator. Over time, as you all enjoy the fruits of your labor, they may thank you for involving them.

Do the Activities in This Book

Find the activity icons throughout the book. These icons indicate movies and books that illustrate a single point covered by a particular chapter or section. Activity icons flag games and exercises that build a skill or help focus your attention on a particular aspect of negotiation. These skill-builders can be as passive as sitting in an airport watching body language, or as active as games that involve your friends or family.

If you plan a birthday party for your child, some of the games in this book are appropriate. We have used the game of telephone (whispering a message person to person) as successfully at a children's party as at a negotiation seminar. Doing the activities in this book is a fun, varied way to build negotiating skills.

Watch some movies

Chapter 22 lists movies that are good for building negotiating skills overall. We believe so strongly in the value of these movies as tools for teaching that we list all ten of them on a tear-out card on the Cheat Sheet in the front of the book, so you can take it to the video store. Some additional movies are mentioned throughout the text that demonstrate more narrow points. *Wizard of Oz,* for example, is mentioned in an Activities icon to illustrate how to deal with the scary individuals you meet along life's path.

Your whole family will enjoy watching most of the films with you (we let you know which films have more adult themes). A new world opens up when you look at films through the eyes of a keen negotiator.

Build your negotiating library

A wealth of books have been written about or involving negotiation. Chapter 23 lists good books to buy or borrow if you want to sharpen your negotiation skills. We believe so strongly in the value of these books that we include a tear-out card in the Cheat Sheet listing all the books in Chapter 23, so you can take it to the bookstore or library.

Books listed in the text itself are recommended for specific skills. Generally speaking, the books listed in the individual chapters are helpful for the subject matter of that chapter.

Keep the Six Basic Skills Handy

The Cheat Sheet in the front of this book contains a tear-out card listing the six basic components. On the back of this card, you'll find your own pause button. Let this serve as a constant reminder to you to maintain your emotional distance at all points in a negotiation.

Remove the card now, if you haven't already done so, and put it in the place where you do most of your negotiating. That place may be on your desk, near your phone, in your wallet, or in a conference room. Put it in a prominent place so that you are constantly reminded to push the pause button and follow these negotiating skills.

Never be afraid that your counterpart may see your list. The beauty of this book is that if the other party also uses the information, the negotiation goes more smoothly, and you reach agreement faster. We view negotiating like a competitive sport — it is much more satisfying when you are playing with someone who is as good as or better than you are. Your own game improves and the results are often better all around.

Debrief Yourself after Negotiations

Self-evaluation is one of the most important activities you can perform after every negotiation — regardless of the outcome.

Think of the most satisfying negotiation you ever handled. Review each step and play it out in an imaginary parallel universe. Think of what you may have done differently and then consider the consequences. This exercise may feel like daydreaming, but devoting a few minutes in a traffic jam or in the shower to reviewing your previous negotiations can improve your performance the next time around.

Evaluating negotiations that didn't end well helps you discover what went wrong. Perhaps you'll realize that it was really better not to have closed the deal. A problem during the negotiation is often an indicator that greater problems will arise if the deal closes. Self-evaluation is as important after successful negotiations as it is after failed ones. Even a winning game has room for improvement. And evaluating a winning game is much more fun.

Know More Than Anybody Else in the Business

Whatever you do for a living, make sure no one on the planet knows more about the business than you do. No matter what your education level, start today to become the best. What you do is important. What you do is worthwhile. What you do helps your fellow human in some way. Be sure the Earth is a better place for the contribution you are making.

We are reminded of the stonecutter who worked long, hard, lonely hours in the rock quarry. He took home barely enough money for his family to live. He toiled in all kinds of weather. He never missed a day of work. Every stone was cut true square. He was always cheerful. When asked what kept him going, he said, "I am building a cathedral." Identify the cathedral you are building and know the work you do is valuable.

Seeing the larger purpose to the work of your life provides the inspiration to become the best and most knowledgeable in your field. This is true no matter how routine your work may seem. Most jobs require regular negotiation on the same type of transactions over and over. Keep good records of the outcomes of these negotiations and evaluate your results. Don't try to rely on your memory. You will soon have a data bank of information that will give you an upper hand in your next negotiation.

Be a Mentor

A *mentor* is a teacher, a trainer, and a helper to someone who is junior to you in your same profession — often, someone just starting out. Always have time to help others on their way up. Rodgers and Hammerstein offer some profound lines about the value of being a mentor in *The King and I*, the musical about the governess who went to teach all the children of the King of Siam (now Thailand). Anna, the governess, is talking to the children who are gathered around her just before she bursts into the wonderful song, *Getting to Know You:*

> *It's a very ancient saying*
> *and a true and honest thought,*
> *that if you become a teacher,*
> *By your pupils you'll be taught.*

As you help someone else grow, you grow yourself. You strengthen your own skills as you hear yourself share them with others. Writing this book has brought positive results in our lives; we read what we've written and correct our life's course and the course of some specific negotiations within our lives. We are deeply indebted to the . . . *For Dummies* people, who have been an inspiration and support in getting it all down on paper, to seminar students across the land who ask such great questions, and to countless clients with whom we have shared so many trials and tribulations. We have grown by sharing with these people, by being mentors to them.

Most of all, we are indebted to the one or two people each year who come into each of our fields under our special mentorship. We find that no activity helps us grow more predictably as helping those who are new to our professions. We urge you to look around your workplace. Find some new person with talent and interest and enthusiasm. Make it your business to be available to that person for any question, any time. Take that person on key appointments when appropriate. Everybody needs a mentor. Your own professional negotiations will benefit as much as those of the person you are helping.

Chapter 19

Ten Personality Traits of Top Negotiators

In This Chapter

▶ Recognizing the qualities of a great negotiator

▶ Developing those qualities yourself

*A*t the beginning of our negotiating seminars, we ask participants what results they want to achieve after the course. Invariably, respondents say they need to be more self-confident, or more assertive, or more patient. Many times, in relating specific incidents, it becomes apparent that they feel they were bested or beaten up in a recent negotiation. They don't want to imitate the bully or the screamer, but they saw that person get results. They ask us what personality traits they need to develop to attain more positive outcomes. So here is a list.

Nobody has all the traits listed in this chapter. As you look over the list, find those that apply to you and develop them further. Find those qualities that you feel are completely absent from your personality and work on them to improve your negotiating style and your life.

You can use all the personal qualities in this chapter, whether you're a shy person or an outgoing person, a nervous person or the most calm person in the world. Fast talkers, slow talkers, and all the talkers in between can benefit from developing these traits. You can develop these qualities as fully as you like, at your own pace, and in your own way.

 It's never too late to work on yourself. You won't get anywhere by blaming your parents or your upbringing or your environment. Awareness is the first step. You can nurture yourself and absorb life's lessons, no matter what your age. As parents, you can consciously set goals for your children. You can model behavior, encourage practice, and reinforce positive behavior. In short, you can train your own kids to be great negotiators.

Empathy

We list empathy as the first trait for a reason. *Empathy* is the ability to partici-pate in another's feelings or ideas, to put yourself in another's shoes. This is the bedrock of all successful communication and a necessary trait for great negotia-tors. The ability to show empathy when someone else is hurt develops and is observable by age three. But without teaching or reinforcement, the ability will not be retained or used. The bully or the screamer in your negotiation may not be a mean person. The screamer may never have developed the capacity for understanding how person on the receiving end of the screaming feels. You can improve your empathetic response by writing out a list of behaviors, values, and goals that you can't possibly agree with, but you *can* acknowledge that *others* feel that way. Next to each behavior, write "but I understand that *they* feel that way."

Some of the traits listed in this chapter are virtually impossible to develop without first honing your sense of empathy. Empathy is the bedrock of win-win negotiating (discussed in Chapter 15). Being empathetic also helps you main-tain your own identity as you experience the views and emotions of others, because it enables you to recognize the differences between you and the person you are talking to. You maintain your own feelings and views while understand-ing the feelings and views of the other person.

Respect

Respect follows close on the heels of empathy. First, you must have respect for yourself and the limits you set. Only then will you be able to respect or consider worthy other people and the limits they set. Respect for yourself is another, more specific way of saying self-confidence. Often, one can exude self-confidence when the butterflies are fluttering furiously inside. Self-respect is a prerequisite for motivating yourself. You want to achieve for your own satisfac-tion — not to please anyone else.

Respect is reciprocal in negotiations: If you give it, you are much more likely to get it. If necessary, be the first to show respect. A good way to improve your respect for people is to listen to people, looking them straight in the eyes. Listen for good ideas and thoughts that make sense to you, and pay a compli-ment to the source. Frequently, respect follows knowledge. The more you know about a person, the more likely you are to respect that person.

Personal Integrity

By *personal integrity,* we mean honesty and trustworthiness. "Honesty is the best policy" is really true in all areas of life. We always think of the humorous adage, "If you don't lie, you don't have to remember what you said." Honesty and trustworthiness are necessary for others to trust you and place their confidence in you in a negotiation. You then are considered a dependable person. How can you develop this right now?

- ✔ Follow the rules of society — even the smallest ones.

- ✔ Keep agreements with yourself and others. If you promise to show up at 9:00 a.m., be there at 9:00 a.m. and not one minute later.

- ✔ Never misrepresent anything in a negotiation. Not replying to a certain question or divulging certain information is completely acceptable; lying is not.

Fairness

Fairness is another trait based on empathy. You must believe that the needs and wants of other people are worth considering, along with your own. Fairness doesn't mean treating people equally or the same. If you have raised children or managed employees, you already know that what is fair in the interests of one is not always fair to the other. One person may need only a stern glance to know what you want; another may need things spelled out with lots of clear words and repetition to even start paying attention.

To develop fairness, consider what your goals are and what the goals are of the other party. Delineate areas of agreement and areas that need compromise. Always keep in mind the ability and experience of the person with whom you are dealing.

Patience

Patience means bearing pains or trials calmly without complaint. It's the ability to tolerate frustration and adversity on the way to reaching your goals — and not give up. This trait allows you to persevere in the face of adversity. You must know that disappointment and setbacks are part of the process of succeeding. Everyone grew up hearing, "If at first you don't succeed, try, try again." It's absolutely true — collecting the "no"s is part of getting a "yes," whether your field is sports, music, science, or whatever. All successful people know that getting knocked down, refused, denied, and blocked is part of life. Success comes to those who are steadfast and keep going.

To develop more patience, look into your past and see how much patience or perseverance you have exhibited. Recall a goal you had years ago that you thought would be impossible to reach. Acknowledge that now you've reached it, or surpassed it. The goal may be a specific yearly income, a healthy relationship, or stature in your community.

If you read biographies of famous people, you're sure to be surprised at how often they were pegged not to succeed. Patience is what allowed these individual to persevere against the odds.

Responsibility

Being responsible means exhibiting reliability or dependability. Being responsible means that you accept the consequences when tasks are completed or neglected. Being responsible doesn't mean that you won't make mistakes; it does mean that you will clean them up when you realize you've made a mess.

One way to improve in this area is to engage in "clearing the decks." This exercise enables you to come to terms with all the little (or big) problems for which you are responsible, so you have a clear space to get on with achieving goals. Examples may include:

- ✔ Apologizing for speaking rudely to a coworker, employee, spouse, or child
- ✔ Scheduling traffic school and/or paying the fine when you have an outstanding traffic ticket
- ✔ Completing a form or application you've been putting off
- ✔ Clearing that pile of papers you've been meaning to file
- ✔ Keeping every appointment on your calendar

Flexibility

Flexibility is the ability to deal skillfully and promptly with new situations and difficulties. If one approach doesn't work, you are able to try another. Life's problems and the problems of a negotiation are seen as challenges to overcome.

When you are in the midst of a problem, brainstorm all possible solutions. *Brainstorming* means listing all the possibilities, without editing. Ignore the little voice in the back of your head that says, "Oh, you *can't* do that." Then decide the consequences of each action. Choose the solution with positive consequences that leads you closer to your goal.

Flexibility is at the heart of closing a deal in a way that satisfies each side and is workable in the real world. You must be flexible in a negotiation in order to fit your goals and needs with the goals and needs of the other party.

Sense of Humor

Having a sence of humor involves looking for the comic quality in a seemingly serious situation — the ability to perceive, appreciate, or express what is amusing or comical. A great teacher once said, "Enlightenment is lightening up" — looking for humor in adversity in order to get on with finding solutions instead of blaming others. A prerequisite is self-respect and the flexibility to take a creative view of an imperfect situation.

To develop this trait, start thinking of the last mistake you made in a negotiation — with your spouse, coworker, client — and step back from it, lighten up, and try to see any aspect that *could* be interpreted as amusing.

Self-Discipline

Self-discipline is at the heart of the ability to lead a self-reliant, self-sufficient life. If you are self-disciplined, you don't need someone "on top of you" to motivate you. You have internal forces that drive you toward your goals, and your rewards come from within you, rather than from people externally reinforcing you. This is another way of expressing the trait of diligence: attacking things in a serious manner. We don't mean serious as in glum and humorless. If you want to become a great negotiator, take on the task with joy, optimism, energy, and a plan — be serious about accomplishing your goals even as you maintain, and use, your sense of humor.

Make your own plan and follow that plan. That is the quality of self-discipline. To improve this trait, live your life as though your life depended on it, because it does. Marcus Aurelius said, "Do every act of your life as if it were your last."

Stamina

Stamina is the ability to keep going when others have dropped by the wayside. Former President Richard Nixon once called Henry Kissinger the greatest negotiator in the world. He called Kissinger a genius and a strategic thinker, and then he launched into a long discussion about Kissinger's stamina. He is indefatigable. He is one of the hardest-working men on Earth. Since leaving public office, he has written eleven books and is still globe-trotting and deal-making in pursuit of peace.

To increase your stamina, do the following:

- ✔ Eat right.
- ✔ Take your vitamins.
- ✔ Sleep enough and well.
- ✔ Try to find balance in your life between work and play.

Stamina is a hallmark of all great negotiators. You can't win the game if you don't have the stamina to stay in the game.

Chapter 20

Ten Common Negotiating Mistakes

In This Chapter

▶ Strategic errors
▶ Worries and distractions

*E*ach of the mistakes listed in this chapter is discussed in greater detail elsewhere in the book. Some of them are discussed in more than one place because any mistake has more than one repercussion. This chapter is a brief review of the ten goof-ups that people ask about most frequently during our negotiating seminars.

At the start of each seminar, we ask everyone to introduce themselves and tell us the single most important thing they want to work on. At the end of the seminar, we ask people to tell us what they are going to work on the most. We keep good records of the beginning and ending portions of the seminars. The beginning part is especially well-recorded, because we use the information throughout the day.

Over the years, we have saved this precious information, not wanting to throw it away. This data is the gold mine from which this chapter was written. If you want to learn from other people's mistakes and discover some things that are not mistakes, this is the chapter for you.

Starting to Negotiate Before You Are Ready

Starting to negotiate before you're ready may be the worst mistake you can make. There is never a good enough reason to start negotiating before you are ready. Avoiding this mistake is particularly difficult when the person pressing you to negotiate is your own client. This person pays your bills. The client wants to hear results. Saying, "No, I need more time before we start this negotiation," is difficult.

No matter whom you are negotiating with, don't start talking until you are ready. If the other side calls, tell the truth: you don't feel fully prepared. Use the occasion to your great advantage by inquiring about the other party's position.

Even if members of the other party don't want to reveal their position, you can ask for the background or history. Often people who don't want to give away their negotiating position feel comfortable giving you their version of the history of the discussions. This is particularly true if you are the designated negotiator for someone else. Lawyer, agents, and Realtors normally know the background of a deal and are usually willing to talk about it even before the negotiation begins. Listening is an excellent way to spend time if you aren't ready to negotiate.

Negotiating with the Wrong Person

Always verify that you are negotiating with the right person right at the beginning. Even when you know the person on the other side, you may want to start by confirming the fact that this person has the authority to close. If your counterpart has the authority to close the deal, you have the right person. In a company setting, your counterpart almost always has superiors higher up on the corporate ladder. This doesn't always mean that a superior is the right person to negotiate with. In fact, negotiating with an executive a level or two too high for the deal you are doing can be worse than negotiating with someone too low on the organizational chart. Top executives may lack the detailed knowledge to deal with all the particulars of your negotiation.

Locking on a Position

When you lock on a position, you insist on a given solution, and you are closed to any other suggestions. You think the solution must be the one you are putting on the table, or the agreement just won't work. This is called *positional negotiating*. When you lock on a position, you destroy the negotiating process. Additionally, you look ridiculous. It is rarely true that the only solution is the one you bring to the table at the very beginning of the discussions.

Locking on a position should not be a problem once you take one of our courses or read this book. Positional negotiating comes from a lack of preparation. If you have problems with this area, read Chapter 2 on preparation and Chapter 4 on setting limits. One step in setting limits is to list all the alternatives you have if you don't successfully close the deal you're working on. The next step is to pick your "or else." That is, decide what you will do if you cannot reach an agreement with your current counterpart.

After you've gone through these two steps, you are much less likely to lock on a position.

A tougher challenge is when the other side locks on a position. When that happens, the other side has failed to fully prepare and probably has not gone through the process of setting limits. You have two choices:

✔ Subtly help them prepare and perhaps get them thinking about their "or else."

✔ Give them a copy of this book with key pages folded down.

We, of course, heartily recommend the second suggestion. But if time doesn't allow, lean back in your chair, stretch a bit, and say something like, "I wonder if we both have the same information." Then start talking about the background of the negotiations. You exchange subject matter. The idea is to bring the other party up to speed. To get somebody off such a spot, you must do the following things:

✔ Abandon your ego.

✔ Abandon your frontal assault.

✔ Abandon all efforts to persuade.

✔ Become a teacher — a gentle person sharing knowledge about the history and background of the negotiation.

Once you open up the mind of the other party, you begin to have an intelligent negotiation. You may or may not get what you want, but at least you increase the possibility of reaching a negotiated settlement, because you will be dealing with someone who is listening — someone who is open to the negotiation.

Feeling Powerless during a Negotiating Session

When we label feeling powerless as a mistake in negotiating, we initially get a great deal of flak. We let the objecting students talk it out. Usually someone in the class is able to make our point for us.

Feeling powerless during a negotiating session is a mistake because_____

_____.

Can you fill in that blank? There is a definite reason that *feeling* powerless during a negotiating session is not a condition of your spirit; it is not dictated by the circumstances; it is not something you have to endure. It is a mistake. If that feeling begins to set in, you need to push the pause button (see Chapter 6). Take a break from the negotiation to figure out why you are feeling that way. Don't continue negotiating.

When you feel powerless in a negotiating session, you are almost always lacking in preparation. Train yourself to hear such feelings ringing like a loud bell — a recess bell. Take a break. Regroup mentally. Come up with solutions. You can even say, "You know, you got me. I'm going to have to give this some more study." If the negotiation is a blast from your boss about something in your area of responsibility, but you are not sure of the answer, just say, "I'm not ready to have this conversation yet, but I can get back to you this afternoon." Or say, "I'll need to get some more information for you on that matter."

Worrying about Losing Control of the Negotiation

We think that the big mistake with losing control is generally the very notion that it *is* a mistake.

This is a perception problem. In our viewpoint, negotiation is not about control. It is about working together to find the best solution to the problem at hand. It is about give and take between people trying to resolve differences. It is about moving forward in life toward well-considered goals that are valued by both sides. It is about building relationships.

So if you have a concern about a tendency to lose control of a negotiation, ask yourself why control is such an important issue. If the problem is a personal loss of control and you feel you may resort to voilence, no doubt the issue needs addressing. However, if your concern is that you are losing control of a negotiation, the question is, "Why do you think you have to be in control every inch of the way?"

You may fear that if you lose control, the other party will run roughshod over you. First of all, if that's true, you may want to rethink dealing with this person. Maybe you should be talking to someone else entirely. Secondly, you need not have this fear if you set your limits (Chapter 4) and you are willing to stick by them.

Wandering away from the Goals and Limits You Set

People too often start a negotiation with a set of limits and goals and then, as the negotiation progresses, ignore them. Without really thinking about it, they modify their goals downward and their limits upward. As time goes on, they seem to lose their way. These people are the most likely to suffer from *buyer's remorse* — that sinking feeling of regret you get the morning after you commit yourself to a deal. Buyer's remorse is similar to a hangover; it comes from getting intoxicated with the deal and ignoring your initial limits and goals.

The best way to avoid losing sight of your limits and goals is to write them down. Let your notes be your guide. Changing your limits and goals as a result of acquiring more data is fine, as long as you're conscious that you're doing it.

Worrying Too Much about the Other Guy

Win-win doesn't mean worrying about whether the people you negotiate with always get everything they want. Unfortunately, many people who aren't too assertive anyway use the wide-spread acceptance of the win-win mantra to justify not looking out for themselves. You must set your own limits and goals and then fight for them to the last (see Part II). The other party should (and usually does) do the same thing.

You do want to negotiate with respect and intelligence. Before closing, take a moment and be sure that you have achieved enough of what you set out to achieve to close the deal, that the other party is getting reasonable benefit from the transaction, that the deal you are about to make is a deal that both parties can live with in the real world, and, in short, that you have a win-win situation. See Chapter 15 for a complete discussion of win-win negotiating.

Thinking of "Just the Right Thing to Say" — the Next Day

It happens to everybody from the President of the United States on down: No one has all the right things to say at just the right time all the time — except in the movies. Life is not a movie. It's not even a good television show. Life is unrehearsed and ad-libbed. The better prepared you are, the more likely you are to come up with the right thing to say at just the right time. But even the best prepared will think of something better to say after thoughtful consideration. The only mistake here is believing that you've made a mistake. Stop being so hard on yourself.

What's important is to be clear in your communications, not to be clever. Clever is fun. Clever feels good. Clever can be satisfying. But clear communications carry the day. If you wake up the next morning feeling that you were not clear enough, it is easy enough to go back and clarify an earlier statement. Just start the next negotiating session with a clarification. Unfortunately, you cannot start the next negotiation session with the announcement that you have thought of a clever put-down. It just doesn't work.

Blaming Yourself for Another's Mistakes

When things go awry, most people blame themselves — even if the problem isn't their fault. Resist that temptation. If you are inclined to blame yourself for the woes of the world, think about why that is so. We think this tendency has a great deal to do with a lack of self- esteem.

Not Focusing on Closing the Negotiation

This is kissin' cousin to worrying too much about the other guy. You must keep all six of the basic skills of every negotiation in mind at all times. Many people are inclined to forget the fact that from the first time you hear about the possibility of a particular negotiation, you should be thinking about the close. Each aspect of closure is driven by the preparation for the negotiation, the goals and limits you set, and the negotiation process itself. Focus on closing during every step of the negotiation.

Every extra moment a negotiation drags on is a moment when something could come up and have a negative impact on the negotiations. We aren't saying that you should rush the close or that you should close before you are ready to do so. Just keep the close in mind at all times. You are in a negotiation to achieve certain goals. When those goals are in reach, go for it.

Chapter 21

Ten Key Negotiations of Your Life

●●

*H*ere are some helpful insights into handling various highly stressful situations in your life. Some of the emotional fallout from the negotiations we list here can cause permanent damage within families. This chapter guides you through these times in a way that minimizes damage to your relationships, while enabling you to stay true to yourself and to your personal values, needs, and wants.

Buying a Used Car

Any car you are likely to buy came off an assembly line. The day the car was built, many other cars just like it were made. Don't fall in love with a car — especially one you have only driven around the block. Another car is always around the corner.

Here are the key points to remember when buying a used car:

- ✔ Know generally what kind of car you want.
- ✔ Don't fall in love with any particular car until you buy it.
- ✔ Know what you can afford to pay and don't spend more.
- ✔ Don't buy a car until a mechanic you know and trust has looked it over — for a price, not as a favor. (You want the mechanic's best professional opinion.)
- ✔ Negotiate the price from knowledge of the marketplace.

The most common source for pricing information is the classified advertising in newspapers or those nifty little magazines (common in most big cities) devoted exclusively to advertising things that private parties want to sell. The next most common source is the *Kelley Blue Book Auto Market Report.* This book reflects a national survey of prices on used cars by manufacturer, year, and model. It has a section in the front that provides tables so that you can add or subtract for the optional features of the car and the car's mileage.

Real insiders use the *Black Book* published on a state-by-state basis by the National Auto Research Division of Hearst Business Media Corporation of Gainesville, Georgia. This book is designed for the people who buy automobiles for used-car lots. If you can get your hands on a current copy of one of these little books, you have the single most reliable information about what the car lot paid for the car you are buying. Add the cost of commission, overhead, and operating expenses, and you have the minimum price for which the car lot can afford to sell the car to you.

See Chapter 1 for a story about how your five-year life plan impacts what kind of a car you should consider. Also read Chapter 17 on closing, so you'll be aware of the continued efforts of the car-lot personnel to close the sale from the moment you express interest in a particular car.

Asking for a Raise

Most people ask for a raise at least once in their lives — some even face this negotiation yearly . . . and dread it every time. Take the dread out of asking for a raise by using the six basic skills outlined in the first six parts of this book:

1. Prepare (Part I).

Before approaching your manager for a raise, prepare yourself internally. You must know that you have earned the right to ask for a raise and that you are valuable to your employer. Gather documentation to prove that you have made an important contribution to the organization and that your absence would be detrimental. If you don't believe that you deserve a raise, no one else will.

After you are emotionally prepared for the negotiation, prepare your case on the merits:

- Know how much your company's budget can afford. Get a feel for how well the company is doing.

- Know, in general, the going rate for your services. The Department of Labor issues statistics each year about pay rates for a large number of categories. You can find these statistics in most big-city libraries and in trade journals for individual industries.

- Know specifically what people in your geographic area are earning for doing the same kind of work with the same number of years experience as you. Ask friends, check the classified ads, go out on some job interviews, or do whatever it takes to get this information.

When you've gathered your data, tell your boss that you want to schedule a meeting about your salary. Don't ambush your boss. Say, "I'd like to talk with you about my salary. I need about 20 minutes of uninterrupted time in your office. When would it be convenient?"

2. Set limits and goals (Part II).

Decide on the minimum amount you are willing to accept and the maximum figure you can hope to receive. Also, decide what you will do if the company does not meet your minimal expectations:

- You may bide your time as you look for another job.

- You may quit on the spot.

- You may just stay with the program . . . and be a less cheerful worker.

3. Push the pause button (Part III).

Keep your emotions in check. Never resort to an emotional plea about putting food in your kids' mouths. Most companies have stacks of evidence that they are in line with the norms. You need to build your case on objective evidence. Make sure that the management knows that keeping you around and keeping you happy will pay off.

4. Listen (Part IV).

You may have to let your boss vent about shrinking budgets, executive compensation, and even personal problems. Letting your boss empty out will clear a space for you when you talk. Ask about your own performance. Listen carefully to be sure that you both view your performance the same way; if you don't, clear up that discrepancy immediately. Going on to talk about more money when the company thinks that you're not performing up to snuff is futile.

5. Be clear (Part V).

Set forth what you think is fair and why. Spend plenty of time on the why. Let your boss know about the research you've done and present all the evidence of the special value that you bring to the company. You want your boss to feel good about the raise you are going to get.

6. Close the deal (Part VI).

This may be the first time your boss has been made aware of your worth to the company. Your boss may have to think about the issue. That's fine, but be sure to set a date for a final decision. You don't want your manager's legitimate need to think about the matter to turn into an excuse to keep you from the salary you deserve.

Where, when, and how you seat yourself when you discuss a pay raise with your boss can impact the entire negotiation. For some helpful hints on how to physically set up the negotiation in your manager's office, read Chapter 3. Chapter 11 discusses the body language of such meetings.

Buying a Wedding Ring

Fortunately for the world's betrothed, the simple gold band remains the standard symbol of love and commitment whether you are Buddhist, Christian, Hindu, Jew, or Muslim. The practice for men varies around the world. More men wear wedding bands in England and its former colonies (including the United States) than anywhere else in the world.

The price of the ring is mostly based on the amount of gold it contains. Unless you happen to be a jeweler, you can't test the *karat* (or purity) of the gold on your own. We suggest that you work with a professional jeweler whom you know, if possible. If you don't know any jewelers and you can't get any great recommendations from friends, at least be sure that you're dealing with someone who has been in business for a while.

The most pure gold is 24-karat gold, which is 99.9 percent pure. By comparison, 18-karat gold is 18/24ths pure gold, and the rest is alloy. The standard in the United States is 14-karat gold, which has a little more alloy and slightly less gold. Be sure 14k is stamped inside the ring, followed by the logo of the manufacturer of the ring. The logo is registered with the Jeweler's Association. In many other countries, including England, Italy, and Israel, the government supervises the gold industry. This is your protection against purchasing anything less than the indicated purity. When you negotiate for a wedding ring, the important thing is to be sure that you are negotiating for the real thing.

In the United States, the use of some decoration on the ring is increasing. Such decoration adds only a relatively small charge to the cost of the band and considering the cost of the overall ceremony, honeymoon, and homemaking, this is one area where you should get what you want. This advice is quite different from the restraint we would urge when you shop for the engagement ring.

Practices surrounding engagement rings vary widely around the world. Our preference, if possible, is to use a family ring to mark the connection of this new life with the past. Chapter 2 has a sidebar that tells how the *Rapaport Diamond Report* (and a certification of the stone) can help you stretch your engagement-ring budget. If you use the *Rapaport Diamond Report,* remember that it represents the cash asking price in New York for single diamonds, meaning that the true price should be lower. And be sure to check the date of the report.

Planning a Wedding

Your wedding may be the most detail-oriented special event you will ever plan. You may become overwhelmed when you look at the total amount of preparation required. Don't go it alone; get a recent issue of any of the magazines on the subject. We bought one issue of *Bride's* and one of *Modern Bride*. These magazines usually include a checklist and sample calendar. The checklists cover every aspect of wedding planning, and the calendar suggests working backward from the wedding date.

Stop now. Before you write anything on the calendar, decide on your total budget and stick to it. Then begin to prepare for the various negotiations, using the budget as your absolute limit.

Break down the big categories into smaller, less threatening chunks. Be aware of which categories involve negotiations and with whom. Obvious negotiations are with the hotel, church or synagogue, food and liquor vendors, and so on. But the real challenge is agreeing on who will take part in the wedding and what role each person will fulfill. Negotiating with your immediate family, your spouse-to-be, and inlaws-to-be can be intense. Use the six skills in this book to stay as objective as you can. Because this is such a personal event, you need to keep your pause button firmly in your grip. (See Chapter 6 for a detailed explanation of this most important tool.)

One special consideration is the role of the children in the ceremony (if you or your spouse-to-be is a parent). We wanted to get the teenaged daughters involved by giving them important roles: They were our only bridesmaids. Each of them was in various stages of accepting the new woman in Dad's life, and this was an important step in building relationships. We let Michelle, Amy, and Wendy choose their own bridesmaid dresses, each according to their own individual taste. We established limits (no cleavage, no black, no micro-mini), but to this day, we're still getting praise from the girls for our sensitivity to their needs.

Buying a Home

Buying a home is the most important buying decision that most people make in the course of their lives. Most people comparison shop a great deal for a house. You search until you find what you want. When you find it, you make an offer and, if the offer is accepted, apply for a loan.

We think that this order of doing things is a bit backwards. Your efforts to get a good deal on the money you borrow should be as complete as your efforts to get a good deal on the house you buy. Most people put the loan-application process off because it seems so daunting, and it also involves the possibility of rejection. Egad!

But this is one of the many times that procrastination can bite you in the behind. Your best bet is to prequalify for your loan before you choose your house. *Prequalification* involves filling out all the forms and getting a commitment from a lending institution that it will lend you a certain amount of money on prescribed terms as long as you pick out your house within a designated period of time. Even if you end up using another lending institution, prequalifying can be a great help for the following reasons:

- ✔ You know what you can afford.
- ✔ You can tell the seller that you are prequalified, which makes you a more attractive buyer. The seller doesn't have to worry about whether or not you can afford the house.
- ✔ You get to shop for the loan and fill out the forms without the time pressures involved when you're afraid someone else will snatch up the house you want.

We understand that going to a bank and asking for a loan is not something most folks enjoy doing. Enter the mortgage loan broker. A *mortgage loan broker* is a professional person who assists you in finding the right loan for your circumstance and helps you fill out the forms. Generally, these brokers are paid by the lending institution for which they work.

We work with a woman we found through the joint recommendation of our accountant and stock broker. She's terrific. You may think that you could get a better deal going directly to the lending institution, but we have not found that to be true. Using a professional loan broker offers definite advantages:

- ✔ Good brokers know the best rates.
- ✔ Good brokers know how to translate all that loan jargon into plain language.
- ✔ Good brokers know which lenders are most receptive to a person in your circumstance.
- ✔ Good brokers help you fill out the forms.
- ✔ Good brokers stay in contact with the potential lender to expedite the processing of the loan.
- ✔ Unlike most people, good brokers enjoy doing all this work. That's why they do it. This fact alone should begin and end the conversation on whether to use a broker.

The rates of various financial institutions are published in the business section of most major Sunday newspapers. Consider the cost of borrowing money to see how important this aspect of your home purchase is. Assume a fixed-rate loan of $100,000 for 30 years. The difference between the monthly payment on a $7\frac{1}{2}$-percent loan and an 8-percent loan is $34.55 per month. That's $12,438 over the life of the loan! The terms on which you borrow money for your home purchase are a significant part of the package.

Chapter 2 contains a great deal of information about preparing to buy a home and the importance of knowing the seller. Chapter 7 explains why you should be open about your enthusiasm for a particular house.

Negotiating a Home Improvement Contract

We have very little sympathy for 90 percent of the horror stories we hear about home improvement projects. We listen politely, but we think that most of the tellers of such tales are blaming the contractor for things that are really a result of their own lack of clarity.

Specifically, we're always hearing about how the contractor didn't show up. Yes, many people in the home improvement business are small operators, who overbook themselves and spend too much time working on the job sites and not enough time planning the work ahead of time. But solutions exist:

✔ Know your contractor before you commit to the project.

✔ Talk through the scheduling issue so that you know exactly what jobs are scheduled. Understand where your job falls on the contractor's list of job priorities. And also find out where the other jobs are so that you can verify the excuses if things begin to unravel.

✔ Build penalties and bonuses into your builder's contract to reward and punish the company for completing work under or over the scheduled time.

The second big complaint we hear is that the project went over budget. Usually, the size of the complaint seems to magically relate to the differences between the project as first envisioned by the homeowner and the final result. Follow these tips to avoid spending more than you want to spend:

✔ Know your contractor before you commit to the project.

✔ Obtain a detailed written bid of the work before you agree to have it done.

✔ Agree that no charges will be assessed unless you sign off on them first.

✔ Always hold a portion of the payment until the work passes final inspection.

Note that the first solution for every problem you can imagine with a contractor starts with the admonition "Know your contractor before you commit to the project." In addition, don't be a stranger while the project is underway. Be on the job site with a cup of coffee for the crew every morning. It takes a little extra effort, but that friendly rapport will make your project first priority over a less pleasant one almost every time.

Most people tell you to check references. Because smart workers don't give references to clients who aren't happy with their work, we suggest another approach. Ask friends or strangers who have been through the process of home improvement for recommendations. We got the best floor refinisher by visiting an open house where the floors had just been redone. We asked the Realtor. The Realtor asked her client, and we had a successful experience. The extra time required to shop for the right contractor is worth it when the work gets done as promised, on time, and at the agreed price.

The importance of knowing the person you are negotiating with is well documented in Chapter 2 of this book. The home improvement project underscores this important lesson like none other.

Negotiating a Divorce Settlement

The trouble with negotiating a divorce settlement is that the laws intended to guide you through this difficult time are, by necessity, based on monetary values, not human values. California law requires couples to divide assets up 50/50. This rule sounds neat and reasonable, but if both parties decide that they want the same painting, another painting of equal value may not do the trick.

The key to dealing with these issues is putting together your support team. The lead person is your attorney. Sometimes, other experts (such as an accountant) are part of that team. If you have children, you may want to include a family counselor. Finally, include the inevitable friend or friends.

Don't leave to fate your choice of friends to include on your support team. Be careful whom you use as your friendly ear during this process. You are very vulnerable at this time. The person to whom you spill your guts about your divorce can just as easily steer you in a destructive direction as keep you focused on the long-range goal of a better life for you and your kids (if you have any). Short-term satisfaction can sometimes create long-term harm.

Be equally careful when choosing a divorce lawyer. Rates charged by these lawyers vary widely. Ask friends and acquaintances who have been through this process to recommend a lawyer. Ask any lawyers you know to recommend a divorce lawyer for you — even if your lawyer friend also handles divorces. Always interview at least two or three lawyers before picking one to use for your divorce. Divorce is a difficult process at best. You want someone who is affable, available, and able.

When children are involved, divorce negotiation is different than most other negotiations. In this special case, you and your soon-to-be ex will have a continuing relationship. Remember the advice flight attendants give you before your airplane takes off. In case of an accident, put the oxygen mask over *your* face first and then give the oxygen mask to your child. This is sound advice. You can't help the kids while you are emotionally untethered, adrift in a stormy sea. Keep your needs and wants in mind at all times so that you and your situation remain as healthy as possible while you tend to the needs of your kids.

In resolving financial matters, never include the children in the process of negotiating or collecting money. Divorce has an adverse effect on children; don't aggravate the situation by adding financial stress to your child's emotional stress. If one parent is truly errant and trying to evade moral and legal obligations, more help for the responsible parent is available today than ever before.

> ✔ Prosecutors are available to enforce local laws that prohibit parents from contemptuously refusing to honor their legal responsibilities.
>
> ✔ For custody and visitation, a uniform custody act has been adopted by all 50 states and the District of Columbia to help in interstate custody disputes.
>
> ✔ A movement exists to make the enforcement and collection of child support easier across state lines.

If you have children that will be affected by your divorce, be sure to choose a lawyer who is a specialist in the areas of child support, visitation rights, and so on.

In every divorce, emotions run high, and anger and resentment tend to bubble over. Add one or more children to the mix, and the situation is even more complicated and emotionally difficult. That's why you should read and reread Chapters 6 and 7 about the pause button and handling hot button issues. These two chapters will be part of your support system during the entire process.

Negotiating about Naptime, Curfew, Dessert, and Other Childhood Necessities

The six steps of negotiating are essential in negotiating with children. The following sections show you how these steps can help you have successful and enjoyable negotiations with your children.

Preparing to negotiate with your kids

Preparing involves knowing what's fair to expect from a child at each age, and setting the stage for success. Ideally, children's responsibility and freedom should increase with age. You get into trouble when you expect too much too soon, or expect too little too late. You need to explore some general characteristics of children at each age by reading books on human development or checking with your pediatrician. In addition, thoroughly understand your own values and priorities so that you can pass these on to your kids.

Setting limits for minors

The limits you set are dependent on the age of the child. A limit clearly tells the child two things: what constitutes acceptable conduct and what substitutes will be accepted. For example, "You may not throw blocks. You may throw balls, but only outside the house."

You should sharply define your limits. Telling your children that they may stay out a little past curfew, but not too much, is inviting trouble. Vague statements leave teens without a clear criterion for making decisions. Instead, state the limit firmly, in a way that says you mean business. And state consequences along with the limit. Setting the stage for success means giving your children advance warning and reminders.

Don't let your warnings and reminders turn into nagging. Make your limits clear and then avoid repeating them unnecessarily. If your child crosses your clearly stated limits, you need to implement consequences. Merely repeating the limit again and again numbs your child to the importance of the limit.

Give children a voice in setting limits and tell them the reasons behind the rules.

Pushing the parental pause button

Knowing when and how to push the pause button is the most important skill when dealing with children. Everyone carries around a lifetime of baggage. Until you become a parent, you may not realize how many things can make you angry. Do any of these examples apply to you?

- ✔ You worry about the kids and express that concern as anger.

- ✔ Certain situations, such as when your children fight, make you feel helpless, and you become angry at your helplessness.

- ✔ You feel either overwhelmed by responsibilities or unsuccessful at taking care of your kids and giving them as much time as you think you should. This perceived failure makes you angry.

Anger is here to stay. All parents get angry at their children. Parents who love cannot avoid anger. It has a purpose; it shows concern.

 Instead of trying to suppress anger, express it in nondestructive ways, without insult. Describe what you see, how you feel, and what needs to be done, without attacking the child's character. Instead of saying, "You are such a slob, leaving wet towels on the floor," say, "When I see towels on the floor, I get angry. I think towels belong on the rack." Express your anger responsibly, with "I" statements followed by a respectful request for a solution. Remember, your most important job is to model how you want your kids to behave. Teach them how to handle their extreme feelings by handling your own.

Listening to your kids

Listening to your children means paying attention. Remember the following tips to create a healthy atmosphere of clear communication between yourself and your children:

- ✔ Don't do other things while your children are talking to you. Give your kids the same respect you give your spouse and coworkers.

- ✔ Avoid the "Mommy, MOMMY, **MOMMY**!!" syndrome by answering your children the first time they call you. Acknowledging your child (even if simply by saying "Just a minute, dear" or "Mommy's talking to someone else right now") shows respect and fosters a sense of empowerment.

- ✔ Don't jump to conclusions. Listen to everything your child is telling you, from start to finish, before responding.

Parenting with clarity

Being clear with children means describing the situation — not evaluating the child's character. Avoid blaming. Restate negative remarks positively. Emphasize what your children *can* do, rather than what they cannot do. Praise your children whenever you can. Describe the specific event that pleases you and your specific feelings; then let your children draw conclusions about their character.

> **Praise:** "Thank you for being early on curfew. I know I don't have to worry about you."

> **Child's inference:** "My parent loves and cares about me. I am trustworthy."

Closing with kids

Closing the deal is as challenging with children as it is in business. You must make sure that both you and your children understand the final agreement the same way. Don't assume that your children automatically understand what you expect of them.

After a negotiation, write the agreement down. Have the kids write it down, too, if they are old enough to print letters. Keep the agreement handy in case the situation resurfaces.

Choosing Medical Care for an Incapacitated Parent

Choosing how to care for an incapacitated parent is a tragic circumstance that visits all too many families. The person that has provided leadership in the family is too ill to make decisions or articulate desires. The loss puts everybody in emotional upheaval. Decisions must be made. At a time when everybody needs love and support, family members begin to argue.

Whatever you do, avoid the "Mama woulda wanted . . ." syndrome. Unless Mama (or Papa) has clearly and uniformly expressed a preference on the subject in a way that applies unmistakably to the situation at hand, don't presume to know what Mama or Papa would have wanted. Even living wills that purport to give guidance are often phrased in such general terms as to leave families without the clear guidelines needed.

With rare exception, those people claiming to know what an incapacitated parent would want are really expressing their own feelings about the subject:

People often say something like . . .	When they really mean . . .
"Mama wouldn't have wanted to be like this. At least let her keep her dignity."	"I'm hurting. It causes me pain to see Mama like this. Let me be free of this suffering."
"Dad always put up the good fight. He would want every chance to beat this thing."	"I can't stand the thought of being without Dad. I want to hang on to him with everything that medical science has to offer."
"What's the matter with you guys? Just decide and quit all this arguing. Mama wouldn't have wanted us to argue."	"I feel that I lost Mama a long time ago. I've worked through that loss. You guys decide at your own pace on a solution that you are most comfortable with and let me know."

Stick with the phrases on the right. By making "I" statements, you get your honest feelings out in the open. By saying "Mama woulda wanted . . ." you mask your honest feelings. If someone else tries to tell you what a parent would have wanted, listen carefully. In 99 times out of 100, what you're hearing is exactly how this person feels about the situation. Let the person speak, pause for a moment, and then verify the true source of the feelings. Say, "Now tell me how *you* feel."

Understand that some people are uncomfortable expressing their own feelings about the sick parent. That's why "Mama woulda wanted . . ." statements flourish. A good question that can help pull out the true feeling is: "In an ideal world, knowing the medical information we have, how would you like to handle this situation?"

There is no right or wrong approach to deciding how to care for an incapacitated parent. The key is to get through this crisis in a way that brings the remaining family members closer, instead of pushing them apart. The important skills here are listening with respect and love to the other members of the family and being clear about your own feelings. We discuss listening in Part IV of this book.

Buying Funeral Services

Good news! Gone are the days when everything about funeral arrangements was a big and baffling negotiation. Around the beginning of this decade, the Federal Trade Commission required morticians and cemeteries to issue written, itemized price lists. They can no longer offer a flat rate and require you to negotiate for the products and services included in the final price.

Some funeral homes in Los Angeles *advertise* that they provide written price lists. Darn right they do. It's the law! Because written price lists are easy to compare, you commonly find a mortuary's lowest prices printed right along with the prices for the fanciest form of service. You also find that the price of specific goods and services holds true to the printed price list, unless you're spending so much money that the funeral director agrees to "throw in" a few extras.

The biggest single item in most funeral services is the casket, which can range in price from under $500 to over $25,000. The current mode of operation for ambitious funeral directors is to gently persuade you that you want the very best (as in the most expensive). So the toughest negotiation you face is with yourself. This is your last opportunity to display your love and affection for the departed; you may have an understandable tendency to overdo it. Restrain yourself.

The most important expression of respect you can offer the departed is the continued love and warm feelings of yourself and other loved ones. Spend your time, energy, and money in getting all the friends and relatives together and sharing memories. That — not the glitziness of the casket — is the heart of the funeral.

Because a little emotional distance from the decision-making process is important during a time of personal loss, we suggest that you carry with you to the funeral home the pause button contained on the Cheat Sheet at the front of this book. If you have time, look over Chapter 6 first. And don't forget that people who cared about you while they lived wouldn't want you to go into debt over their deaths.

Chapter 22

Ten Videos to Rent,
Watch, and Enjoy

● ●

In This Chapter

▶ Videos that profile negotiating techniques

▶ Getting the most out of these movies

● ●

*T*hroughout this book, we mention films that demonstrate some point about negotiation. They are marked with the Activity icon because watching a film is an activity you can do with family or friends. The films listed in this chapter have three qualities in common:

✔ The films are about negotiating in general, as opposed to some narrow aspect of negotiation.

✔ The films are likely to be suitable for the whole family.

In the main body of this book, we have referenced several other great films that profile negotiating principles. However, some of those movies contain some rough language or graphic sexual scenes. While personal tastes vary, the films listed in this section fall within the viewing range of most of America. Even the first (and best of the films) — an early Al Pacino classic — is not a violent film. The tension is terrific, but the movie is not violent.

✔ The films are high in quality.

You will like some more than others, but there isn't a clunker among them. We often hear back from students about how valuable and enjoyable the films were.

Do the following right now:

1. **Turn to the Cheat Sheet in the front of the book.**

2. **Tear out the card that has the names of the ten films listed in this chapter.**

3. **Mark the ones you are most eager to see.**

4. Put the card in your wallet.

5. Rent and watch the films at your convenience.

If you have already seen one of the films listed, you may want to watch it again, keeping in mind the information in this book.

Dog Day Afternoon

Millions have seen a very young Al Pacino and Charles Durning turn in virtuoso performances as captor and cop in the classic film *Dog Day Afternoon* (Rated R). Based on the true story of a bank robbery that turned into a hostage situation, the film shows each member of the police team move quickly into action and negotiate with skill and training. Granted, some slight dramatic distortions occur — but no actual fabrications. The events were recreated accurately. I won't spoil the ending, but you see the police procedures carefully followed.

Each of the six basic principles of negotiating is clearly demonstrated in this film. Here is a friendly guide through the negotiation without ruining the film.

- ✔ **Prepare:** Note how the police immediately and throughout the film try to gather information about the man holding the hostages.

- ✔ **Set limits:** The police set limits before they ever start talking. Their goal is to get the hostages out safely. When a hostage is hurt, they find out how the injury happened. If it was an accident, they continue the negotiation. If it was an execution, they make a frontal assault on the site.

- ✔ **Push the pause button:** The police have a firm hold on the pause button. One officer's sole job is to observe everyone's emotional state. His or her job is to keep a check on emotions and remove officers before the strain of the situation overcomes them.

- ✔ **Listen and clarify communications:** This is a constant. Note in the barber shop that someone is always in the background with headphones. That officer is monitoring all the communications both ways to be sure that they are clear.

- ✔ **Close:** The authorities keep the goal constantly in mind. Notice how many times the police try to close this negotiation. Our advice to attempt to close negotiations early and often is well demonstrated in this film.

You can watch this film more than once. Each time you notice something new about the way the skills in this book apply to this type of high-stakes negotiation.

The Taking of Pelham: One, Two, Three

The Taking of Pelham: One, Two, Three (Rated PG) is a film about a hostage situation on a train, a situation that gives rise to the title of the film and a disastrous negotiation. You can clearly see the mistakes in this negotiation every step of the way. Deaths result. You can watch wisely from your armchair and study all the ways in which the negotiation went off track. Because the team led by Walter Matthau's character broke every rule in the book, a favorable result was virtually impossible.

Again, follow the model of the six basic ingredients of all negotiations.

- ✔ **Prepare:** Not only is the negotiating team completely unprepared for the highjacking of a train, they miss almost every opportunity to prepare during the negotiation. They sit around guessing about the highjackers when they could be asking many questions.

- ✔ **Set limits:** No limits are set. Nothing the captors do decisively changes the situation.

- ✔ **Push the pause button:** These officers never heard the words nor do they have a grasp of the concept. They eventually turn on each other when they should be focused on the captors.

- ✔ **Listen and clarify communications:** Watch for failures in this important area of negotiating.

- ✔ **Close:** The authorities simply don't have this basic element in mind. They just keep going.

Both this film and the one listed previously are shown at the FBI school at Quantico, Virginia, as examples of how to and how not to negotiate a hostage situation.

Kissinger and Nixon

This made-for-television film originally aired on December 10, 1995, on the TNT Network. Beau Bridges plays Richard Nixon; Ron Silver plays Kissinger. They are both brilliant.

This extraordinary film examines Kissinger's efforts to negotiate a peaceful settlement to the Vietnam War. It is based on Kissinger's biography and other sources that aren't necessarily consistent with Kissinger's own diary.

You witness the face-to-face discussions between Kissinger and the North Vietnamese. You see the more difficult negotiations with U.S. allies in South Vietnam and the toughest negotiations of all—those with the President of the United States.

First, observe the negotiations between Kissinger and the North Vietnamese. This is a classic, well-tuned negotiation. Both sides were well prepared. Both sides set certain limits. Both listen and communicate clearly. They are able to agree rather quickly.

Kissinger could not sell the agreement to the South Vietnamese, and Nixon was furious. Watch this more than once to see how difficult multisided negotiations can be. This film shows first hand what is so true in many real-life negotiations: Reaching an accord with the opposing party can be easy; the most difficult negotiations are often between people on the same side of the table.

The other members of what was supposed to be the same team outmaneuvered Kissinger at every turn. In the White House, Kissinger was the odd man out. He was valuable to the President, but the President had a hard time accepting him into the inner circle. Nixon had an even harder time with those who trusted and respected Kissinger — Nixon's mortal enemies — the press. Nixon believed Kissinger earned some of that trust and respect by revealing confidential conversations.

South Vietnam presented different problems. Kissinger underestimated the President's unwillingness to sell out the South. Nixon didn't think any more of the leadership of that country than Kissinger did. Kissinger was a little blindsided by what appeared to be Nixon's loyalty to the South. Nixon didn't want to be seen by the American public as abandoning our ally, no matter how unworthy they may be or how practical it was for him to do so.

In order to seal the deal, Kissinger needed the President's personal assurance to the South Vietnamese. The President had to sign secret side letters to convince the South that the United States would not abandon them. Of course, in the end, America did.

Finally, the film depicts Kissinger and the press. Kissinger risked revealing some of his problems to the press. Even with Kissinger's skills and long-term relationship with the press, this gambit had mixed results. Kissinger and Nixon received *Time* magazine's man of the year award jointly.

Ruthless People

Any film with Danny DeVito and Bette Midler is bound to be fun. *Ruthless People* (Rated R) is no exception. It's about a young couple who kidnap an heiress (Bette Midler) and demand ransom from her husband (Danny DeVito). However, they make the most common mistake of any negotiation: They forget to find out about the person with whom they are negotiating. Mr. Stone (DeVito) is ecstatic to have his wife out of the house. In fact, he was planning to murder her anyway.

The movie demonstrates the basic problem with all kidnapping negotiations. There really isn't another option for getting the money if the obvious target doesn't come through with the desired cash. The negotiations — and the movie — take a wonderful twist when Mrs. Stone takes on new value. Value is a matter of perception; it's in the eyes of the beholder. Have a good laugh as you see how value and power are perceived and misperceived in this situation

High and Low

High and Low is a film based on the novel *King's Ransom* by American novelist Ed McBain. It's another movie about kidnapping and a misassessed situation. See how this subject matter is handled in the hands of one of the greatest directors in the world, Akira Kurosawa of Japan.

This classic movie features one of the great living actors of our day, Toshiro Mifune. He plays a wealthy businessman who must work through his moral, ethical, and financial dilemma when the son of his chauffeur is mistakenly kidnapped. What a negotiation! And even though the film has subtitles, you will have no trouble following along. The film is letterboxed, which means that it is left in its original form (much wider than it is high). This leaves a nice black bar across the bottom of your screen for the translation, which means that you will have no trouble reading the subtitles.

Notice, first, how the professional negotiator — the senior law enforcement official — begins the process by pushing the pause button. Everybody has to settle down and wait. The next step is to gather more information about the kid who was kidnapped and information about the demands. When the phone rings, the professional negotiator dons a pair of earphones and begins to listen. They record the message so that they can listen again and again. This way, clear communications are ensured.

The kidnapper is very bright. He never stays on the line long enough to be traced. He knows Japanese law, which he recites during the conversation. One of the detectives calls him the "smartest crook I ever saw." But they still don't know much about him and don't seem to be trying very hard to gather information about him. You quickly note that this lack of preparation — which leads the police to speculate — hurts the negotiation. The police should have read Chapter 2 of this book.

You think you are headed for a *Dog Day Afternoon* kind of movie focusing on a hostage situation. Instead, the plot turns into a negotiation between the wealthy industrialist and everyone else in his life to decide whether or not to pay the ransom. The movie then turns into a fast-paced detective movie. When the surprising culprit is found, the story goes into high gear. The police not only want to catch him, they want to convict him of a capital offense. Each time the movie ends one phase of the story, it moves to the next level.

Kurosawa is a master filmmaker, and this is one of his master works.

Broadway Danny Rose

Broadway Danny Rose (Rated PG) is one of Woody Allen's best. You don't have to like Woody Allen to like this movie. It is all about some very senior stand-up comics (has been, borscht-belt guys) sitting around New York's famous Carnegie Deli reminiscing about the life story of a renegade agent named Danny Rose (played by Woody Allen).

During the movie, note that Woody Allen never pushes the pause button. He talks nonstop without ever stopping to think what he is saying. But he does hang in there. Give that man points for tenacity. His negotiating success is purely accidental from a technical point of view. He never uses any of the negotiating skills in this book. You may wonder why in the world people spend the time and effort becoming good negotiators when people like Broadway Danny Rose can succeed without skills. The movie demonstrates just how accidental his success is. Life is sweeping this man along. He just keeps talking and talking as events play out. This is a fun movie to watch and very instructive.

Naked Spur

James Stewart and Janet Leigh star in the classic film *Naked Spur,* made in the days when cinemas were still advertising "Made in Technicolor," because not all movies were. The movie was shot in the beautiful Colorado Rockies.

This film is one great negotiation scene after another. Then the plot slides neatly into a life-and-death negotiation between the lawmen, led by Stewart as an upstanding marshall, and the man they hope to bring to justice.

Slowly, the negotiation that forms the center point of the film emerges as the lawmen take the outlaw back to Kansas. Watch this guy. He is good. He has his objective in mind and he does not miss an opportunity to advance his cause. Everything he does is designed to close the deal on his terms: He wants his captors to let him go.

As the overall negotiation nears its end, notice all the little deals between various characters that contribute to the main negotiation.

This film is not so obviously centered on negotiation as most listed in this chapter, but your family will enjoy this old-fashioned Western.

Patterns

Patterns is actually the January 12, 1955, edition of the Kraft Television Theater performed live — no starting over if someone makes a mistake. This performance won an Emmy for the brilliant and prolific television writer, Rod Serling. It is available in many video stores today as part of the series called *The Golden Age of Television.* And what a golden year 1955 was! *Lassie* debuted, *Peter Pan* came to television in living color, the *$64,000 Question* was launched, and *Your Hit Parade* was also introduced.

In *Patterns,* Ed Begley (the father of popular actor Ed Begley, Jr.) plays a senior executive who is unwillingly replaced by a very young Richard Kiley. At the end of the first scene, my client, the late Elizabeth Montgomery, plays a young secretary who proclaims "Wow, you never know when you are going to hit a nerve." At that point, you know you are off on a great ride as a student of negotiation and communication.

This production demonstrates how important it is to know all you possibly can about the person with whom you are negotiating. The boss, Mr. Ramsey, and the new executive, Mr. Staples (Richard Kiley), don't know each other very well at the beginning of the film. You get to know them and all the other well-drawn characters during their interaction in the corporate world.

The film ends in one of the most incredible negotiations you will ever have the pleasure to witness. Like a fly on the wall, you watch the powerful and ruthless executive locked in verbal combat with a bright and sensitive young executive. You see that both men are well prepared and have set certain limits. They both drew lines that they are not willing to cross. These lines seem to prevent any kind of effective compromise.

We saw this film for the first time and almost immediately watched it again. It is a great lesson in effective negotiation.

Lilies of the Field

The classic film *Lilies of the Field* is not usually thought of as a negotiation film, but it is. Sidney Poitier won an Academy Award for his on-screen negotiations with a group of nuns who need his services to build a chapel.

Poitier is first shown driving in the desert. When he needs some water for his car, he stops at a convent. The nuns need some help in the fields. Poitier is having none of it — or so he thinks. He has never negotiated with such a determined group.

In addition to the differences in religious outlook, skin color, and cultural background, most of the nuns don't speak one word of English. Thus, the first misunderstanding: Poitier thinks he has been hired for one day for wages to be determined in good faith. The nuns don't have wages, but they do have food and a bed and a million ways to put the brakes on Poitier's departure.

Note how Poitier's actions are not consistent with his statements. He keeps saying he is leaving, but he stays. He obviously needs the milk of human kindness more than he needs to continue his westward trip. This lesson is somewhat accidental, but the negotiating principle is clear. Often people ask, even insist, on logical terms and overlook their own human needs.

Poitier and the nuns finally make a deal to build the chapel, and they shake on it. For the first time, there is a meeting of the minds. He bonds with the nuns. He connects with these women. That connection is what he really needs.

The deal came together because Poitier met his needs. He said his needs were financial, but they were actually a bit more universal — human connection, appreciation for his worth, and positive feedback for his purposeful goal. He is proud, intelligent, skilled, hard-working . . . and all alone.

If you can find out a person's real needs, you will close a deal every time. This is a powerful negotiating lesson. Near the end of the film, Poitier's character prints his name very unobtrusively — Homer Smith — at the very top of the chapel's spire. When he leaves, he is happy and satisfied. He got what he wanted.

Columbo: Murder by the Book

Okay, I know *Columbo* is a television show, but this episode is on video! This famous detective, performed so consistently by Peter Falk, is one of the best examples of the key skills of a good negotiator: listening and communicating clearly. He also has incredible integrity. He sets his goal and never wavers. His steely determination brings victory in the toughest of circumstances.

The big lesson to learn from Columbo is how to ask questions. You can read the sections in Chapter 8 on asking questions and listening. You will find Columbo demonstrating every type of question and listening to the answer. No single source better demonstrates how to ask questions. Court TV presents the question-asking process in the unnaturally structured environment of a trial setting. You can learn a great deal about how to ask questions by watching court proceedings on television. You can learn much more from Columbo. Study the man. Let him be your mentor as he entertains you.

You can find *Columbo* regularly on The Family Channel, which is carried on most cable television systems.

Chapter 23

Ten More Books to Add to Your Library

• •

In This Chapter

▶ Some of the best books on negotiation

▶ What to look for in each book

• •

*T*o become a skilled negotiator, fill your bookshelf with the best books published about negotiating. Why? Because negotiating is more constant in your life than any other activity except breathing. Love, sex, and eating are less frequent activities in your life than negotiating. And, in fact, love, sex, and eating also involve a certain amount of negotiation. So gather together the widest ranging group of books possible on this most pervasive of topics.

This chapter starts off with two works of total fiction. Most people think of going to the business section of the bookstore when they want to buy a book to increase negotiating skills. They think of fiction when they want to read just for the fun of it. We believe that improving your negotiating skills should be fun, so we direct you to some top-notch recreational reading as the first two choices.

Our list also includes books by or about the negotiators themselves. Reading about real-world negotiations is fun. You get the participants' version of the facts. These books take you inside the negotiation.

Our list ends with three obvious choices about the techniques of negotiating. This book gives you all the basics you need to negotiate successfully. However, you may find that when you begin focusing on negotiations in your life, you want to read more. Our recommendation is to avoid books that promote fad theories. These tried-and-true books stick with basics.

Reading books about the particular field in which you do most of your negotiating is also helpful. If you are the mother of young children, buy books for and about children and child-rearing. If you run a small manufacturing company, read all about small manufacturing, in general, and your business, in particular. It is often said about negotiators that the one with the most knowledge wins.

The Negotiator by Frederick Forsyth

Frederick Forsyth is one of the giant writers of our time; he is a master of the international thriller. *The Negotiator* is a long book, but it's a real page-turner. It made the best-seller list by being exciting — not because it was a good book about negotiating.

At one point or another in the book, every negotiating principle in our book is brought out in this well-told tale about a high-stakes negotiation. The story is about a man of immense power and a conspiracy to crush the President of the United States. The kidnapping of a young man on a country road in England is but the first brutal step in the explosive plot to engineer the president's destruction. Only one man can prevent the plan from succeeding. This negotiator must draw upon his deepest strengths and skills to save not only the victim, but the entire free world.

A Maiden's Grave by Jeffery Deaver

Jeffery Deaver knows how to write. *A Maiden's Grave,* Deaver's ninth thriller, is about a 12-hour siege — a war of nerves between a captor and the FBI senior hostage negotiator. The book puts you in the middle of a delicate and dangerous hostage negotiation. Deaver describes the perverse bonding that takes place between a captor and the negotiator. If you ever doubted the importance of Chapter 6 of our book, this love affair between two adversaries should convince you otherwise.

Deaver also describes the inner workings of the FBI hostage rescue team as they try to rescue eight deaf school girls and their teachers. The captors are three heartless prison escapees with nothing to lose. The clock never stops ticking. Anything could happen as this book builds to a heart-stopping climax.

The Late Shift: Letterman, Leno, & The Network Battle for the Night by Bill Carter

The Late Shift is the true story that began May 23, 1991, when Johnny Carson stepped out on the stage of New York's Carnegie Hall at the annual meeting of NBC affiliate stations. Carson was there to dazzle the affiliates with the power of the network's programming. Instead, he announced, without warning or fanfare, that he was leaving *The Tonight Show* — NBC's flagship late-night program and the most profitable television show ever.

Fans were surprised. Executives were stunned. The press reacted with a flow of ink about one of the most incredible stories of show business infighting. Few retirement announcements have drawn such a strong reaction.

Bill Carter, the author of this book, covers the television industry for *The New York Times*. He tells the behind-the-scenes story of two giant corporations and two quirky comedians with dreams and ambitions of their own: Jay Leno and David Letterman.

This is a big story and an intense negotiation. It takes you step-by-step through a high-stakes negotiation with some of the most skilled negotiators in Hollywood. It also reveals, with surprising honesty, the mistakes and missteps of some of the most highly placed executives in television.

Barbarians at the Gate: The Fall of RJR Nabisco by Bryan Burrough & John Helyar

Barbarians at the Gate is another totally true book that reads like a novel. It is as exciting as any whodunit you've read, and was on *The New York Times* best-seller list for six months.

This book tells the inside story of the largest corporate takeover in American history — a deal that caused a frenzy that overtook Wall Street in October and November of 1988. It's the story of dealmakers and the deal, of boardrooms and bedrooms. The authors allow you to be a fly on the wall during the highest levels of negotiation.

Ninety-five percent of the material in the book was taken from a hundred interviews around the country. Because the authors also covered this hot story for the *Wall Street Journal,* they had tremendous access to the people who actually made the deal. The dialogue is as accurate as the memories of the people they interviewed. This reality adds to the book's excitement.

This book served as the basis for the HBO movie of the week we mention in Chapter 2.

Kissinger: A Biography by Walter Isaacson

This is first full-scale biography written about Henry Kissinger, the former Secretary of State. The author, Walter Isaacson, is an editor at *Time, Inc.* and the author of several other books. He interviewed Kissinger and 150 other people who played a role in Kissinger's life.

The book covers Kissinger's life from growing up as a Jewish child in Nazi Germany to his tortured relationship with President Nixon to his present-day success as an international business consultant. Don't be put off by the bulk of the book; you can jump into any chapter that interests you and read it without plowing through the whole book cover to cover. What makes the book valuable to us is that Isaacson devotes a separate, highly readable chapter to each major negotiation of Kissinger's career.

The book also tells the story of how Kissinger's whirlwind approach to negotiating spawned the phrase *shuttle diplomacy.* Kissinger is often referred to by world leaders as the greatest negotiator on the planet. He has written 11 books himself, and countless other books have been written about him. Kissinger is featured in two recent movies. Even if foreign affairs isn't your normal area of interest, you can learn a great deal by reading about this man.

This book was the basis for the Turner Network television movie, *Kissinger and Nixon,* which focused purely on the negotiation to settle the Vietnam War at the end of Nixon's first term.

Talking Peace: A Vision for the Next Generation by Jimmy Carter

Former President Carter has been involved in some of the most interesting negotiations of modern times. Most recently, he went to Haiti in a high-stakes effort to avert an escalation in the conflict there. Because he is still in the news, following President Carter is particularly interesting.

Talking Peace was originally intended to introduce children to the peace process. We recommend the book for its simplicity and the way Carter explains negotiation, mediation, and how to achieve win-win settlements. Carter founded The International Negotiation Network (INN) to seek peaceful ways to reduce civil conflicts and to prevent smaller-scale disputes from escalating into wars. The INN links different peacemaking resources across the globe. It includes 22 individual experts who give of their time and talents to improve the process as well as the prospects of peace.

This book includes some stunning charts about the use of force by the United States. It also lists conflicts around the world during recent times. You won't believe how much serious conflict exists in the world until you read through this simple, straightforward book.

Carter talks a great deal about negotiating skills in this book, with a special emphasis on the importance of preparation. Preparation includes the procedures that will be used for the negotiating sessions themselves.

This Side of Peace: A Personal Account by 'Ha'nan Ashr'aw'i

'Ha'nan Ashr'aw'i is the highest-ranking woman involved in the Middle East negotiations. She is a Christian Arab woman in a Muslim, male-dominated world. She is also a working mother who is a pivotal peacemaker in the most monumental negotiations of our lifetime.

The Middle East negotiations are as tough as negotiation gets. We think that no single situation tests the negotiation skills so thoroughly as the struggle for peace in the Middle East. Ashr'aw'i has a great deal to tell us about the Middle East. With honesty and clarity, she shares her inside view of Middle East diplomacy, Arafat, the PLO hierarchy, and the Palestinians. She also discusses the basic principles of negotiation. In her every word, Ashr'aw'i demonstrates a commitment to the human — not the political — elements of nation building.

Before you read this book, look over the chapter on the personal traits of good negotiators. Ashr'aw'i has every one of them.

Getting Ready to Negotiate: The Getting to Yes Workbook by Roger Fisher and Danny Ertel

Believe it or not, this workbook, with its forms and exercises, is one of the best-selling books on negotiating. We never thought that so many Americans would buy a workbook. This book's success is one of the most exciting indications of the public thirst for self-improvement that seems to be sweeping the land.

The workbook follows the best-selling book on negotiating, *Getting to Yes: Negotiating Agreements Without Giving In* by Roger Fisher and William Ury from the Harvard Negotiating Project, which has been a best-seller for a long time. The book is lively and well written and has the tacit endorsement of one of the world's great institutions of higher learning (Harvard). The authors explain the Harvard Law School BATNA theory — the Best Alternative to a Negotiated Agreement — an important concept that helps you set your limits. The book pays as much homage as we do to the importance of solid preparation and helps you see the lack of it in others when you encounter positional negotiating — what we call the take it or leave it offer.

Selling For Dummies by Tom Hopkins

Selling is a special form of negotiating. I first learned of the . . . *For Dummies* series in a bookstore in Toronto, Canada, when I was speaking at the Toronto International Film Festival. This small store had both Tom Hopkins' book, *Selling For Dummies,* and Dr. Ruth Westheimer's book, *Sex For Dummies.*

Hopkins' book covers some of the same ground as this one, but in different ways. *Selling For Dummies* is a good companion book to this one, regardless of your profession. The book is essential if your profession is selling. In addition to discussing many of the topics in this book (such as the importance of preparation, goal setting, and closing), Hopkins offers many solid tips about developing leads, keeping your spirits up as you experience rejection, and time planning. We highly recommend this book for everyone.

Swim with the Sharks without Being Eaten Alive by Harvey Mackay

Buy this book and put it where you can read it often. Mackay gives you valuable snippets of advice on negotiating, selling, and life — and he does it with humor and style. What a great way to start the day. In fact, this may be a case of saving the best for last. We have been fans of this book for a long time. Pick any page at random and read it. Somehow, you feel as though you can take on the world. That is probably why *Swim with the Sharks* was on the best-seller list for so long.

Our book covers all the fundamentals of negotiating — in an organized and thorough manner. Harvey Mackay's book takes your mind to a new level of enthusiasm and optimism about negotiating. Combine our book with the energy and optimism of Mackay's book, and you feel unbeatable in your business and in your life.

Chapter 24

Ten Internet Resources for the Modern Negotiator

In This Chapter

▶ Going online for the first time

▶ Where in the Web you can find out about negotiating

▶ Using search engines to find the topic you want

▶ Chatting with other Internet users

*O*ur fabulous editor, Shannon Ross, thought that it would be a good idea to include a list of Internet resources, seeing as how the . . .*For Dummies* series got its start with computer books. We liked the idea but didn't have a clue about how to use the Internet.

We soon learned that the first step to using the Internet (after buying a computer with a modem, that is) is to choose a service provider. Some of the more common services are America Online (AOL), CompuServe, and Prodigy. (You can also get a direct link to the Internet and avoid paying for all the bells and whistles of a full-fledged service, but then you have to figure out a great deal of technical stuff for yourself.) Most of the services offer a free introductory period to get you hooked on using their program. Be sure to negotiate for some free time up front.

We first installed America Online when we started the editing process for this book so that we could send and receive changes and comments electronically. America Online has the most users (including Shannon, our fabulous editor) and is great for sending attachments back and forth.

Installing the program is amazingly easy. We could not believe that we didn't have any problems with the installation, because neither one of us has much experience when it comes to computers. We installed AOL using the oh-so-simple instructions on the disk and the prompts on the screen as the installation proceeded.

After you install your Internet service provider's program, look around for a gateway to the Internet (on AOL, this gateway is a button called Internet Connection). You may have to install additional files to be able to "surf the Web" (as our kids say), but this installation is a one-time inconvenience and is worth the initial investment of time and/or money.

When you step into the Internet, you have access to a maze of electronic sites — or, if you will, a *World Wide Web* of pages. Each page has its own address (called a URL, for Uniform Resource Locator). In this book, we write these addresses like this.

How you move from page to page depends on the type of service you're using. But one thing that's universally critical is that you type the precise Internet address for the site you want to visit, including all the periods and slashmarks. Any discrepancy whatsoever produces an annoying message to the effect that you screwed up, and you end up back where you started.

After you type the URL, your computer begins its search. Eventually, the Web page you want appears on your screen, or you get a dreaded message telling you that the site you're trying to access is busy or that you didn't enter the address correctly — aghhhhhhhh!!!

The Internet is a vast warehouse of information. Use the following resources as a starting place. Notice that the title of this chapter isn't "The Ten *Best* Internet Sites." That's up to you to decide. This chapter is just an alphabetical list of ten really good resources out of thousands currently on the Internet. The last two sections in this chapter show you ways to find additional information on the Net.

Many people who have Web sites are trying to sell something. That's not bad if you're trying to buy something, but it can be annoying if you just want information. All the sites listed in this chapter have value for you as a negotiator, regardless of whether you buy any courses or materials they may be pedaling. We tried to choose sites that put information before commerce.

DiploNet

DiploNet is a network of diplomats focusing on conflict management and resolution, peacemaking, and multilateral diplomacy. Use this site as a springboard to other valuable negotiating resources, including these three:

> ✔ **WIN (Washington Interest in Negotiation) Group:** Link to this page to plug into international negotiation issues.

✔ **MIT PMNM (Massachusetts Institute of Technology's Program on Modeling for Negotiation Management):** Connect to the Sloan School of Management, where Professor J.D. Nyhard heads up efforts to develop an online system to support all aspects of negotiation, from general negotiation advice to case-specific information.

✔ **Linkages (Sustainable Development Negotiations):** Linkages is a spiffy Web site that discusses current environmental issues and can hook you up to the *Earth Negotiations Bulletin.* The topic is pretty specific, but browsing this Web site can give you insight about how to negotiate — as well as new ways to save the Earth!

Look for DiploNet at `http://www.clark.net/pub/diplonet/DiploNet.html`.

Institute for Global Communications

The Institute for Global Communications (IGC) Web site is really five different directories in one:

✔ PeaceNet

✔ EcoNet

✔ ConflictNet

✔ LaborNet

✔ WomensNet

Browse the different directories to find the negotiation information and strategies you're after. ConflictNet, for example, provides links to a worldwide conflict resolution community and current information on legislation, conferences, training, and so on.

The IGC Home Page is located at `http://www.igc.apc.org/`.

International Communications and Negotiation Simulations

Link up to this University of Maryland College Park project designed to provide educational simulations of international negotiations. If you're interested in becoming a world-class diplomat, or just being able to negotiate like one, try out the ICONS project at `http://www.bsos.umd.edu/icons/icons.html`.

Marriage and Relationships

This site is an excellent resource for negotiating with a loved one. Look here for general information about relationships, a discussion of conflict in marriage, and rules to fair fighting. The Web address is http://www.webcom.com/pleasant/sarah/marriage/marriage.html.

Peacemakers

Peacemakers is an online organization that strives to help individuals resolve their conflicts peaceably and outside of the courtrooms. If you're interested in joining or just getting more information, check out http://spider.lloyd.com/~fdelmer/.

The Program on Negotiation at Harvard Law School

Harvard Law School is a hotbed of negotiation theory. This site links to a journal and a newsletter specifically about negotiating. Figure 24-1 gives you a peek into this Web site. Find out more at http://www.harvard.edu/vine/providers/program_on_negotiation/.

Rutgers Center for Negotiation and Conflict Resolution

Rutgers is a small Web site put up by the Center for Negotiation and Conflict Resolution located at the State University of New Jersey. Check it out at http://info.rutgers.edu/RUSLN/cdispres.html.

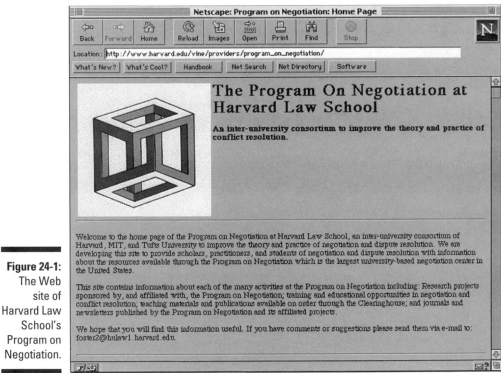

Figure 24-1:
The Web
site of
Harvard Law
School's
Program on
Negotiation.

United States Institute of Peace

The United States Institute of Peace has a Web site that offers resources for conflict resolution, negotiation theory, and peace studies. Among the useful tidbits you can find at this site are general reference links, news clippings, mailing lists, Usenet groups, networks, search objects, and more. See Figure 24-2 for an idea of the cornucopia of information housed at this site.

Reach this Web page at http://witloof.sjsu.edu/peace/conflict.html.

Search Engines

Isn't this cool? Our fabulous editor (Shannon Ross) introduced us to these sites, and they may become our best tool for preparing for a negotiation. Notice that Shannon (our f.e.) really knows this stuff, so she suggested a real techy term for this section — search engines. *Search engines* are just programs on the Web that enable you to search for different Web sites based on a keyword or subject matter. In fact, we used search engines to find all the entries in this chapter.

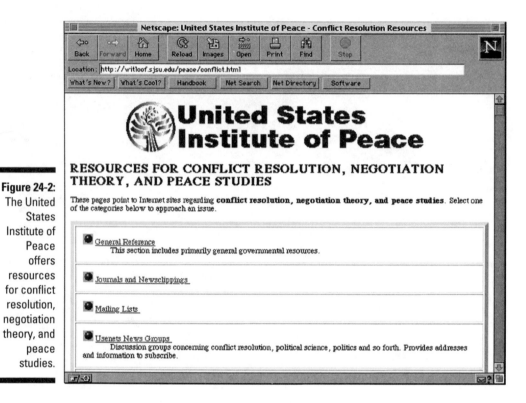

Figure 24-2:
The United
States
Institute of
Peace
offers
resources
for conflict
resolution,
negotiation
theory, and
peace
studies.

Suppose that you don't have an address for a certain Web site (the way you do for the preceding eight sites), but you do know the general subject area you want to explore. With most search engines, all you have to do is type a keyword to indicate the topic you're interested in and then tell the search engine to do its thing. Up pops a list of sites containing your keyword and enabling you to link directly to any site that interests you.

The search engines are free to use, and they all work about the same way. Here are some of the more common ones:

- ✔ **Alta Vista** (http://www.altavista.digital.com)
- ✔ **Inktomi** (http://inktomi.berkeley.edu/)
- ✔ **Lycos** (http://www.lycos.com)
- ✔ **WebCrawler** (http://www.webcrawler.com)
- ✔ **Yahoo!** (http://www.yahoo.com)

If you're still a little computer shy, you can search for using an Internet directory similar to the Yellow Pages. only a fraction of the Internet sites available are listed in the those that are listed tend to change their addresses more ofte can update their books. On the other hand, the feel of pages betw fingers can be comforting, and these books can spare you some of t work by sorting through mountains of Web sites for you.

Whatever your business or area of interest, you'll find plenty of relevant information on the Internet. But you can use the Internet to prepare for more than just the *topic* of your next negotiation — you can prepare information about the *person* with whom you'll be negotiating. Chapter 2 discusses the importance of preparing for the individual as well as the subject. In that chapter, we mention the Six Degrees principle, which states that you are only six persons removed from any other person on the planet. Well now, in the computer age, you're only six *keystrokes* away from anybody on the Internet.

The Internet contains so much information about individuals, it's scary. For curiosity, we searched for the name of a person at IDG Books Worldwide with whom we negotiated the contract for this book. We were stunned by the sheer volume of information, most of which we would have considered confidential. In this particular case, having that information would have been helpful in breaking the ice — for example, we found out that she had grown up a mile from our house!

Just as helpful would have been information on the *company* that publishes the . . .*For Dummies* series. We found this information by simply typing the word "dummies" in the Yahoo! search engine.

We learned a great deal of information about IDG Books Worldwide, including some surprises. We already knew that they started the business based on publishing information about computers. When they branched into business books like this one, they became the fastest growing publishing company in the world. Having worked with their various staff members, it is easy to see why. We gathered much of this information the old-fashioned way before starting our negotiation with IDG, but using the Internet would have been much faster and more complete.

Chatting, Forums, and E-mail

If you can't find the answers you seek on the World Wide Web, try asking one of those faceless folks also using the Internet. The Internet enables you to get in touch with all kinds of people who are interested in the same subjects you are. Odds are, someone out there has the answer you need for your next negotiation.

you can chat with other Internet users:

.rvice provider: Most service providers offer a
to communicate with other members. Choose from
ou and other members can carry on a real-time
yping messages back and forth), *forums* (where you
read messages on a given subject), and a mail area (where
nd private messages to other computer junkies). Experiment
call your service provider, or pick up a book about your service.
turally, we recommend a . . .*For Dummies* book.)

Through a Bulletin Board System (BBS): BBSs are like forums but are not
monitored by any commercial online service. Instead, moderators (called
Sysops for System Operators) keep the conversation going and make sure
that everyone's on the up and up. How to join a BBS is beyond the scope of
this book, but if you're interested, pick up your very own copy of *BBSs For
Dummies* by Beth Slick and Steve Gerber.

✔ **Sending e-mail:** Many of the Web sites you visit provide an Internet
address to which you can send electronic messages (e-mail). If a particular
Web site catches your interest but you still have more questions, find the
Internet address of the person responsible for that Web site and begin a
personal, one-on-one dialog.

Obviously, if you're getting information from anonymous sources, you have to
evaluate what they tell you for yourself. But online chatting can turn up some
really interesting tips, leads, and directions to more information on and off the
Internet.

Index

IDG BOOKS WORLDWIDE REGISTRATION CARD

RETURN THIS REGISTRATION CARD FOR FREE CATALOG

Title of this book: **Negotiating For Dummies™**

My overall rating of this book: ❑ Very good [1] ❑ Good [2] ❑ Satisfactory [3] ❑ Fair [4] ❑ Poor [5]

How I first heard about this book:

❑ Found in bookstore; name: [6]   ❑ Book review: [7]

❑ Advertisement: [8]   ❑ Catalog: [9]

❑ Word of mouth; heard about book from friend, co-worker, etc.: [10]   ❑ Other: [11]

What I liked most about this book:

What I would change, add, delete, etc., in future editions of this book:

Other comments:

Number of computer books I purchase in a year: ❑ 1 [12]   ❑ 2-5 [13]   ❑ 6-10 [14]   ❑ More than 10 [15]

I would characterize my computer skills as: ❑ Beginner [16] ❑ Intermediate [17] ❑ Advanced [18] ❑ Professional [19]

I use ❑ DOS [20] ❑ Windows [21] ❑ OS/2 [22] ❑ Unix [23] ❑ Macintosh [24] ❑ Other: [25]_____
(please specify)

I would be interested in new books on the following subjects:
(please check all that apply, and use the spaces provided to identify specific software)

❑ Word processing: [26]   ❑ Spreadsheets: [27]

❑ Data bases: [28]   ❑ Desktop publishing: [29]

❑ File Utilities: [30]   ❑ Money management: [31]

❑ Networking: [32]   ❑ Programming languages: [33]

❑ Other: [34]

I use a PC at (please check all that apply): ❑ home [35] ❑ work [36] ❑ school [37] ❑ other: [38] _____

The disks I prefer to use are ❑ 5.25 [39] ❑ 3.5 [40] ❑ other: [41]_____

I have a CD ROM: ❑ yes [42]   ❑ no [43]

I plan to buy or upgrade computer hardware this year: ❑ yes [44]   ❑ no [45]

I plan to buy or upgrade computer software this year: ❑ yes [46]   ❑ no [47]

Name: _____ Business title: [48] _____ Type of Business: [49] _____

Address (❑ home [50] ❑ work [51] /Company name: _____)

Street/Suite# _____

City [52]/State [53]/Zipcode [54]: _____ Country [55] _____

❑ **I liked this book!** You may quote me by name in future
IDG Books Worldwide promotional materials.

My daytime phone number is _____

IDG BOOKS

THE WORLD OF
COMPUTER
KNOWLEDGE

☐ YES!

Please keep me informed about IDG's World of Computer Knowledge.
Send me the latest IDG Books catalog.

BUSINESS AND
GENERAL
REFERENCE
BOOK SERIES
FROM IDG

Negotiating For Dummies™

Cheat Sheet

...For Dummies: The Best Selling Book Series for Beginners

Phrases to Avoid

- ✔ "Trust me."

- ✔ "I'm going to be honest with you. . . ."

- ✔ "Let's split the difference and be done."

- ✔ "Take it or leave it."

- ✔ "I'm not sure about this, but. . . ."

- ✔ "Am I right?"

- ✔ "kind of," "sort of," "probably," and "seems like"

- ✔ "Ummm," "like," and "really"

Tips for Better Communication

- ✔ Know your subject before you open your mouth

- ✔ Write down the points you want to cover

- ✔ Clear off your desk or turn off the T.V.

- ✔ Sit up straight (or stand) to stay alert

- ✔ Don't interrupt

- ✔ Look the other person in the eye

- ✔ Count to five before responding

- ✔ Restate or paraphrase what you heard the other person say

Videos to Rent

These movies are not only fun to watch, but (if you aren't careful) they can teach you a lot about negotiating as well.

- ✔ *Dog Day Afternoon*

- ✔ *The Taking of Pelham: One, Two, Three*

- ✔ *Kissinger and Nixon*

- ✔ *Ruthless People*

- ✔ *High and Low*

- ✔ *Broadway Danny Rose*

- ✔ *Naked Spur*

- ✔ *Patterns*

- ✔ *Lilies of the Field*

- ✔ *Columbo: Murder by the Book*

Your Very Own Pause Button

Press here whenever you need a break. Take a moment to think through the negotiation, remember why you're negotiating at all, and cool down.

BUSINESS AND
GENERAL
REFERENCE
BOOK SERIES
FROM IDG

Negotiating For Dummies™

Cheat Sheet

Books to Read

Add these fiction and nonfiction books to your library to sharpen your negotiating skills:

- ✔ *The Negotiator* by Frederick Forsyth
- ✔ *A Maiden's Grave* by Jeffrey Deaver
- ✔ *The Late Shift: Letterman, Leno, & The Network Battle for the Night* by Bill Carter
- ✔ *Barbarians at the Gate: The Fall of RJR Nabisco* by Bryan Burrough & John Helyar
- ✔ *Kissinger: A Biography* by Walter Isaacson
- ✔ *Talking Peace: A Vision for the Next Generation* by Jimmy Carter
- ✔ *This Side of Peace* by 'Ha'nan Ashr'aw'i
- ✔ *Getting Ready to Negotiate: The Getting to Yes Workbook* by Roger Fisher and Danny Ertel
- ✔ *Selling For Dummies* by Tom Hopkins
- ✔ *Swim With the Sharks Without Being Eaten Alive* by Harvey Mackay

. . .For Dummies: The Best Selling Book Series for Beginners

Your Key to Reading Body Language

Get to know the signals that tell you whether the person you are negotiating with is receptive to what you have to say or is resisting your words.

Signs that a person is receptive

- ✔ Leaning forward
- ✔ Increasing eye contact
- ✔ Uncrossing legs
- ✔ Touching the forehead or chin
- ✔ Cocking the head

Signs that a person is resistant

- ✔ Twisting to face the exit
- ✔ Reducing eye contact
- ✔ Locking ankles
- ✔ Making fistlike gestures
- ✔ Fidgeting nervously

The Six Basic Skills of Negotiation

- ✔ Preparing
- ✔ Setting goals and limits
- ✔ Maintaining emotional distance
- ✔ Listening effectively
- ✔ Speaking clearly
- ✔ Knowing when and how to close